SCANNER
SOLUTIONS

Winston Steward
with
Martin C. Brown

Scanner Solutions

Library of Congress Catalog Number: 99-068482

ISBN: 0-9662889-7-1

5   4   3   2   1

Educational facilities, companies, and organizations interested in multiple copies or licensing of this book should contact the publisher for quantity discount information. Training manuals, CD-ROMs, and portions of this book are also available individually or can be tailored for specific needs.

MUSKA&LIPMAN

Muska & Lipman Publishing
2645 Erie Avenue, Suite 41
Cincinnati, Ohio 45208
www.muskalipman.com
publisher@muskalipman.com

This book is composed in Melior, Columbia, Helvetica, and Courier typefaces using QuarkXpress 4.0.4, Adobe PhotoShop 5.0.2, and Adobe Illustrator 8.0. Created in Cincinnati, Ohio, in the United States of America

About the Author

Winston Steward has written or co-written more than a dozen computer books, on topics ranging from business applications to graphics, digital art, and Web design. He designs marketing materials for a fiber optic modem company in Chatsworth, California, and lives with his family in Los Angeles.

Dedication

For Louna, "a little bit of everything. . ."

Acknowledgments

I would like to thank Andy Shafran, Elizabeth Agostinelli, Al Valvano, Hope Stephan, and everyone at Muska & Lipman for the opportunity to contribute to such an interesting and exciting book series. I'm always glad for a chance to ease people's transition into the alternately fascinating and frustrating world of PCs. Special thanks to my agent, Margot Maley Hutchison at Waterside Productions, for remembering me when it counts; to my family, for patience in the face of such tight schedules; and to Louna, for reminding me that words still matter.

Credits

Publisher
Andy Shafran

Editorial Services Manager
Elizabeth A. Agostinelli

Managing Editor
Hope Stephan

Development Editor
Al Valvano

Copy Editor
Bill McManus

Technical Editor
Audrey Grant

Proofreader
Shauna Pope

Editorial Assistant
Cary Jasper

Cover Designers
Dave Abney
Michael Williams

Production Manager
Cathie Tibbetts

Production Team
DOV Graphics
  Michelle Frey
  John Windhorst
  Kevin Vollrath

Indexer
Ellery Albert

Printer
C.J. Krehbiel

Contents

9—Special Effects Photo Editing 147

10—OCR and Working with Text 165

11—Desktop Publishing 181

12—Scanning Documents for Business and Other Uses 199

13—Graphics and Web Design. 219

14—Family Fun 237

Introduction

In *Scanner Solutions,* you'll learn everything you need to know about your scanner in short order. There's a little about how your scanner works, tips for a successful installation, how to operate your scanner, and how to obtain various software applications to run with your scanner. You'll learn about photo editing, scanning documents and converting them to text, even creating forms and spreadsheets from your scanned files.

Scanner Solutions is designed to be read cover to cover or used as a reference. If you've not yet purchased a scanner, you may want to start with Chapter 2, where various types of scanners are discussed and certain models and makes are recommended. If you own a scanner, but feel it's being underutilized and ignored, glance through chapters 4 through 12 and see the various ways a scanner can fit with your particular household. In this book, we move through a bit of everything—for example, scanning and special photo effects, desktop publishing, business applications, and scanning programs for kids.

This book is part of Muska & Lipman's Solutions series. Just like others in the series, *Scanner Solutions* provides specific steps to acquaint you with some aspect of the world of computer technology. You'll learn the hows and whys of scanning and scanning applications without getting bogged down in details. This book starts from the beginning—buying a scanner, installing it, and getting up and running—but before long, you'll be enjoying your scanner in ways you may never have thought possible.

What You'll Find in This Book

This book is a broad look at all the different ways you can use a scanner, including tips for purchasing a scanner you'll be happy with. You'll learn, for example, a lot about editing photos, extracting text from documents, publishing with your scanner, and how to prepare your images for the Web. Lots of skills are covered in these pages, with tips on when to apply them.

Who This Book Is For

If you own a scanner and suspect there's lots more you can do with it—but aren't sure where to begin—this book is for you. Likewise, if you are considering buying a scanner, but fear it may lie dormant with the other toys in the electronic gadget graveyard, this book can help. You will be amazed what these machines can do!

How This Book Is Organized

This book includes fifteen chapters and two appendixes:

▶ Chapter 1, "Scanner Possibilities: An Overview." Learn what's in store in the book and get a glimpse of the breadth of what we'll cover.

▶ Chapter 2, "How Scanners Work." An informative but jargon-free look at what makes a scanner do what it does, emphasizing what you need to know to get the most out of your scanner.

▶ Chapter 3, "The Right Scanner for You." We'll look at specific scanners, models, types of scanners, and the varieties you are most likely to see at the electronic store. You'll learn the differences between them and come away with something you'll really use.

▶ Chapter 4, "Installing and Configuring Your Scanner." This chapter will supplement the installation guide that came with your scanner and help you through any bumps and glitches in the setup process.

▶ Chapter 5, "What Software is Right for You?" You'll get a good look at the programs available for your scanner and determine what's the best investment of time and money. Then you'll learn how to locate, download from the Internet, and try out all kinds of programs that make your scanner a more useful tool than you'd ever imagine.

▶ Chapter 6 "Scanning Successfully." A close look at the scanning process, what makes a good scan, and how to get good results every time.

▶ Chapter 7, "Saving Your Scans." You'll learn about graphic file types, what each of them offers, and when to work with one over the other.

▶ Chapter 8, "Basic Photo Enhancements." There's so much you can do to bring new life to a scan of a damaged photo and to make a good picture even better. This chapter explores the best photo editing techniques for all occasions.

▶ Chapter 9, "Special Effects Photo Editing." There are many surprisingly simple software operations that can turn your scans into truly artistic expressions or simply are lots of fun to experiment with. This chapter starts your imagination down that road.

▶ Chapter 10, "OCR and Working with Text." Scanning is not just for photos but for letting you edit text documents in an unprecedented way with surprising ease. You'll see how any text document can become electronic in a matter of minutes.

▶ Chapter 11, "Desktop Publishing." With a scanner, any photographic idea can end up in your document. You'll learn how to create well-designed brochures, pamphlets, and other publishing projects.

▶ Chapter 12, "Scanning Documents for Business and Other Uses." With a properly configured modem and printer, your scanner can function as a fax machine and copier. You'll learn how your scanner can become quite a convenience for the home office or small business environment.

▶ Chapter 13, "Graphics and Web Design." Scanned images bound for the World Wide Web need to be optimized to load quickly and look their best. You'll learn about how the Web uses color and displays your pictures and about preferred file types.

▶ Chapter 14, "Family Fun." Kids can safely scan if you lay down a few guidelines first. You'll also learn about using your scanner to create family projects, developing your own games and rainy-day activities. We'll look at some software programs that are especially good for bringing young children into the world of digital design.

▶ Chapter 15, "Arranging and Archiving Your Files." Once you've scanned more than a handful of photos or documents, you'll see how essential it is to have a plan to keep track of your scans, as well as temporarily store the images you don't need for the moment. This chapter also explores how to retrieve any picture on your computer with a few mouse-clicks.

▶ Appendix A, "Scanning and the Law." There are limits to what you can legally scan and what you can do with those images when you've scanned them. This appendix is a primer on the legalities of scanning, and the hows and whys of copyrighting intellectual property and photographs.

▶ Appendix B, "Your Scanner and Your Mac." Although many of the features of Mac scanners are the same as those on PC scanners, some important differences exist that haven't been covered yet that you need to be aware of when installing, setting up, and using your scanner on the Mac. Those differences are covered in this appendix.

Conventions Used in This Book

Although this book covers a broad territory, not emphasizing one product over another, there are times when specific instructions and steps are invoked. In such cases, my instructions will guide your mouse step-by-step. Instructions will begin with the menu at the top of the screen, down through the submenu, dialog box and specific data area for typing in a number or clicking a button. Let's take, for example, "From the File menu, click Print Preview. The image appears in the preview screen. Click the Zoom button to magnify your view of the image area." Such instructions guide you from the first menu option you click, down to where data is entered and your image is edited.

The book also features the following special displays for different types of important text:

TIP
Text formatted like this will provide a helpful tip relevant to the topic being discussed in the main text.

CAUTION
Warnings about actions or operations that could make irreversible changes to your image or that might lead to consequences that are potentially confusing will be displayed as a "Caution." Be sure to read Caution text—it could help you to avoid some very troublesome pitfalls!

NOTE
Notes highlight other information that is interesting or useful and that relates to the topic under discussion in the main text.

Keeping the Book's Content Current

For updates, corrections, and other information related to the content of the book, head out to:

www.muskalipman.com

1

Scanner Possibilities: An Overview

Not long ago, scanners were a high-end tool for graphics professionals only. They cost a king's ransom, and the money required for a scanner-ready computer would also bankrupt a few royal purses. Most computer users didn't have scanners unless they made their living with them. I remember quite clearly digging deep into my spending money just to have a "few" pictures scanned, because buying a scanner myself was completely out of the question. There were few software programs capable of running a scanner, and those that did were far too complex for the computer novice.

So what has changed? Why do we see them now at the electronic store, going for the price of a few tanks of gas? Well, scanner technology has improved and costs have come down. Also, many, many companies are lined up ready to sell you a scanner. The scanner interfaces have become more user-friendly, and everybody stands to gain from you, the consumer, having a positive experience your first time out with a scanner.

Tapping Into Your Imagination

Take a deep breath, let your imagination run wild, and consider all that you can do with a scanner. Start with this thought: any image you see can now be put on your computer. Once there, images (or other documents) can be altered with digital art programs for all kinds of uses or saved and archived as simple text, freeing up file cabinet space. Images that you like can be saved on your computer and posted on a Web page, made into a customized greeting card, or incorporated into a product brochure for a small business. (However, see Appendix A, "Scanning and the Law," for guidelines on what is allowable.) Newspaper articles, family memorabilia, legal documents, photographs, artwork, elementary school yearbooks that are starting to show their age, "classic" album covers or magazine art that you may want to rescue from the ravages of time—any and all images are ripe for scanning.

The Artist Within

Using the art tools covered in this book, scanned images can be combined with other images in interesting montages, "painted" with digital art software, cropped, restored, and otherwise edited to your own liking. You can then create your own calendars, invitations, and posters or simply enjoy an old photograph restored to its original luster.

Document Preservation

If your file cabinets are overflowing with documents that you can't quite seem to part with, scan them. They'll take up far less space on your hard drive than they do on your shelf. Study materials for your personal use, such as passages from classic literature, can be scanned, saved on disk, and printed on regular paper, allowing you to freely mark up the margins without destroying something valuable. If you are in the legal or medical profession or any other line of work where the ability to retrieve segments of old documents is a must, a scanner can be your best friend.

Becoming a Publishing Wiz

Desktop publishing programs can incorporate your scanned image into all kinds of documents, such as product brochures, menus, flyers, special event announcements, and wedding invitations, as well as educational tools such as timelines and school reports. If you've created the perfect business logo and want to use it on business cards, company stationery, letterheads, or a corporate Web page, all you have to do is scan it. Once an image is scanned, you can do virtually anything with it.

What's Ahead

In this book, we'll get you started with your scanner, making sure that you purchase the right one for you, get it plugged in, and up and running, then explore just how images are scanned, saved, and later retrieved on your computer.

We'll talk a little bit about scanner purchasing choices: not all scanners are created equal. If you "go for the cheap one," what features will you have to do without? Are they essential? What tradeoffs can you expect? Will you end up wishing you had spent a few more dollars, or will you be happy with a true bargain? Making a good choice here really depends on what you want to do with your scanner, and we'll explore all of those issues in the early part of this book.

Software Needs

You'll need to evaluate not only which scanner to buy, but also the software required to manipulate the images you scan. Most scanners come with simple image editing software that may have all the features that you need, and thus you won't need to buy anything else. However, if you find yourself drawn into the world of graphic design, perhaps the free program that came with your scanner is just not up to the task. Well, then, what should you buy? In this book, we'll discuss guidelines to help you avoid both overspending and the frustration of trying to coax professional results out of nonprofessional software. We'll talk about image editing, text extraction, desktop publishing, and all kinds of software that maximizes your scanner's value.

Troubleshooting and Tips

Unfortunately, getting your scanner to work correctly with your computer may not go as smoothly as you'd like. Setting up a scanner for the first time is not as easy as plugging speakers into a CD player. Your scanner has to be configured to work with your PC. Sometimes, this process is automatic, goes forward without a glitch, and you can be up and scanning in no time, but for certain computer configurations, a little finesse is required. While this book is not meant to replace your scanner's *User's Manual,* we will explore some solutions to common setup problems that you may encounter.

Just the Right Amount of Information

Like everything else in the computer business, you'll find that the scanner choices are endless. Every step of the way, you'll have to decide what is right for you. Is this image destined for a Web page? A printed, four-color document? Or will it be converted to text and archived with other important papers? This book helps you step through those choices and eliminate the frustrating trial and error you'd endure if you were on your own.

Working with a scanner requires that you understand a little terminology. Knowing a little bit about color modes, screen and print resolution, and pixels will help you get the best results from your images. Images bound for the World Wide Web require different treatment than pictures you'll be including in a professional brochure, printed up at great expense. In this book, you'll learn which set of options applies to each situation. You'll also want to know why an image that appears so large on your computer screen is so small when printed, or what to do about the little dots or "railroad" tracks that show up out of nowhere on your scanned pictures.

Storing Your Scans

Another issue this book addresses is how to retrieve your images after you save them, particularly how you can organize them so that you can quickly access them later. This may not seem like much of an issue now, but after you've been scanning for a while, you'll appreciate a handy way to retrieve archived images. Related to this issue is the huge amount of disk space scanned images and documents can require. Once you've owned and enjoyed a scanner for a few months, you may be amazed at how quickly the hard drive space can disappear. We'll take a look at methods for storing images and documents "for the long haul," taking up minimum space, but being handy enough for quick access.

Faxing and Copying

We'll also discuss faxing with your scanner. Configured correctly, a scanner can function quite nicely as a fax machine, saving you the expense of another purchase, as well as a trip down the hall and having to play with another set of buttons. (To use your scanner as a fax machine, note that you also need a modem on your PC.) Once an image is scanned, you can fax it from your computer, meaning that you never again have to retrieve that original paper document, which is quite a convenience.

Finally, we'll address the capability to use your scanner as a copy machine, skipping the process of saving an image to your hard drive and going straight from scanner to paper output. This functionality requires a printer attached to your computer, as well as a scanner.

Naming Names

In this book, we are not out to push one particular hardware or software solution. We all have our favorites and, when applicable, we'll happily tell you what those are. However, so many types of PCs, scanners, and related software packages are available today—and so many ways to creatively implement a scanner solution—that we'll simply tell you all about the particular solutions we have found to be the most rewarding, from both a results and a time-saving point of view. Regarding software discussed in these pages, we do not want you to go out and spend money needlessly. Therefore, we'll largely (but not exclusively) discuss software packages that are available for free trial on the Web. It's very nice to be able to get an idea of what solutions work for you, without incurring additional expense. Whenever possible, we'll point you in that direction.

Putting the Power of Scanning at Your Fingertips

Although we do have a bit of technical ground to cover, the most important resource to tap here is your imagination. Let's state one more time the power that a scanner puts at your fingertips: the ability to acquire, alter, and transmit any photograph or document in any way imaginable. Grab a picture with your scanner, and it can be on its way to the other side of the world in a matter of minutes. Alter that picture, add text to it, change its colors, or add elements to it before you send, print, fax, or save it as part of a project you may develop later.

Technological advances in recent years have conspired to make scanners cheaper and easier to use, and the software to manipulate the output of your scanner has plummeted in price, even as those software packages have grown more powerful and easier to use. Additionally, the computer power required to run a scanner used to cost a king's ransom, but no longer. It's just about impossible to buy a new computer that lacks the resources to run a scanner. The computer firepower that used to be available only to professional graphic designers is now standard in almost every commercially available PC. Bottom line: if you've bought a computer in the last few years and are intrigued by what a scanner can do, you'll be limited only by your own imagination. Let's take a quick preview of what you'll be learning in this book. In the next few pages, we'll peek ahead at the type of projects and skills you'll acquire, and show you what some of the results will look like.

TIP

Some amazing software is available for you to download from the Web and try out for free. You can try out programs of all kinds and practice many types of scanning skills without initially having to spend more money than what you spend on your scanner. The software packages available for you to try out just by downloading are sophisticated and quite powerful and will give you a real taste of what you can do with your scanner. Throughout this book, we'll refer and point the way toward many shareware and *trialware* programs. Trialware is software that you are free to try out for a limited time and then must either purchase or remove from your computer. Often, programs you download and "test run" from the Internet are trialware. The basics of downloading software are explored in Chapter 5, "What Software Is Right for You?

Photo Retouching and Graphic Design

Figure 1.1 shows a photograph with uneven exposure. When trying to photograph a scene in limited light that includes light and dark subjects, a camera can miss subtleties, leaving one face bleached or the other shrouded in darkness.

Figure 1.1
A photo in need of more balanced lighting.

Figure 1.2 shows the corrected photograph after applying graphic editing techniques that we will cover in Chapter 8, "Basic Photo Enhancements."

Figure 1.2
The photo with the lighting corrected via software

You'll also learn how to edit and alter photos, creating interesting photo montages and including them in cards (See Figure 1.3.) In these cards, banners, brochures, and such, you can design your own color schemes, add customized text and special effects, or just "go with" one of the design ideas generated by the graphics software you are using.

Figure 1.3
A card created with a
scanned photo.

Graphic design schemes you create can be deployed in many ways, using
the same photographs, text, and design concepts in each type of project.
Figure 1.4 shows a PowerPoint presentation for an art school.

Figure 1.4
A PowerPoint
presentation using a
color, photo, and font
scheme.

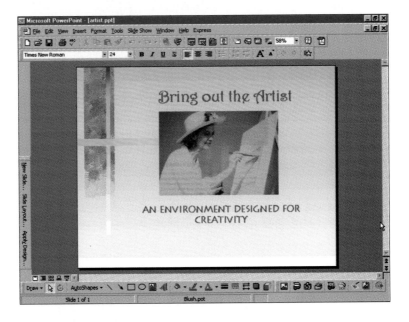

A three-fold brochure is shown in Figure 1.5, using the same text elements, color scheme, and central photograph as in the previous figure. In this book, we'll explore how to scan and plan your projects using the same design sense consistently throughout.

Figure 1.5
The same design scheme applied to a brochure.

Applying Special Effects to Photographs

Figure 1.6 shows a card that includes two photographs that have been "feathered" around the edges. Feathering causes the borders of photographs to appear to fade in, making them fit more naturally in the card's color scheme.

Figure 1.6
A card made from photos treated with a feathering effect.

Another, more obvious, example of feathering, or fading two images together, is shown in Figure 1.7, a cover for a syllabus for a product seminar. We'll explore that technique and other photo-editing tips and tricks in Chapter 9, "Special Effects Photo Editing".

Figure 1.7
Fading two scanned images into one composite piece.

Figure 1.8 shows a family photograph with a "painterly" impressionistic effect applied to the background of the photo, while the main subject matter is untouched. This also did not require too much elbow grease or wild amounts of artistic talent—just a little experimenting.

Figure 1.8
A family photograph with an effect applied to the background, leaving the main subject untouched.

Before   After

Something Different for a Change

In another section of the book, we'll look at a computer program that slices a photograph into a puzzle and then times how long it takes you to reassemble it (see Figure 1.9), and another program that scans regular sheet music and compiles the results into a MIDI file that can be played through your computer speakers with the click of the mouse.

Figure 1.9
You can create a puzzle from a scanned photo.

Scanning Forms

Have you thought it might be possible to scan some of those forms you use, and perhaps print them as needed, with names and addresses already included? You can. Figure 1.10 shows a scanned form. After the scan, the form fields and headings are imported into a program that "recognizes" the form's components and saves the scanned form into a flexible, editable document. Later, you can apply a database to the form, printing copies with names, purchases, and other contact information in place (see Figure 1.11). You'll learn more about these features in Chapter 12, "Scanning Documents for Business and Other Uses."

Figure 1.10
A scanned form.

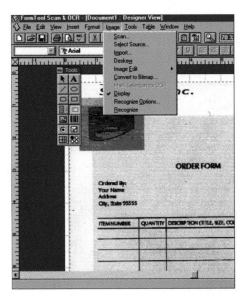

Figure 1.11
Applying a database to information from the scanned form.

Scanners and Word Processing

Scanners have lots of applications for programs such as Word and WordPerfect. You can use your scanner and a word processing program to reformat an old document, sprucing up the information and making it more useful. Figure 1.12 shows a scan of an old magazine article (words that the OCR program does not understand are highlighted in green). Without photographs, the information in the magazine article is uninviting and hard to absorb.

Figure 1.12
An old magazine article scanned.

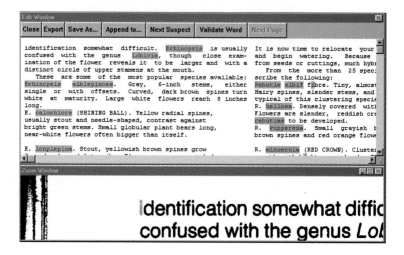

Figure 1.13 shows the same information imported from the scanner into a Word document, with photographs added.

Figure 1.13
Information from the scanned article used in a Word document.

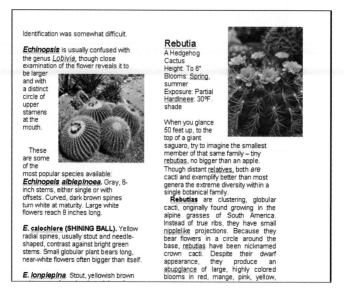

No matter how the text was organized in the original document, once you scan it, the words can be reformatted to suit your purposes. We'll look at this and other similar features in Chapter 11, "Desktop Publishing." You'll learn a bit about programs such as Copyshop 2000, which brings scanning and optical character recognition (OCR) power right into Word, as you can see from the toolbar shown in Figure 1.14.

Figure 1.14
The Copyshop 2000 program brings scanning controls right into Word.

Also in this chapter, you'll get a taste of creating practical items from scanned photographs, such as CD labels and jewel case inserts, as shown in Figure 1.15.

Figure 1.15
Creating a CD label from scanned family photos.

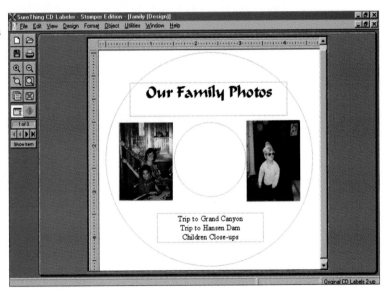

Web Design

If your photos and scanned documents are destined for the Web, you'll be happy to learn how easy it is to add pictures and text of all sorts to Web pages, enabling you to design elaborate Web sites without having to learn HTML or delve into a world of complexity. But to whet your whistle with something a little different, here is a glimpse of a program that turns your pictures into 3D online "worlds" that visitors to your site can navigate through, zeroing in on any picture they choose, or just cruising through, taking in the entire tour (see Figure 1.16).

Figure 1.16
An online 3D virtual tour created from scanned photos.

You'll get a good look at how to create interesting online galleries in Chapter 13, "Graphics and Web Design." Making online photo albums is as easy as choosing which pictures to save to your Web page and posting the results (see Figure 1.17).

Figure 1.17
An online photo album, viewable by visitors to your Web page.

We have lots of practical ground to cover as well, including choosing a scanner and software that are right for you, organizing your pictures, and even legalities such as determining what's okay to scan and under what circumstances. We'll start with a brief look at what a scanner does. Scanners are powerful tools, so it's good to have an idea about what's going on "under the hood."

2

How Scanners Work

This chapter will not make you a Ph.D. in scanning, but it will give you a basic understanding of the process, how the image is reflected from the picture surface and electronically recorded and saved on your computer. We'll discuss how digital images work and the variety of media you view them on. As a result, you'll know the essential difference between an image's printed size and how it appears on your computer monitor or online. You'll also learn enough about image resolution to make a good scanner purchase choice or understand the capabilities of the scanner you do own.

We'll look at types of scanners (sheetfed, flatbed and film scanners) and the special abilities of each. You'll learn that scanners come with one of three types of data ports—parallel, SCSI or USB. We'll talk about the significance of each.

What Is a Scanner?

The job of a scanner is to transform a printed image into something your computer can use. A photograph, or any other printed media, is a long way from the world of bits and bytes inhabited by your computer. It's quite miraculous that all the colors of an image you can see with your eyes are accurately converted to digital data, to be saved and manipulated by any means you and your computer are capable of. It's a long journey from the printed page to the digital image. Here's how it works:

Images reach your eyes as waves of light, and each color and shade of color is actually a wave of a specific amplitude and frequency.

Your eyes know what to do with such data, but a computer does not. Light waves are analog data, whereas a computer requires something digital to work with rather than analog. Enter the scanner, which converts the light reflected off a picture from analog data into digital data (zeros and ones). These binary digits then are stored on your computer and can be manipulated later.

The essential element in a scanner is a *charge-coupled device (CCD)*, which is an array of multiple tiny sensors—photosensitive cells—that move vertically across your page, converting light levels reflected off your page into digital data. These sensors move across your document line by line, recording as much data as possible (see Figure 2.1).

Figure 2.1
A scanner's parts revealed.

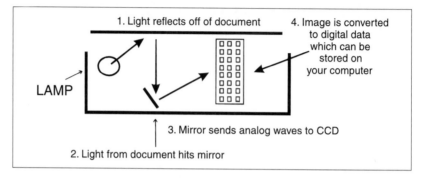

One of the main factors affecting the quality of a scanner is the quality and number of photosensors that the scanner's CCD employs (known as a scanner's *optical resolution*). Most affordable scanners used to have a 300 dot-per-inch (dpi) CCD, meaning that the scanner can obtain 300 samples of color for every inch that it travels across your page. These days, 600 dpi CCDs are more common, which enable twice as much optical data to be recorded by your scanner. This is why, when shopping for a scanner, you should look for a model with a 600 dpi optical resolution.

Older scanners had CCD chips with a single row of sensors. These scanners have to make three passes across the document, picking up one color per pass (red, green, and blue). Newer scanners have three rows of sensors that simultaneously pick up data from the image. Since the CCD has three rows, one for each primary color, they can record all colors in a single pass.

Inside your scanner, the CCDs send charges representing the analog light levels to an *analog-to-digital converter (A/D converter)*, which converts the electrical charges to digital data. This digital data is then stored on your computer. A newer bit of technology, another silicon chip called a *contact image sensor (CIS)*, performs the same function as a CCD, but is lighter, less expensive, and has the A/D converter built right onto the chip itself. This is why newer "entry-level" consumer-grade scanners are also lighter and less expensive. However, the CIS does not quite deliver the same quality of image as a scanner with a CCD, because the chip's architecture doesn't support as many photosensors, thus making the image less accurate. As the technology improves, the disparity between scanners with CCD and CIS chips should diminish. For the time being, though, you may want to make sure that the scanner you purchase has a CCD chip.

Scanner Components

A flatbed scanner's main components are as follows (see Figure 2.2):

Figure 2.2
A flatbed scanner.

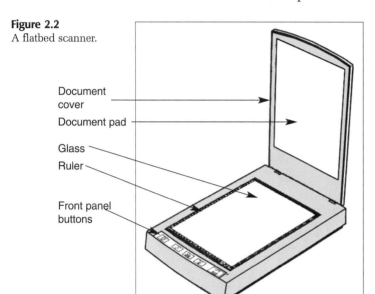

Document cover

Document pad

Glass

Ruler

Front panel buttons

▶ **A glass screen**—You place your document face down across the glass.

▶ **A lamp**—A scanner's "moving part." It travels along the bottom of the screen, illuminating the document. Light from the document is reflected to a set of mirrors. (This is why flatbed scanners only work best with reflective material, such as photographs and magazines, rather than transparent material, such as film and overhead transparencies.)

▶ **A set of mirrors**—Light reflected from the document is transmitted to the mirrors, which pass the light waves along to a lens.

▶ **A lens**—Focuses the image information onto the CCD.

▶ **Charge-coupled device**—Registers the analog charges—the color light waves—and directs them as voltage to the A/D converter.

▶ **Analog/digital converter**—Converts the voltage to digital information, which can be stored on your computer.

Scanning: Getting Enough Dots

Let's take a minute to learn the measurements that indicate a good, clean scan, so that you can make sure that the scanner you purchase is capable of such a feat. Some tips for applying that knowledge are provided, too.

When you look at a picture that you scanned on your computer monitor, it's a bit like looking through the glass bottom of a submarine at the rocks beneath. The rocks are just rocks, but many factors determine how they appear to you. Let's look at the course of a simple 4×5-inch photograph as it is scanned, edited, and then printed.

When you scan a full-color 4×5-inch photograph for printing from your desktop printer, scanning at 150 dpi is more than adequate (you'll learn why in Chapter 3). Let's figure out what the file size of this image will be, or how much room it will take on your hard drive. If your scanner is scanning at 150 dpi, you multiply 600 (4 inches × 150 dpi) × 750 (5 inches × 150 dpi), arriving at a figure of 450,000 pixels. When scanning in full color, however, each color channel (red, green, and blue) uses one byte of space (we'll look at how this relates to the number of colors shortly). This means that each pixel uses 3 bytes of space—one byte for each color. So, you must multiply the number of pixels (450,000) by three to get an indication of how much space the file will take up on disk. So, we can say that a full color version of our photograph will take up 450,000 × 3 bytes, or 1,350,000 bytes, which is perhaps better written as 1.35mb of disk space.

How a Monitor Interprets Your Image

On the other hand, your computer monitor displays between 72 and 75 dpi rather than 150 dpi. So, to be viewed on your monitor, only 72 dots are used to fill up one inch of image space. But the image still is going to display all the dots it was scanned with, even if its definition of an "inch" has changed. So, the image will appear more than twice as large as the original you scanned on your scanner (see Figure 2.3).

Figure 2.3
Your monitor displays at only 72 dpi, so an image scanned at 150 dpi will appear twice as large as the original.

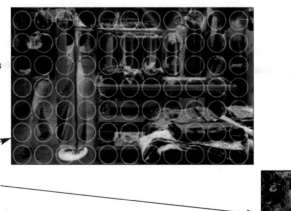

Appearance on Monitor

Original Scan

How a Printer Interprets Your Image

Conversely, an inkjet printer can print well over 150 dots per inch. When you print an image, many hundreds of dots go into filling up one inch of printed space. However, the image still has the same number of dots to work with. The image has dots to distribute. It doesn't care what an "inch" is. It only cares about how thinly or thickly it should be printing those dots, and lets the "inches" fall where they may (See Figure 2.4).

Figure 2.4
Your printer requires more dots per inch to print an image, so a picture scanned at 150 dpi will appear smaller than the original.

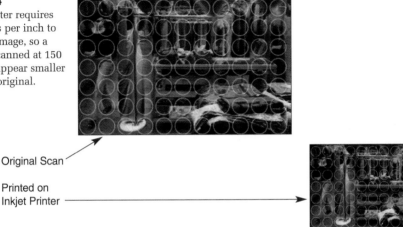

Original Scan

Printed on
Inkjet Printer

The inkjet printer's focus on how it should print the dots is the reason your images appear in different sizes, depending on the media you view them on. However, your goal is to get a good scan. When you scan an image, you want to provide yourself with enough information to work with later. You may want to print that image immediately, or perhaps edit, enlarge, recolor, or add text to it. Any of these processes require that your image be scanned with *adequate detail.*

Scanning for Image Detail

We've touched on why an image appears so large on your monitor compared to the much smaller printed image. In later chapters, you'll learn how to exert control over the printed, posted, and displayed image sizes. For now, it's important to understand how your scanner captures an image digitally, the measurements it uses, and how that image information can be of use to you later.

To achieve image detail, a scanner records and saves each image as a series of thousands of basic *picture elements,* or *pixels.* However, you don't see the pixels. Just as your eyes see a drop of water, not the individual atoms that make up that drop, your eyes see an image as a seamless combination of millions of colors (more than 16 million), not as the individual pixels in that image. For a scanner to simulate this vast array of visible colors, the rows upon rows of barely visible dots that make up your image, a scanner builds your image, one dot at a time, using bits. Bits are the most fundamental binary measurement (think of bits as the electrons and protons that make up a single atom of water) Because there exists such a wide variety of colors, your scanner needs to work with a huge array of digital combinations to build colors with. Hence, your scanner must combine 8 bits of digital data to create only a single accurately colored pixel— this pixel being one tiny dot in the vast ocean of color that comprises the photograph you are scanning. Figure 2.5 shows a scanned photo (top) and a detailed closeup of the image broken down into pixels.

Figure 2.5
A scanned photo (top) and a zoomed in image showing pixel detail (bottom).

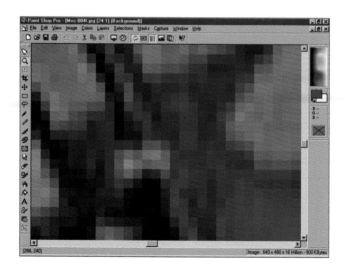

Higher Bits Are Better

So, bits are the building blocks required to create one accurately colored dot on your page or screen (pixel). How does this knowledge help you buy a good scanner? The scanner that you buy should be a 24- to 36-bit scanner. Look for that number on the scanner box. The higher the bits, the better, as explained next.

A 24-bit scanner can sample 8 bits of color information for each of the primary colors—red, green, and blue—to create 1 pixel. Because $8 \times 3 = 24$, at least a 24-bit scanner is required to render color correctly.

Well, then, if 24 bits (8 bits for each of the primary colors) is sufficient, why would a higher number be better? After all, most scanners today are 30- to 36-bit. The explanation is simple. Due to imperfections inherent in electronic data transfer (electrical interference, a poor signal-to-noise ratio), not all the color information obtained by each of the 8 bits will be accurate. Some scanned data bits will not be very usable. That's why standard 24-bit scanned images tend to be a bit shadowy. Some of the bit data just isn't that accurate. Therefore, to ensure that a fully accurate color sampling is obtained, and that each pixel represents a color as close to the original as possible, newer scanners employ a *bit depth* of 10 or 12 bits per color channel (red, green, and blue). Adding the extra bits creates a more representative sample, a more accurate pixel, and, by extension, a more accurate image.

So, you really should buy a 30- to 36-bit scanner. As of this writing, 40- and 48-bit scanners are making an appearance as well. If the prices come down somewhat, that added amount of detail provided by the extra scanning bits would be worth the investment. Nonetheless, for scanning family photos and home office use, a 24-bit scanner should be sufficient for your needs. If you find yourself becoming a bit of a perfectionist, however, higher than 24 bits may be what you need.

Understanding Resolution

Purchasing a scanner based on its advertised "resolution" is a bit like buying a stereo based on its peak wattage. Those 100-watt speakers really deliver more like 50 watts most of the time. Although the term "resolution" has myriad definitions (I'll clarify each as the need arises), for now, just remember that the *important number* is optical resolution, which refers to the resolution at which you will be scanning your image.

This section explores the ways that scanner manufacturers can play fast and loose with the term "resolution," and how you can avoid being deceived.

CHAPTER 2

Use the Lower Number

A scanner receives image data row by row, and the larger the number of dots, the more detail a scanner can record. A 600 dpi scanner yields more detail (and thus, a more accurate image) than a 300 dpi scanner. The lamp moves forward one step per row, causing light to be reflected from the image to the CCDs a row at a time

However, when looking at a scanner's specifications, have you ever noticed that the vertical number is twice as high as the horizontal—for example, 600×1200 dpi resolution? That's because the scanner's transport mechanism takes half a step between the rows of dots it is measuring. To meaningfully use the measurement taken between rows, the scanner uses mathematical averaging. Don't use this extended vertical resolution setting (in the preceding example, the 1200 dpi figure) as as major scanner purchasing criteria. Instead, make your purchase based on the true optical resolution—the lower number (600 dpi in the preceding example).

Disregard Interpolated Resolution

Scanner boxes and spec sheets also report a dizzyingly high "interpolated resolution." Sometimes a scanner with an optical resolution of 600×600 dpi will be advertised as having an interpolated resolution of 9600×9600 dpi. But remember: new detail can be added to an image only by increasing the true resolution at which it is scanned, giving you more measured dots to work with. *Interpolated resolution,* on the other hand, increases the image's size and complexity by averaging the colors in between the image dots that it actually measures. If the scanner measures and records a blue dot of color, and then a yellow dot next to it, it will stuff a few pixels of green in between, giving you more "resolution" to work with, but it won't add any data actually recorded by the sensor's scanners. In some instances, for example, when a photograph is simply too small, and an increase in scan size is a must, using software interpolation can be helpful. However, if used in the upper ranges, software interpolation can make your image look muddy and indistinct.

Scanning vs. Printing Resolution

This discussion appears very early in the book to prevent all of you racehorses from going out and buying a 1200 dpi scanner, then rushing home to scan an image at 1200 dpi, and then being left to wonder why your computer crashed. Here's a bit of important information:

When purchasing a scanner, the maximum resolution is important, of course. However, this does not mean you should plan on scanning at the maximum resolution.

When scanning an image that will be printed on your home inkjet printer, one common assumption is that you should scan the image at the same resolution that the printer advertises. Most inkjet printers today boast a dpi resolution of 600, 740, or even 1400. But, most often, scanning an image at 150 dpi is sufficient for inkjet printing. In Chapter 4, "Installing and Configuring Your Scanner," we'll explore the differences between image resolution and printed "dpi" more thoroughly, but for now, keep the following maxim in mind: Although an inkjet printer can indeed print 600 or even more dots per inch, it takes many dots to accurately simulate all the colors of your scan. Therefore, scanning at 150 dpi is more than adequate for most printed material. Why the discrepancy between printed resolution and scanned resolution? Read on:

Your computer's video card can generate more than 16 million colors. Your monitor can display all of them seamlessly. There is no need to "mix" or combine pixels to make pink look *a little more pink* than the *other pink,* for example. It simply displays *exactly* the color called for in the image.

But does your inkjet printer print 16 million colors? No. It has cartridges capable of printing between three and four colors. So how does it re-create what you see on your monitor? It combines primary colors, that's how.

Your printer creates a blend of dots that, when put together, will resemble the true color from your scan. Thus, several "printer dots" are needed to recreate a pixel of genuine color from your original image. This fancy footwork of combining printer dots to make one true color dot from your image means your actual image will be smaller. Therefore, if you scanned your image at 150 dpi, your printer may need 600 dpi to simulate all the colors used in the image you scanned and spread the image across the same distance as would appear on your screen with the lower resolution.

When to Scan at a Higher Resolution

The following few paragraphs are for those of you who need to absorb quickly as much information as possible and don't want to wait to get the whole story on image resolution.

Although I'm recommending in this book that scanning an image at 100 to 150 dpi resolution usually is sufficient, here are some exceptions:

▶ When you scan a line drawing that uses only one color, such as a black-ink drawing, scanning at your printer's actual resolution will produce better results. That's because the printer doesn't need to combine many dots to simulate shades of color. After all, the line drawing is only black, right? So, the printer can lay down a single dot for every pixel that was scanned in your original image. The ability to match your scanned image "dot per dot" allows your printer to make use of its full printed-resolution possibilities.

▶ When you plan to do heavy editing to your image (for example, use filters to stretch, blend, combine images, and otherwise get wild and crazy), you may want to scan at 300 dpi. However, if your image is going to be posted on the Internet, and not printed, there is truly no reason to scan above 100 to 150 dpi.

▶ If you plan to increase the printed size of your image, scan at a resolution proportional to its eventual printed size. For example, if you plan to scan a postage stamp and print it at four times its original size, don't scan at 150 dpi. Scan at 600 dpi instead.

Scanner Types

Table 2.1 describes scanner types, their significant features, and when one would use one type over another. Briefly, scanners can be categorized by the following characteristics:

▶ **Media type**—Scanners can scan either reflective media (magazines and photos) or transmissive media (negatives and transparencies). Some scanners can scan both types. This means a scanner would either shine light *through* the media source (film or transparencies, which are transmissive media), or shine light that reflects off the media source (magazines, photos and newspapers, which are reflective media).

▶ **Document feed type**—A scanner can provide a glass surface for positioning the media (flatbed scanners), an entry port for inserting fed media (sheetfed, slide and film scanners), or a large cylinder that the media wraps around, secured by tape or temporary glue (drum scanners).

▶ **Media transport mechanism**—How does the document come in contact with the light source? In flatbed scanners, the light moves, while the document is stationary. In film scanners, the film cassette is positioned inside a small transport, where the film is unwound and exposed to the scanner lamp. In drum scanners, the document is fastened to a cylindrical drum, which rotates rapidly around the light source. In sheetfed scanners, paper is loaded vertically at the top of the scanner, much like an inkjet printer, and each sheet is fed through the scanning mechanism and the light source.

▶ Price Range—Drum scanners are into the tens of thousands of dollars. Film scanners can be over a thousand but are often seen for below $400. Flatbed scanners are less than $700 and even below $100. Sheetfed scanners are quite often less than $100.

Table 2.1
Types of scanners and their features.

	Media Type	Document Feed	Media Transport	Popular Use	Cost	Most Suitable Environment
Flatbed Scanners	Reflective media	Document lies on scanner bed surface	Bulb moves across media. Document is stationary	Scanning photos, text documents, magazines and newspapers	$99-$700	Home or small office
Drum Scanners	Transparency and Reflective media	Document is fastened to cylindrical scanner drum, and rotates at high speed	Document rotates around drum, which shines very bright laser light at document	Scanning high-quality photographs and artwork for professional use	Above $10,000	Professional graphic design and print facility
Film and Transparency Scanners	Transparent media	Slides or film canisters are inserted into transport mechanism which moves the slide to the light source	Slide or film moves across light source.	Specially designed camera film, and slides generated from regular film	$399 to $1299	Home or office where higher quality scanned photos are needed, such as real estate or medical photography
Sheetfed Scanners	Reflective media	Pages load vertically into scanner interface like an inkjet printer	Paper moves downward across scanner sensors	Scanning large amounts of text from pages	$69 to $200	Home or office where high volume of text documents need scanning

CHAPTER 2

Sheetfed Scanners

Sheetfed scanners scan multiple documents, one after another, much like the output from an inkjet printer. They are ideal for scanning multi-page documents for text extraction. Most often, sheetfed scanners are used with an OCR (optical character recognition) program. Usually, the scanner quality is sufficient for text, but less than ideal for photographs or complex graphics. Sheetfed scanners often cost less than $100 and take up very little space on a desk. They are ideal for environments where text-based documents need to be scanned routinely, but no photos. Figure 2.6 shows a sample sheetfed scanner from the Visioneer Web site (**http://www.visioneer.com/products/sheetfed/nt**).

Figure 2.6
A sheetfed scanner.

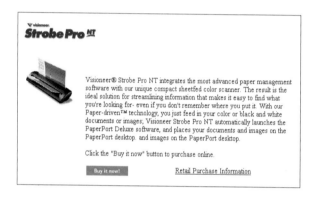

Flatbed Scanners

Flatbed scanners are the most popular household scanners. They scan photographs and other documents. The document is placed on a flat glass scanner bed, while the scanner lamp travels from one side of the document to the other. The resolution and photograph scanning quality can be suitable for near-professional use. Text can be scanned and extracted with flatbed scanners as well. Some models are small enough to take up a corner of space on a desk. Figure 2.7 shows a sample flatbed scanner as shown on the Mustek Web site (**http://www.mustek.com/Imaging/products/catalog/1200-cp.htm**).

Figure 2.7
A flatbed scanner.

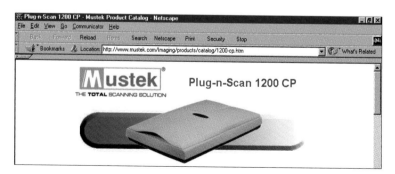

Film Scanners

Film scanners are used to scan transparent, or transmissive, media, such as transparencies or film. Film scanners project light through the film or transparency to the CCD sensor on the other side. Price depends on resolution and capacity. They work differently than flatbed scanners because you insert the photograph or film negative into the scanner, instead of laying it on top.

If you intend to scan only photographs and would like a bump up in quality from what flatbeds can do, then a film scanner is probably your best bet. They are smaller than flatbeds, taking up about half the space on a desktop.

How Film Scanners Work

With film scanners, the film is moved, not the light source. Film scanners can produce images with resolutions above 2000 dpi. Compare that figure to a typical flatbed scanner, which scans at 300 to 600 dpi. Some employ the camera's own advanced photo system (APS), which allows you to keep the scanned images offline, saving them in the APS unit rather than on the hard drive.

Don't mistakingly believe that because you scanned a film of a photograph, you can print it only within the same size and dimensions of a photo. Film that you scan with your film scanner can be treated with the whole array of graphic editing tools, just as any other type of image can be manipulated. And because film scanners scan images at such high resolutions, you can print them larger than photo size without losing any detail.

Printers Especially Suited for Film Output

Being able to scan an image at such a high resolution isn't of too much value if you don't have a reasonable means of printing it. Fortunately, photo printers such as the HP PhotoSmart and the Epson Stylus Photo print photos at extremely high resolutions. Both printers can approximate a true color value on one single dot, instead of spreading several similar color tones across several dots to make up the difference. This allows them to utilize more of the image's true resolution. That way, photos that you scanned at such high resolutions can be put to good use.

Business Card Scanners

Business card scanners are for extracting contact information from an associate's business card and storing the data in a way that's accessible, perhaps on a laptop or palmtop computer. Business card scanners run independently of your computer. Like the palmtop computer, they are small enough to take on business trips.

CHAPTER 2

Understanding Data Ports

The scanner you buy will have one of three types of ports: SCSI, parallel, or USB. These ports determine how data is transmitted from the scanner to your computer. Each type of data port technology has its up and down side, and your knowledge of these will aid you in selecting the right scanner for you.

First, let's talk a bit about what data ports are, and how they work.

A scanner can convert your image into digital form, but the result is a huge amount of data. How does your scanner transfer so many bits and bytes to your computer for safekeeping? That's where *data ports* come in to action. In fact, the job of moving large amounts of data between a PC and an external device (such as a printer, modem, or scanner) has always been daunting.

Serial Port Technology

In the first PCs, serial ports were used, which moved 8 bits of data at a time, followed by 1 bit of data that said, "Did you get that?" The PC would then reply, in essence, "Yes, I did, thank you." Then 8 more bits of data would be sent, all in a row, one by one. When it came to sending a large print job to a printer or scanning a document, imagine how inefficient a serial port was. Newer PCs still have serial ports, but they are used largely for pointing devices and external modems—never for scanners.

Parallel Port Technology

In the 1980s, parallel ports were developed, which allowed 8 bits of data to be transmitted simultaneously, a big improvement over serial ports. Today, printers, scanners, Zip drives, external hard drives, and CD-ROM drives all can connect to your PC through your parallel port. The results are still a little slow, even with improvements in parallel port specifications that have been implemented since the mid-1990s. Scanners that plug into your computer through your parallel port can be annoyingly slow. Additionally, parallel port scanners require your CPU to allocate system resources to transmitting scanner or printer data. This means that while your scanner is scanning, you can't use your computer for much of anything else. And to top it all off, since your parallel port is most often reserved for your printer, having a parallel port scanner requires that both devices work together. Such compatibility is not always easy to come by, though.

SCSI Technology

The fastest method for attaching a scanner to your PC is the SCSI (pronounced "skuzzy") interface. SCSI, which stands for *small computer system interface,* is not merely a port that allows data to pass through certain channels along assigned pathways. Instead, SCSI comes with its own train tracks. The SCSI is a "bus" interface, an electronic pathway that escapes the limitations of sharing data through the computer's own data channels. These data channels, as explained below, can easily get overtaxed, no matter how powerful your computer is. The SCSI bus interface, however, manages the data itself, without draining your CPU.

Since SCSI is a more complete hardware solution, you must open your computer and insert a SCSI card into one of the available slots. These slots are standard, meaning that all newer computers will support a SCSI card, but be forewarned that setting up a SCSI scanner involves this minor bit of technical prowess (beyond that, you simply need a screwdriver). SCSI installation is dealt with thoroughly in Chapter 4.

The SCSI Advantage

Another advantage that SCSI-connected scanners have over other connection systems is the ability to link several external devices together and use them somewhat simultaneously. For example, you can use a SCSI Zip disk, CD-ROM drive, and scanner, and each device, if properly configured, will send and receive data along its own designated pathway. Although some parallel port devices, such as Zip disks and printers, do allow one device to "pass data through" to the PC and back, the results are unpredictable and not smooth at all. Print jobs and file transfers can easily get lost. Often, if two devices try to pass data through your parallel port simultaneously, your computer can "freeze up," forcing you to reboot.

SCSI Pitfalls

Configuring a SCSI card or a SCSI device can be far from automatic, though. Although eight devices can be chained together to your computer through a SCSI port, each device needs to be assigned its own ID number. Some SCSI devices assign themselves one specific ID number, and that number cannot be reassigned. This can be a problem if you have two devices that require the same number.

Additionally, the last device in the SCSI chain of peripherals must be *terminated,* because the SCSI card must have a way of knowing which device is "last in the chain." Often, this termination step is accomplished by placing a large connector plug over the available SCSI port on the final device. Or the same task sometimes can be accomplished by software, by placing an "X" in a checkbox to indicate which device is last in the chain and thus should be "terminated."

CHAPTER 2

USB Technology

The newest method for connecting a scanner to a computer is the *universal serial bus (USB)* port. Most computers commercially available since 1998 have USB ports. Devices plugged into USB ports are almost always immediately recognized by the computer (meaning that USB ports truly support plug-and-play functionality after the proper drives are installed). USB ports are very fast and can support 127 external devices chained together through one computer. However, only scanners with USB connectors can work with USB ports, although USB-enabled scanners are not nearly as rare as they once were. Nonetheless, USB port technology is far more user-friendly and problem-free than parallel ports and SCSI-based options. Data travels much faster through USB ports than their predecessors. Expect to see more USB scanners and other USB-based PC and Macintosh options in the near future.

Now that you've had a general look at how scanners work, the following chapter provides information that will help you select the right scanner for your purposes.

3

The Right Scanner for You

Before you buy a scanner, consider carefully what your needs and interests are. What are your priorities? Desk space? Not much room available for another electronic gizmo? Then size is a major consideration for you. You'll want a scanner with a "small footprint." How about convenience? Some scanners have single-touch e-mail, fax, copy, and scan command buttons right on the front panel. After you configure your scanner the first time, you'll seldom have to work with software dialog boxes. Are you buying this scanner to copy numerous pages at a time? Then perhaps a scanner with an automatic document feeder is in your future. Do you have an eye for color detail, and thus want quality at any price...well, *almost* any price? So, how much is too much to pay for such quality?

In this chapter is a table that matches the requirements you may have with a particular scanner that meets those requirements. But first, we'll get started by discussing some recommendations, hardware requirements, and a definitive number called *Dmax,* or *dynamic range.*

NOTE

If you've already purchased a scanner, this chapter need not be an exercise in hindsight. Read through and see if some of the features discussed here are available on your scanner. You may be surprised at what you already own.

Some Up-Front Advice

In an effort to help you avoid wasting time and money, the following are some major points to consider when you are deciding which scanner to purchase:

CHAPTER 3

Buy USB

Strongly consider purchasing a scanner with a universal serial bus (USB) port connector. Of course, your computer needs to have a USB port, as discussed in the previous chapter, but *peripherals* that utilize USB port connectivity truly have done much to reduce the pain and suffering experienced by computer users trying to get their scanner, printer, or digital camera to work as advertised. Although parallel port scanners also do not require you to install an internal interface card, they are slow and can create problems when you try to use your printer. And although SCSI-based scanners are fast, they require an internal card, meaning configuration can be a hassle.

Check the Software

Make sure the scanner you buy has a good selection of software to work with. Look for name-brand optical character recognition (OCR) software thrown in, such as Caere OmniPage, Presto!, or TextBridge. Look for editing software by Adobe, Ulead, or Corel. Scanning utility packages such as Paperport, ScanWise, and ScanWizard can help you get started quickly. Don't buy a scanner for $39 and then find out you need to purchase a $90 OCR program just to make it do what you want it to do.

Understand Your Hardware Requirements

To run the type of scanner you are likely to buy at an electronics store these days, the following is a minimum set of requirements:

▶ A Pentium 100 processor

▶ 16MB of RAM

▶ 50MB hard drive space

▶ A 24-bit true color video card

▶ A SCSI, parallel, or USB port

▶ A modem, if you intend to use your scanner as a fax machine (optional)

▶ A printer, if you intend to use your scanner as a copier (optional)

Know the Dynamic Range (Dmax)

Dynamic range is a rating that determines a scanner's overall ability to deliver the cleanest, most accurate scans. Besides your own eyes and satisfaction level, a scanner's dynamic range figure (Dmax) tells you the most about how well a scanner scans. If available, the Dmax will be listed on the box or on the specifications sheet of a scanner. A Dmax value above 2.2 is considered acceptable, and a Dmax higher than 3.1 is considered very good.

Such a number is sometimes needed, because the usual indicators of a good scanner (resolution and bit depth) do not always tell the whole story. Here's why:

▶ A scanner's active component, the charge-coupled device (or its less expensive cousin, the CMOS image sensor) is electrical, and subject to *circuit noise* (interference by fluorescent lighting and other nearby electrical activity). A manufacturer will build a CCD to meet a certain signal-to-noise ratio, but the most effective ways of doing this can be expensive.

▶ Not all CCDs are created equal. Some fail or lose their sensitivity.

▶ Some scanners simply have brighter bulbs than others, which makes for brighter, more lively images.

Most scanners costing less than $400 are not going to list a Dmax value, because it won't be very flattering. Producing a scanner prototype that meets the most rigorous specifications takes time and money, and scanner profit margins these days are slim. A Dmax spec is critical, however, if you are planning to produce 11×17-inch full-color photographic artwork and need it to be perfect. Most desktop scanners with true optical ranges above 1200×1200 dpi provide a Dmax number in their specs. However, if the most you are planning to do with your scanner is create birthday cards, post photos on the Web, or even make smaller-sized product brochures, the unavailability of a Dmax spec in itself shouldn't deter you from buying a particular scanner.

Know Your Purpose

Why are you buying a scanner? Here are some purchase suggestions based on what you want to do with it:

▶ **Small Office-Home Office scanner**—If you will be mostly scanning text documents, and desk space is at a premium, think about a sheet-fed scanner, such as the UMAX PageOffice and the Visioneer Paper Port series scanners. Sometimes called personal document scanners, they are smaller than most inkjet printers, and paper loads from the top, allowing you to scan many pages unattended. These scanners are usually grayscale and are suitable for faxing, e-mail, scanning text, and other office chores.

Sheetfed scanners are a bit hard to find on the market because extra-small flatbed scanners can perform more functions while taking up little space. You can buy a flatbed scanner with a document feeder option. Good examples are the HP ScanJet 6350 Cse and the Astra 2400S. The Microtek ScanMaker series has an optional ADF (automatic document feeder) that allows automatic scanning of between 10 and 50 pages of text . Automatic document feeders will add about $100 to the price of your scanner.

▶ **All-Around Family Scanner**—The UMAX Astra 2000U is less than $200 and comes with a solid software package that has a little something for everyone in the family (fun and simple photo editing software and a good OCR package). The Umax Astra 2000U scans at 600×1200 dpi at 36 bits for good photo reproduction. Good for a novice, the Astra 2000U comes with a very easy-to-learn scanner interface that quickly puts most of the scanner's functions at your fingertips.

For a little more money, look into the Epson Stylus Scan 2500. It prints, scans, and makes copies, printing at 1400×720 dpi and scanning at 600×2400 at 36 bits. The extra printing and scanning resolution make your pictures look better at both ends of the process. The Epson Stylus Scan 2500 has a very easy-to-use interface and a broad, well-rounded software package.

▶ **High-Quality Photo Scanning with Affordability**—If you want near-professional scanning quality for not that much more money, look into the Epson Perfection series. Scanning at 1200×2400 dpi, the Epson Perfection provides a true "bump up" in quality compared to less expensive scanners. The scanner comes with a transparency adapter for scanning transparencies and Adobe Photoshop 5 LE for professional image editing power. Also check out the HP ScanJet 690 Cse. It scans photos, transparencies, standard documents up to 8.5×14 inches and comes with the full version of Adobe Photoshop 5. Though both of these scanners cost twice as much as the more budget-minded scanners, the results will show in the finished product.

▶ **Saving Contact Information**—Business card scanners, such as the Seiko Smart Business Card Reader, are small devices that read business cards and retain the contact information for saving into a palmtop or laptop computer, and organized by a Personal Information Manager for later use. They are single-purpose devices that perform a single task and do it well. Not only is contact information extracted and stored by the scanner, but the business cards are saved as complete images as well. This allows you to save each card intact and later view each by "flipping" through the collection of all card images.

▶ **Working Exclusively with Photos**—If you are only going to be scanning photos, and you'd like those photos to have a bit more quality than the average scanned image, look into a film scanner. They scan canisters of film quite conveniently, at a resolution far higher than the average 600×1200 dpi flatbed scanner.

Why is So Much Resolution Necessary?

You may recall from Chapter 2 that scanning at 150 dpi is most often sufficient for everyday scanning. Why, then, am I recommending that you buy a scanner with at least 600 dpi? Because you never want to push a machine to its limits. You want a scanner that is capable of scanning *well above* what you are asking of it. For example, when scanning for OCR, it's essential that you get a very good 300 dpi scan, with as few errors as possible. A scanner that can scan 300 dpi at a maximum may not be up to the task of doing an exceptionally clean 300 dpi scan.

Additionally, you may have instances in which you want to scan close to 600 dpi, or even 1200 dpi. If you are scanning a wallet-sized photo and want to print it to a full 8.5×11-inch page, you'll need to scan that photo at a dpi that is at least four times its size (see Figure 3.1). That means you'll need to scan it at 600 dpi, not 150 dpi. Also, line drawings can—and should be—scanned at the printer's resolution. So if your printer can print 720 dpi, go ahead and scan your line drawings at 720 dpi.

Figure 3.1
To print an image at a size larger than its original size, it should be scanned at a higher dpi.

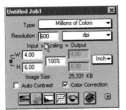

Recommendations

Table 3.1 should make shopping much easier for you. In the left column are the features that you may want. The center column includes some general points to keep in mind while you shop. The right column has recommendations for some actual scanners that fullfil the requirements listed in the left column. Please note that prices likely will have fallen since the time this book was published.

CHAPTER 3

Table 3.1
Recommendations for Different Scanner Requirements

Requirement	General Features	Specific Recommendations
Top-quality scans	A dynamic range (Dmax) rating of 2.1 or higher. 36-bit color depth or higher. True optical resolution of 600×1200 dpi or better	For good optical resolution and high dynamic range, the Epson Expression 800 ($699). Consider a scanner that does both reflective media (magazine pages and photographs) and transmissive media (film and transparencies) **Suggestions:** Agfa DuoScan ($679) Microtek Scanmaker 4 ($599)
Scanning photographs only	Film scanner for scanning rolls or cartridges of film	Film scanners that use Advanced Photo System (APS) film cassettes **Suggestions:** The Minolta Dimage Scanspeed or the Nikon Coolscan III, both of which are above $700 currently. More affordable film scanners are the HP PhotoSmart, the Olympus ES-10, and the Kodak Advantix, both at less than $400.
Convenient operation	Scanners with one-touch buttons on the front panel Scanners with intuitive and user-friendly software packages	Scanners that include a wide array of software packages, including photo editing, desktop publishing, OCR, e-mail and fax software if applicable. **Suggestions:** The Visioneer 5300 and 7200 have scan/e-mail/fax/copy buttons on the front, as does the HP 4200. Agfa and Epson scanners have especially easy-to-use software interfaces.
Scanning speed	USB or SCSI port Check whether the included SCSI card is a known manufacturer, such as Adaptec. Look for an advertised scanning speed of at least 10ms per line.	Just about any scanner with a USB port connection. USB scanners are generally as fast as SCSI-based scanners and far easier to set up. If speed is at all a priority, avoid parallel port scanners. **Suggestions:** Epson Perfection 636 ($299) Microtek ScanMaker X6EL ($199)

Continued on page 43

Table 3.1 continued from page 42

Requirement	General Features	Specific Recommendations
Text recognition, scanning many pages of text	Look for a scanner that features well-known OCR software, such as Caere OmniPage or Text Bridge. Look for a scanner with an affordable document feeder option.	**Suggestions:** UMAX Astra 2100 comes with Caere OmniPage LE, as does the Agfa SnapScan. Microtek Scanmaker X6EL and other Microtek scanners come with TextBridge. The Epson Perfection series comes with an excellent software selection. Microtek offers 10-page autodocument feeder add-ons for under $150. UMAX's Astra series offers 50-page feeders for under $300.
Ease of installation	Any scanner with a USB port will have a far less complex setup than a SCSI system. Additionally, USB scanners are much faster than scanners that connect via a parallel port. Look for name-brand software packages, such as Adobe, Caere, Ulead, and Text Bridge. Included software is usually listed on the box.	**Suggestions:** Agfa, Epson, and Visioneer scanners excel at quick setup and scanning right out of the box. Scanning options are presented on the screen in a clear, easy-to-interpret manner
Top photo editing software	All scanners include some type of photo editing packages. If you want near-professional editing power, look for Adobe PhotoShop LE, Corel Photopaint or Printhouse, or Ulead PhotoImpact.	**Suggestions:** Scanners above $300 tend to include higher-level photo editing software. Some scanners below $200 that include Adobe PhotoShop LE or Photo Deluxe are the Microtek Scanmaker series and the UMAX Astra series.
Fun projects, cards, banners, calendars	Look for scanners with software that automatically inserts your scanned pictures into ready-made projects.	**Suggestions:** The Canon FB series scanners have a decent resolution (600×1200 dpi) and very easy-to-use "family fun" software. HP Scanjets come with a CD full of many "get you started" projects. HP has a big marketing campaign that promotes a CD of projects (that all encourage you to buy more HP items).

Continued on page 44

CHAPTER 3

Table 3.1 continued from page 43

Requirement	General Features	Specific Recommendations
Low, low cost	A decent scanner with 600×1200 dpi resolution and 36-bit color depth can be bought for less than $100. You may not get USB connectivity or much of a software selection at that price. The ability to scan film, slides, or transparencies won't be found at that price range for a while. All scanner manufacturers are scurrying to release high-featured models hitting the $89 mark.	**Suggestions:** The Microtek Slimscan and ScanMaker X6 series are often found for less than $100, as are the Visioneer One-Touch models, the UMAX 2000U and the Mustek Plug & Scan EP scanners.
Scanning oversized material	Look for scanners with 8.5×14-inch, or even 11×17-inch, scan beds. These involve some quality trade-offs, however. Scanners with top-quality resolutions that also scan 11×17 inches or larger can run into the thousands of dollars.	Mustek A3 EP scans up to 11.7×17 inches. It only has a 300 dpi resolution, though, and connects via parallel port. Microtek ScanMaker X6EL scans up to 8.5x14 inches, as does the Agfa DuoScan series.
Minimal desk space	You have only a tiny corner on your desk for a scanner.	Look for sheetfed scanners to really save space. The Microtek SlimScan and Visioneer One-Touch series are particularly compact.

NOTE

You may notice that your scanner doesn't have an on/off button. The reason is that totally removing power from a scanner isn't advisable if even a slight chance exists that you may use it momentarily. If the bulb has to heat up all the way from a cold state (no power), you have to wait a few minutes before scanning, or suffer an image that might look a bit dull.

After you purchase a scanner, the following chapters will help you learn how to install and configure it, as well as use the software package that comes with it.

4

Installing and Configuring Your Scanner

In this chapter, we'll cover most aspects of setting up your scanner for the first time. If you have a SCSI scanner, you'll need a screwdriver and a steady hand. That's because the computer's cover must be removed and the SCSI card inserted. But if your scanner is a parallel port or USB type, no technical prowess is required.

We'll be discussing plugging in the scanner, installing drivers, the basic scanning interface, and setting up the photo editing program that came with your scanner. Most of the long, step-by-step instructions in this chapter relate exclusively to the SCSI installation process, so otherwise, the entire installation experience can be done with very quickly.

Installing a Scanner: An Overview

Installing a scanner has four steps. Your role in this setup process basically is to plug in the scanner to a power source and to the appropriate port, put the installation CD into your drive, and let the setup program do the rest. However, spending a few minutes understanding the installation process will make it all seem a bit less confusing and mysterious. Here's the short version of the requirements of proper installation:

▶ The scanner must be "recognized" by the computer

▶ Drivers must be installed

▶ A basic scanning interface must be made available

▶ Full-featured graphic editing and OCR software must be set up

NOTE

If your scanner is a small computer system interface (SCSI) device, you need to install the SCSI card, which is discussed in the section "Installing a SCSI Scanner," on page 52.

CAUTION

Read the manual. Yes, you've heard that one before, and you may be thinking "Why do I need to read the manual if this book will tell me how to install my scanner?" Well, the fact is that each type and make of scanner installs slightly differently. Some have critical startup procedures that must be followed exactly. This chapter is meant to supplement and add a little clarity to the installation process and make it easier to wade through the product manual jargon. Make sure you take a good look at the scanner's installation instructions before implementing the steps explained here.

The following sections go a bit deeper into each step.

"Recognizing" the Scanner

Scanner recognition is the process of getting the two electronic devices, the computer and the scanner, to acknowledge each other. Device recognition begins as soon as you plug in your scanner and turn on your computer. This recognition must happen for an important reason, described next.

Your computer sets aside specific data routes through which it can exchange information with other devices, such as scanners, printers, and Zip drives. Rules control which device gets to send data first, how many bytes of data can be sent at a time, how fast that data can be sent, and where that data should temporarily be stored. Your mouse, keyboard, CPU clock, hard drive, and any other devices all need access to your CPU, which acts somewhat like a traffic cop (see Figure 4.1). Because of this CPU access requirement, when you first plug in your scanner, a bit of handshaking and introduction has to occur. Essentially, your scanner says to your computer: "Hello, I am a scanner, and I am configured to use *this exact* memory address as my route." The computer may respond, "Well, that route is not available, but I can see that you are also configured to use *this other* memory address, which is available. I am ready to receive data from you along that route. Welcome aboard."

Figure 4.1
Data flows from the
scanner to the
computer via an
assigned port.

Next, new rules of the electronic transfer of data are established. The device is ready to send bits of data, and the computer is ready to receive them. Half the battle is already won.

Installing the Drivers

The next component of scanner installation is to set up the drivers. *Drivers* are small "libraries" of files that your scanner refers to in order to do its work. As previously mentioned, a scanner appropriates memory (RAM), hard drive space, and CPU power to get its job done. For example, as your scanner is scanning an image, it needs to display that image on your monitor. It does this by temporarily storing data on your hard drive, and getting permission to display that data by using the resources of your video card. After that process, the computer gives you the option to save the image permanently to your hard drive. Installing the software drivers clears the way for this to take place.

All scanners have a special set of drivers, called *TWAIN drivers.* While exploring your graphic editing software, you may see this term, TWAIN, in reference to running your scanner. TWAIN stands for *technology without an interesting name,* and represents a standard developed by scanner manufacturers to make sure that any TWAIN-compliant scanner you purchase will run correctly on any commercially available PC.

You simply need to know that the term TWAIN found in the menu of a software program means that you can open your scanner from within that program (see Figure 4.2).

Figure 4.2
The reference to TWAIN means that your scanner can be accessed from this program.

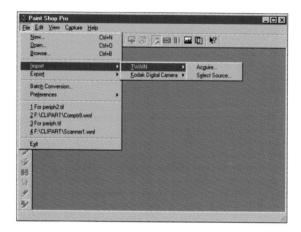

TIP

If you are planning to install several *peripheral* devices, such as writable CD-ROM drives, Zip drives, or digital cameras, an understanding of how drivers work may be essential if your computer setup becomes complicated. Peripheral devices–scanners, printers, external CD-ROM drives, and Zip drives, for example–are run by your computer but connect via an external port.

When your scanner is working, it creates temporary files to perform its many tasks. These files are created and later destroyed in a very specific sequence, according to what the scanner is doing at the moment. So, when you install your scanner, it sets up small "libraries" of files in your Windows/System directory. These are tiny but powerful programs that do specific, behind-the-scenes chores. It's quite elegant, really. Think of those Disney movies with the tiny creatures in the shadows creating elaborate feasts out of thin air, and you'll get the idea.

When you install your scanner, you can see the progress of these files being installed, by watching the blue "progress bar" display on your screen during installation. As the installation process progresses, the blue bar grows from left to right. Watch the words underneath as they quickly whiz by. Notice that many of the files being installed end with the file extension .dll (which stands for *dynamic link library*). Those are the driver files that actually run your scanner. If you ever need to *uninstall* your scanner, it may be hard to remove these files, which remain behind after the scanner is uninstalled and may conflict with other similar devices that you try to install later. Make sure, then, that you use the Add/Remove Programs feature to fully uninstall files left over from an uninstalled scanner's software.

NOTE

Computers today can become graveyards of unused software clutter, full of programs that you never intend to use, but you may feel you lack sufficient knowledge to uninstall them. If you are quite sure you are not going to use a particular program, you should fearlessly get rid of it. Unused programs not only take up hard drive space you could use for something meaningful, they prolong your computer's startup process. That's because the program must be identified and configured in the Windows System Registry when booting.

So, if you don't use it, uninstall it. Select Settings from the Windows Start menu and choose Control Panel. Click the Add/Remove programs icon and locate the program you want to uninstall. Then click Uninstall.

Setting Up the Basic Scanning Interface

The third step of scanner installation is setting up the basic scanning interface. Each scanner comes with a program that provides dialog boxes and toolbars to scan with (see Figure 4.3). For example, you'll see an interface for determining how large your image should be, how much resolution to scan with, and what color mode to use. You'll also see a screen where your image appears after it is scanned, as well as options for saving or editing the image. Microtek's ScanWizard or Agfa's ScanWise are examples of basic scanning interfaces.

Figure 4.3
A scanner interface from Paint Shop Pro. This interface would look the same if accessed from any graphics program.

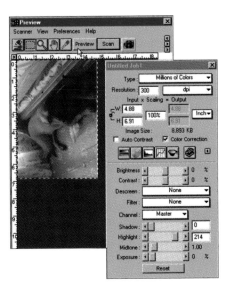

After installing your scanner and running the CD setup program, the basic scanning interface will be available from any program on your computer that recognizes TWAIN drivers. Some examples include Paint Shop Pro, Adobe Photoshop, Corel Photopaint, and even Word 97 or 2000. Most newer graphics, desktop publishing or word processing programs will probably have a menu option for scanning directly into that program. So, after basic scanner installation, you may be able to use your scanner without installing anything else.

To find out whether a particular application is TWAIN-enabled, try the following:

1. Open the program, and select File>Import (or Acquire or TWAIN).

2. Choose Select Source, and then choose Scanner.

3. Alternately, click the Edit menu in a program, and chose Insert, or Insert Picture. There should be an entry something like: From Scanner, or From TWAIN Source.

4. If you see such an option, you can scan directly from this program (the scanner interface, discussed later in this chapter) will appear directly in this application whenever you select a TWAIN or Scanner menu item.

Installing Software

Finally, your scanner CD more than likely contains installation instructions for a full-featured software program that not only displays your image but also allows you to edit it and provides options for resizing, cropping, altering its colors, and any other tinkering that may occur to you.

Although having the basic scanning interface available from a graphics program is all you really need to operate your scanner, scanner manufacturers tend to throw in the following types of programs:

▶ A limited edition of a more elaborate graphics editing program (such as Adobe Photoshop or PhotoDeluxe).

▶ An organizer that automatically retains all of your scanned documents indefinitely, presenting them to you in thumbnail views (such as Visioneer PaperPort).

▶ Optical character recognition (OCR) software for text recognition.

Automatic or Optional Installation

Your scanner CD may install these programs automatically, in which case you'll notice several new programs in your Windows Startup menu after you reboot your computer, according to the scanner installer's instructions. The scanner installer sets up all of these other programs to enhance the value of your purchase, providing lots of editing power at your fingertips, without requiring any more decisions on your part.

Some scanning setup programs automatically install only the basic scanning options (the TWAIN drivers and the simple scanning interface), letting you decide whether you want to install other extras provided on the CD. If the scanning installer lets you determine how many features to install, you have some decisions to make.

More May Not Be Better

To begin with, always keep in mind that more software on your computer is not necessarily a good thing. If you *already have* a favorite graphics editing program installed on your computer, then do you need another? Perhaps not—but make sure that it runs the scanner interface. To do so, open the program, click File, and see whether an Import or Acquire feature is available.

Unless you already have a favorite full-featured OCR program in mind, you probably should let the scanner installer set up its own OCR software. Optical recognition of text is almost never 100-percent accurate, so it may be wise to go with the OCR program packaged with your scanner, which quite possibly is the OCR software most suited for the scanner.

Before installing an application from the scanner CD, make sure you don't already own something similar. For example, there's no need to install the scanner CD's version of Adobe PhotoDeluxe if you already own a full-blown graphic editing program like Micrografx Picture Publisher or Photoshop. Just because it comes on the scanner CD doesn't mean there is some magic relationship between the two.

Scanner Installation Tips

The installation tips below are not meant to replace the manual that comes with your scanner but to make the process go a little more smoothly if you encounter snags and save you from the hassle of calling someone in technical support.

Before installing your scanner, consider how it should be positioned. Place it so that you can easily open the scanning bed cover and lay documents over the glass, adjusting them conveniently. You may notice that the scanner does not come with a long cable, especially if you bought a SCSI scanner. This is intentional, because a long cable distance between the computer and scanner will diminish the scanner's performance.

A Trouble-Free Installation

A trouble-free installation of your scanner depends on these factors:

▶ **Your port must be properly configured.** This is usually a no-brainer, but problems can arise. For example, if you've purchased a parallel port scanner that requires a high-speed parallel port (EEC or EPC specifications), and your computer cannot provide the high-speed parallel port connection, installation might be hampered until adjustments are made. Also, remember that if you've purchased a SCSI scanner, you first need to install the SCSI adapter card, and then you can worry about plugging in the scanner. Even USB port scanners can run into glitches. For example, occasionally a USB scanner will not initially be recognized until you "refresh" the port. This is done by opening the Windows Device Manager, clicking the USB port icon in the Device list, and clicking the Refresh button.

▶ **Drivers must be properly installed.** Drivers are automatically installed when you run your scanner's setup program (usually from the CD or floppy disk that came with your scanner). But some driver files refuse to install themselves if files by the same name are already on your computer. Or your computer may not be currently configured to recognize certain drivers. Driver installation usually is problem-free, but if not, read the Tip on drivers earlier in this chapter.

▶ **Your computer must meet your scanner's system requirements.** Refer to the previous chapter on hardware requirements. These requirements include sufficient free disk space, adequate RAM, and compliance with monitor and video card specifications.

SCSI, USB, and Parallel Port Scanner Installation

The port that your scanner uses often determines the ease of installation. This section looks at the installation issues that you are likely to encounter with each type of device.

Installing a SCSI Scanner

Let's begin with the hard stuff. If the scanner you purchased doesn't have a SCSI connection, you may skip this section. But if your scanner is a SCSI device, then read on. Again, note that this segment isn't meant to replace the instruction manual that came with your scanner; this simply is a guide to some basics. If you haven't yet installed your scanner, reading through this segment could save you a little grief.

If you've ever installed a sound or video card, installing a SCSI card will be quite similar. As mentioned in the previous chapter, a SCSI card is a bus. It provides extra pathways for SCSI-enabled devices to exchange information with your computer's other components. SCSI-powered scanners are some of the fastest, because they do not drain your computer's own internal memory resources to the extent that parallel port scanners do. They utilize the same type of slot that a sound card or video card would (see Figure 4.4).

Figure 4.4
SCSI cards are placed in slots set aside for devices such as video cards, sound cards, internal modems, and SCSI cards.

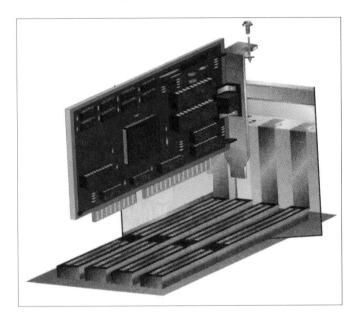

Installing a SCSI Card

To insert a SCSI card into a slot on your computer, you only need a screwdriver. Do the following:

1. Turn off the computer, unplug it from its power source, and then remove the computer casing. You'll probably need to unscrew four or six screws in the back that are holding the casing in place.

2. The slots should now be accessible. Your computer may have several types of slots, such as some PCI, API, and AGP slots. Check the interface to make sure that the card's point of contact *exactly matches* the intended slot.

3. Position the card over the slot so that there is no horizontal or vertical angle between the card and slot. The card will fit in the slot only if it is pushed in perfectly straight. When the card is in correct position, you'll notice that the screw hole on the bracket matches its corresponding hole on the computer case.

4. Even when correctly positioned, the card will require a good shove. It should fit very tightly. Pressure is required, but again, make sure the card is perfectly perpendicular with the card's interface.

5. Once inserted, wiggle the card in place, to make sure it is truly inserted correctly. Screw the slot screw into place, fastening the card into position.

6. Replace the cover and plug in the computer and all of its components.

A new interface slot is now available on the back of your computer. That's the connecter for the card that you inserted. Notice that it looks a bit like a parallel port. When it comes time to plug in your scanner (or plug your printer into the parallel port), make sure you do not confuse the two interfaces.

Powering Up the Scanner and Computer

Now you are ready to turn on the scanner and then the computer, by following these directions:

1. Plug one end of the scanner cable into the scanner, and the other end into the SCSI interface on the back of your computer. Then connect the computer's power cord.

2. If you have more than one SCSI device on your computer (such as a scanner, CD-ROM drive, and Zip drive), then carefully read the section in the scanner manual about assigning *SCSI device numbers.* In a SCSI environment, each device must be assigned a unique number, identifying it to the SCSI card. This number will be automatically assigned and should only be an issue if several SCSI devices are present.

3. Many scanners do not have an On button. When they are plugged in, they are on. The purpose of providing constant power to the scanner is to reduce the scanner warm-up time when you want to make a scan. If your scanner does have an On button, power it on now.

4. Turn on your computer.

5. Watch the startup sequence that appears on the screen. You'll see a brief notification that a SCSI card was found. This message will occur early in the bootup process, when there is only a bit of white text against the black screen. At this time, the computer is looking for installed components, before you see the green Windows Startup screen. You'll also see a message saying "No SCSI boot device found. Press Ctrl + A." You may ignore this message.

6. When Windows starts to load, you'll see a message "Windows has found new hardware and is looking for drivers to install for it." Next you'll see the Add New Hardware Wizard, as shown in Figure 4.5. You'll be prompted to tell Windows where the files can be found.

Figure 4.5
When Windows first detects the scanner, you'll see this message after booting your computer.

7. Insert into the appropriate drive the CD or floppy disk that came with your scanner, and then consult the scanner manual for further installation instructions. It's quite possible that Windows has already detected the CD and displayed the setup screen (for an example, see Figure 4.6). If not, more than likely you'll be required to open the CD in Windows Explorer and click the Setup icon. The installation program will take over at this point.

Figure 4.6
A typical scanner setup screen, displayed after inserting the CD that comes with your scanner.

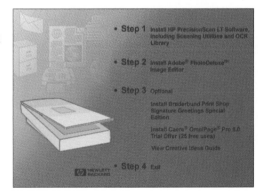

Installing a USB Scanner

To review the basic USB technology and appearance, see the previous chapter. You may recall that a USB-port-enabled computer can manage more than 100 external devices. The port transfers data quickly, most often with fewer *device conflicts* than parallel ports or SCSI devices. However, this section specifically discusses USB installation issues.

One main advantage of USB scanners is that, as a new technology is developed specifically for modern plug-and-play applications, your computer recognizes them as soon as they are plugged in to the USB port. You can usually proceed immediately to the driver, scanner interface, and advanced software installation. If you plug in your USB scanner and get no message that the device was "found," do the following:

1. Right-click the My Computer icon and select Properties.

2. In the System Properties dialog box, click the Device Manager tab.

3. Make sure an entry exists that reads universal serial bus controller.

4. Click the plus sign next to that entry. Look for two additional entries: one identifying the USB controller, and another that says USB Root Hub (see Figure 4.7).

    —If you do not see them, you need to enable USB through your computer's BIOS. Consult your CPU manual for how this is done.

    —If you do see them, click the Refresh button, close the dialog box, and reboot your computer with the scanner plugged in and turned on. After rebooting is complete, you should see a message that the scanner has been "found."

Figure 4.7
Device Manager will show USB port components. You can refresh your USB port from this screen.

Installing a Parallel Port Scanner

When you plug your scanner into your parallel port, nothing much happens. Insert the scanner installation CD into the drive and wait for the installation program to appear on the screen. (If nothing happens, see the section later in this chapter, "Working with the Installation CD.") Allow the installation program to install the necessary drivers and check the parallel port for the presence of a scanner. Here are some points to keep in mind:

▶ Normal setup for a parallel port scanner is to plug the scanner into the same port that your printer plugs into, momentarily unplugging your printer from the computer. You'll probably find sharing parallel ports to be inconvenient after a short time. There are two ways to solve the need for an additional parallel port:

—Purchase a parallel port *A/B switch,* a small box that allows two parallel port devices to be plugged into a single parallel port. A toggle switch activates one device or the other. These devices are available at most computer stores and are a breeze to set up.

—Install a second parallel port on your computer. The port must be configured (one port will be LPT1 and the other will be LPT2) and should be done by someone who has experience setting up the port configuration on computers. The process is similar to installing a SCSI card, but because of the need to match IRQ and addresses and such, the procedure can be frustrating.

▶ Even if your printer has a pass-through parallel port, do not try to use the printer at the same time as your scanner. Parallel ports cannot reliably support two data streams simultaneously passing through the port. Your print or scanning job will probably be lost, and your computer may freeze, forcing you to reboot. In particularly large scans, the scan may stop in the middle (freeze up and not continue scanning) if it is plugged into your printer's pass-through port. You may be forced to unplug the printer from the computer while you scan and not use the pass-through port at all.

Working with the Installation CD

Once your scanner is connected and detected by Windows, the CD that came with the scanner will continue to load all scanner-related software. Scanning setup software behaves in two basic ways:

▶ In some instances, after putting the scanner installation CD into the drive, it automatically loads the drivers for the scanner and then requests that you reboot your computer. After the computer is rebooted, you can then load the more advanced features.

▶ Some scanning software CDs load everything all at once, without any say-so from you, other than asking you to identify the drive and folder where all of the software should be installed.

CHAPTER 4

Software Installation Tips

As always, consult the manual that came with the scanner for details. However, here are some general tips to keep in mind:

▶ The CD that comes with your scanner should start as soon as you insert it into the CD-ROM drive. If it doesn't, open My Computer and right-click the CD icon. Select Open, and the CD's folder will open. Click the Setup icon (see Figure 4.8. The icon could also be called Install.exe). The installation program should start.

Figure 4.8
If your scanner software CD does not start automatically, open it through My Computer, and click the Setup icon.

▶ If you are given the choice regarding what software to install, don't feel compelled to install everything. Installing too many programs on your computer can slow down bootup time. Your startup menu can also grow to a ridiculous length, requiring you to scroll down to view all of your programs, and making you wish that you'd been a bit more selective. More is not necessarily better. For example, if you already have a good graphics editing program, you may not need another one, unless you are in the mood for experimenting. If you do "overinstall" and decide you don't need all the programs, don't forget that you have the Windows Add/Remove Programs feature available in the Control Panel.

If you decide later to install some of the software from the installation CD, you need not repeat the scanner installation process. The following steps usually work when you want to install only a portion of a CD's contents, without activating the autostart Setup program.

1. Put the CD in the drive, and if the Installation screen appears, click Close or Exit.

2. Right-click the CD icon in My Computer and select Open.

3. Look through the list of folders for one that more than likely contains the program you want to install (for example, to install Caere OCR software, look for a folder called OCR, or Caere. To install Extensis PhotoEnhance, look for a folder called Extensis or Photo tools).

4. After you locate the right folder, right-click it and click the Setup icon. Only the specific program that you clicked will install, not the entire scanner installation program from scratch.

Limited Edition Software

Many of the programs that come on the scanner installation CD will be limited editions, "special" or trial versions of the full-blown programs. These programs often don't have all the features of the full version. For example, the limited edition of Adobe Photoshop found on some scanner installation CDs does not have color calibration and registration features and other high-end tools. Some limited edition programs don't have a full tutorial or don't include templates and forms designed to get you started quickly.

Scanner Registration

At the end (or occasionally at the beginning) of the installation process, you'll be requested to provide your name, address, and other contact information to register the scanner. Doing so may make it easier to receive technical support for your scanner, should a problem arise, and speed the return process, should you need to invoke the warranty. You aren't required to register immediately, even though the registration message appears with a good deal of urgency. It's often difficult to exit Registration without completing it. Registration is strongly encouraged by the manufacturer to "lock in" your purchase. However, if you think that you may not keep the scanner, you can always fill out the information later if you decide to keep it.

Conducting a Test Scan

After you install the scanner and the software, make sure all is well by doing a test scan. Although the process of scanning is covered in the next chapter, here's how to do one simple scan to make sure all systems are go.

1. Open the scanning interface. To do so, do one of the following:

    —Start the scanning program that was installed with your scanner. (Click the scanner icon that appears in the lower-right part of the Windows desktop).

—Start a scanning session from within a graphics editing program, such as Paint Shop Pro (Select File>Acquire>Source and then click the scanner name).

—In either case, the scanning interface should appear.

2. Make sure the scanner is on, open the scanner cover, and place a picture to scan face down on the surface. Since you are only verifying operation, scan only a small picture. You'll notice an arrow pointing to the corner where the picture should be placed (Figure 4.9). Make sure the corners are even with the sides of the scanner glass.

Figure 4.9
Most flatbed scanners provide this arrow as a guide, letting you know where the scanned document should be placed.

3. Slowly place the scanner cover back over the glass. If you move too quickly, you'll create a burst of air that may push the picture off-center.

4. All scanner software interfaces have a Preview button that enables you to check the position of the image and crop the scanned area so that only the image itself is scanned and not the entire scan bed. We'll discuss all the scanning tools in the following chapter, but for now, we'll shorten the process and simply verify that the scanner is working.

5. Leave the resolution and color mode values at their default levels.

6. Click the Preview button with the mouse. You'll hear the scanner operation begin, and a bar will appear on the screen, marking the progress of the Preview.

7. When the Preview is finished, your picture will appear on the screen. A rough scan of the image appears, displayed as a guide to see whether the image needs to be repositioned before final scanning. The image will not look particularly clear at this time. Only when you open the image in your graphics editing program will it look like something worth paying for.

8. Click the Scan button with the mouse. If you hear the machine operating, see a progress bar, and see the image again appear on the screen (it won't look any different than the Preview did), then you can be sure that the scanner is working. Installation was successful.

Scanner Installation Troubleshooting

If the test scan does not work, or if other problems occur during installation, you can use the following troubleshooting tips to help you determine and fix the source of the problem:

▶ If installation suddenly aborts partway through, make sure you have enough free hard drive space. The scanner box should report how much free space is needed. To insure correct installation, you should have at least an additional 50MB above that stated amount.

▶ If the scanned picture looks grainy and blotchy, make sure your computer is set to display 65,000 colors (High Color mode) or more, preferably 16.7 million colors (also known as True Color mode). To verify this, right-click your desktop and select Properties. Click Settings. In the bottom-left corner, check the Colors drop-down menu (see Figure 4.10). If you see 256 colors or less, click the drop-down menu and select 16.7 million, or True Color mode. You may be prompted to restart your computer. After you change the color mode, you'll notice that your grainy picture looks better. You won't have to rescan your image. The image itself is fine; the viewing mode simply limited how it was displayed.

Figure 4.10
To view and change your computer's Color mode, right-click your desktop, choose Properties, and then choose the Settings tab.

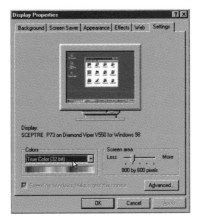

▶ If you try to open the scanner interface and get a message that the scanner is not present (or "not found"), check cable connections and power. If those are in order, then reboot your computer. Sometimes a hard reboot is needed for Windows to detect the scanner, clearing the parallel port or USB port of old data or enabling the SCSI adapter.

▶ If you are using a SCSI scanner, make sure no device conflicts are present. SCSI devices must be assigned a unique number (0 through 7). Look in the Windows Startup menu for a SCSI setup panel (something similar to Figure 4.11). The SCSI setup menu will have an option for choosing a number. For more details, check your scanner manual, specifically the section on SCSI connections.

CHAPTER 4

Figure 4.11
Some SCSI devices have a setup screen for assigning a unique number, especially major brands like Adaptec. You'll not need to invoke a SCSI Id interface unless you have more than one SCSI device.

▶ If you are using a parallel port scanner, printer activity can interfere with your scan. With some printers, even previous print jobs can cause the parallel port to not recognize the scanner, because some printers don't "give up" the parallel port after they are done printing. The port incorrectly detects that a printer is still present, and thus won't recognize the scanner. The solution is to reboot your computer. Additionally, there may be a "fix" for this problem on the Web. Glitches like the one described above are often solved with a small downloaded software "patch" (like a patch for a leaky bike tire). Go to either the scanner or the printer company's Web site and look in the technical support section for a solution to this problem. If there is no patch, there may be a document describing the problem and a solution.

▶ When scanning, hard drive space is a big issue. Scanners will not work well unless at least 10 percent of your hard drive space is free. If you have a hard drive less than 500MB, you'll need more like 20 percent free.

▶ If your scanner is offline (it is turned off, or you've removed it for the time being), and you notice that your mouse is not moving smoothly across the screen or the keyboard ignores your typing, and then your typed words suddenly appear, the reason could be the following. Sometimes, when your system expects to see a scanner inline and up and running, it will send an electronic message out to "search" for that device. While it searches, computer operation can temporarily freeze up. Not finding the scanner, the computer essentially says "Oh, well, I'll try again later." Then, in a few seconds, it sends out its "search" prompt again, temporarily freezing computer activity. The solution? When you take your scanner offline, do it in such a way that the computer knows what you are up to. For example, click the scanner icon at the bottom right of the Windows desktop, if there is one, and select Close; or open the scanner program from your Windows Startup menu and select the Going Offline option, or something similar.

▶ When installing a parallel port scanner, you may have to uninstall older printers first. Some printers, especially older HP 600 series printers (and a few Lexmarks, I've noticed) do not "give back" the parallel port after they are done printing, which would allow your scanner to use the port. Additionally, some printers permanently reserve certain memory addresses set aside for the parallel port (they are supposed to hold onto these memory regions only while printing, not keep them permanently). Hence, if you notice that your parallel port scanner freezes while scanning (or if suddenly the printer that has worked so well for you freezes while printing), go to the Printers menu (from the Windows Start menu, select Settings>Printers), right-click any printer you are not using, and select Delete. Doing this will remove that printer from your system and free up resources it was hogging. Reboot your computer and try scanning again.

Returning the Scanner to the Store

Everyone makes regrettable purchases, which is nothing to be ashamed of. Just take the scanner back. Everyone does it. Why shouldn't you? Perhaps you've purchased a scanner that is very powerful but difficult to set up. Go ahead and return it, and instead purchase a scanner with simple one-touch features, such as the Visioneer series or the HP 4200. Or perhaps you were a bit too penny-wise and bought a scanner with a mere 300 dpi resolution. If the images are not as good as you expected, take it back and make sure you get a scanner with at least 600×600 dpi, with 36-bit color depth. Or if you bought a scanner that doesn't include adequate software, and perhaps you did the math and realized that the extra amount you'd have to spend to go out and buy the necessary software would greatly exceed the price of the scanner you *should have bought,* then exchange it for that other scanner. Live and learn. Always hang on to the receipt.

Now that you have your scanner up and running, Chapter 5 will explain how to select the right software for your scanner and even download it from the Internet so you can get a taste of what kind of programs may be right for you—without spending money unnecessarily.

5

What Software is Right for You?

Setting up your scanner is only half the battle. What do you want to accomplish with your new scanner, and what's the best way to meet that end? In this chapter, we'll talk about choosing the right software to meet your needs.

What Kind of User Are You?

The scanner is a tool. Like a Swiss army knife, it can be used for many tasks. Your scanner can be an artistic tool, an office tool, a tool of imagination, or a tool simply to reduce drudgery. Think for a moment what you bought this thing for. Then, read through this chapter and determine what suits your goals.

Let's start by putting some of those amorphous purchasing intentions into words. You probably bought your scanner for one or more of the following reasons:

▶ You want to scan family and personal photos, create computerized photo albums, and then e-mail them to friends and family, or to include personal photos in other "fun" projects. You have no interest in becoming a scanner expert or in learning all there is to know about photography, lighting, or other highly technical aspects of creating electronic documents. You just want to have fun.

▶ You want to create brochures, good-looking postcards, calendars, or perhaps make a Web site with some of your scanned handiwork. You'd like to learn enough to give your scanned work some polish, invest a little time learning photo editing, and be able to create a nicely designed document. Maybe someday you'll start a business incorporating graphic design skills. Nonetheless, you have not quit your day job. This definitely is still a hobby.

▶ You have a business that requires scanning documents, scanning a logo, or perhaps scanning photos of a product line, and these scans have to look businesslike. Still, you don't have all year to become a graphic design artist. Although you are not trying to make a splash in the art world, the documents you create with your scanner need to look professional.

▶ You want to scan text, such as household or business documents (perhaps tax-related records or other financial records). You'd feel more secure if these papers didn't exist only on paper. Your scanner is meant to help you accomplish that.

▶ You are writing a thesis, term paper, or some other lengthy paper document. Or perhaps you want to design a magazine or create a book with your own scanned illustrations or graphic artwork. In any event, you are making something people will read on paper, and you want your scans to play a role in it.

▶ Your office requires some scanning, copying, and faxing, and if all of this can conveniently be accomplished with one machine, then that's what your office wants.

▶ Art and photography are your life. The scanner is one tool to help you realize artistic creations. You want to learn the ins and outs of digital design and are interested in this stuff only if it makes you a better artist.

How Much Time and Patience to Invest

Once you pick a type of application that becomes your scanner's mainstay, how long will it take for you to truly feel you are accomplishing something? This section talks about the scanner software *learning curve*.

Assess Your Needs

How much time do you want to spend mastering scanner skills? Learning the essentials about a computer peripheral device like a scanner can take up more evenings than you probably care to imagine. Keep your goals in mind, and remember the following:

▶ If you buy a program that has lots of features, expect to spend many evenings and weekends mastering it. Powerful programs that can do a zillion things tend to be more complex. Often, people new to the software world will initially spend lots of money on a program, believing part of what they are paying for is ease of use and convenience. That is not so. Higher-priced programs are feature-rich and geared to the professional who needs versatility and power.

▶ If you are a beginner, you don't need to spend lots of money on a program unless you are sure that a feature you require is missing from a less-expensive package. For example, if you know that you'll need to adjust text size repeatedly during the course of a project, then you need a versatile program such as CorelDRAW. If you know you need prepress options, such as printing registration bars, calibration marks, and proof sheets, then you may need Adobe Photoshop or something similar. Otherwise, an entry-level graphics program costing less than $100 should suit you just fine.

▶ Be selective and keep coming back to how a particular program will enrich your life, not how many free features you can tack on to your computer. Since I will be leading you into the cornucopia of free software, I must warn you how easy it is to go a little crazy. Don't download everything just because you can.

Picking the Right Program

Your job is to strike a balance between what you want a program to do for you and the amount of time and patience that you have available. You'll have to decide whether you want a program that can't do everything possible or whether you are willing to learn the ins and outs of an extravagant piece of software.

Table 5.1 on page 75 identifies at least two programs for each type of application previously described. I'll point out at least one complex and full-featured product for those of you who want to learn all the ropes and at least one program for those of you whose needs are fairly simple and who just want to get up and running quickly. From looking at the table, you may very well determine that the software that came with your scanner is exactly what you need at this stage. Why spend money if you don't have to? Programs that often are included with scanning software are designated with an asterisk.

Almost every program mentioned in the table directly supports your scanner. That means you can scan an image by using the program's own menu. Likewise, almost every program is downloadable from the Web as trialware. Although some of the products mentioned are not exactly household names and may not be available on the shelves of all software stores, that shouldn't deter you from trying them out. Many of the programs mentioned will be explored in detail in later chapters.

Program Types and Recommendations

Now that you are focused on what you want to use your scanner for, this section looks at a rough outline of the types of programs you may want to use. We'll look at three types of software that make nice companions to your scanner: image editing, publishing and design, and file management programs.

Image Editing Software

Let's take a glance at some image manipulation and editing programs. We'll look at basic and advanced photo editing and at family-fun, project-based programs.

Basic Photo Editing Programs

These are programs that help you resize, rotate, crop, sharpen, and clean up your pictures. They are simple, have only a few menus, and can be learned in a few minutes. They also are a tool for *converting file formats,* which can be necessary for sharing images with others who want to edit them or for posting them on the Web. Figure 5.1 shows Paint Shop Pro, an excellent, easy-to-use photo editing program.

If you are interested in the simple task of preparing photos for the Web or in cleaning up images for an online photo album, brochures or cards, consider Paint Shop Pro.

Figure 5.1
One of the very best basic photo editors: Paint Shop Pro

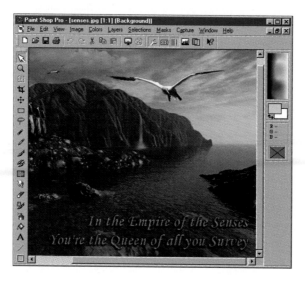

Advanced Photo Editing Programs

These programs do all the tasks previously described, as well as create montages by layering and pasting images one over another or by applying special effects filters. They give you more editing control, enabling you to add artistic text or soften the edges of one picture before combining it with another. Advanced photo editing programs prepare your photo for professional printing and can create an exact outline (called a mask or a selection) around a precise segment of your image, making it easy to edit one segment of your image while leaving the rest untouched. Figure 5.2 shows Adobe Photoshop, the world's most popular advanced photo editing program.

Consider Photoshop if you want to manipulate images as a graphics professional and perhaps make your living as a graphic designer.

Figure 5.2
The main Photoshop screen.

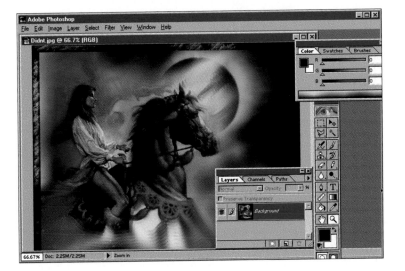

Fun and Project-based

These programs create cards, posters, banners, and calendars. The resulting documents are usually very colorful and stylized. Fun programs make it easy to turn your pictures into theme-based projects for major holidays and events and are usually not very hard to use. Text and background art are automatically added to your document, and the photos you scanned are just one element in the project being designed. Some will lead you by the hand, asking you simple questions about what you want to create, requiring only that you click Yes or No. You are encouraged to experiment, by adding special effects to the text, by changing background artwork, or even by adding a sound to your project if it is going to be sent as an e-mail or posted online. Figure 5.3 shows Broderbund's The Print Shop Deluxe 6, a behemoth, eight-CD family publishing center.

Buy a program like this if your main goal is to have fun with your family and make holiday and household-event centered projects.

Figure 5.3
The Print Shop Deluxe 6 has everything for any type of family-oriented printing project.

Desktop Publishing Programs

Now we'll glance at a page design program like Microsoft Publisher. Desktop publishing programs are used to make books, magazines, brochures, and other paper documents in which you want control over each page's appearance. They allow you to change the way your words appear paragraph by paragraph, customize headlines, add various kinds of artwork to each page, and insert your scanned photos into any page of your document. Microsoft Publisher is an easy-to-use desktop publishing program.

Buy Microsoft Publisher or a similar program if you want to make semi-professional documents and do lots of things with paper creativity.

Word Processing Programs

Word processing programs are used most often for essays, for thesis, research, and term papers, or for any type of document in which the text on each page looks relatively the same. Unlike desktop publishing programs, which concentrate on making adjustments on each page, such as for a magazine or a brochure, word processing programs focus more on how the text flows uniformly from page to page. Some word processing programs enable you to scan your photos right into the document.

Word processing programs are best for thesis papers, essays, reports, monographs, manuscripts, and product manuals.

Digital Art Programs

Digital art programs aim to simulate real-life artistic media, creating images with realistic brush strokes, pencil sketches, or charcoal drawings, enabling you to create on a backdrop that looks like a real canvas rather than a flat computer screen. These programs manipulate your photo to appear "painterly." You can paint over your photo with your mouse, leaving dabs of paint, chalk, or watercolor designs beneath each brush stroke, while the photo still resembles what you started with. Figure 5.4 shows Fractal Design Painter, the premiere natural media digital art program.

Purchase Painter, or perhaps Corel PhotoPaint or Micrografx Picture Publisher, if you want to develop fine art skills with your scanned photos.

CHAPTER 5

Figure 5.4
Fractal Design Painter provides imaginative and truly unique natural media painting tools.

Illustration and Design Programs

Illustration and design programs actually provide drawing tools, enabling you to manipulate and transform shapes and text into true works of art. It's common to combine a very precisely drawn illustration with a scanned image, using, for example, an illustration program to design a backdrop for a photograph. Figure 5.5 shows CorelDRAW, the most popular program for creating artistic text and precision shapes.

Use illustration and design programs if you will be creating logos, projects with very precise artistic text, and artwork that will be resized for various uses.

Figure 5.5
CorelDRAW can edit illustrations and even resize text easily.

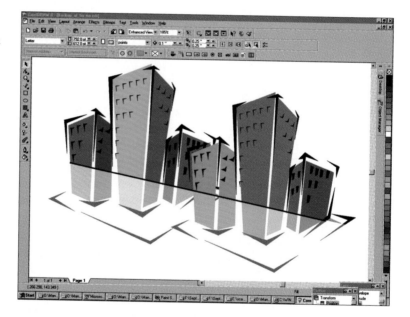

Web Site Design

Perhaps you bought your scanner to help create images for your Web site, using either your existing photos or photos you have yet to take. Either way, to get them up on the Web, you need your scanner.

Document Management Software

Your scanner also provides you with a way to store documents and files electronically. This software can save images of important documents (like birth certificates or mortgage info) or convert them into text that you can edit directly on your computer (recipes, bills, and the like). This section introduces the different categories of document storage software.

OCR Programs

Optical character recognition (OCR) programs convert your scanned text into text that you can use in a word processing program. Normally, when you scan text, you cannot edit it. It's just a photograph of words that you can't change. But when you apply OCR to your scanned text, it becomes *editable.* You can add words, fix spelling, use new fonts, or otherwise change the text any way you like. Figure 5.6 shows the Caere OmniPage Scan Wizard for extracting text.

Figure 5.6
Caere OmniPage trial version is an OCR program that comes with many scanners.

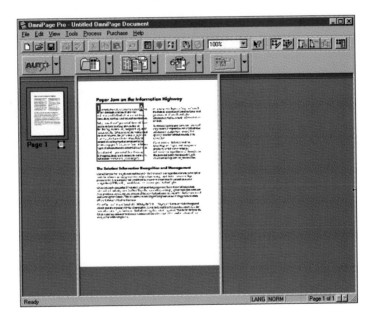

Faxing and Copying Programs

Faxing and copying programs enable you to make a printed copy of a document and then e-mail or fax it from within your scanner with a single mouse click. These programs provide a convenient interface for quickly taking care of these tasks.

Thumbnail and Archiving Software

You've probably noticed that all the files on your computer are visually represented by small icons. These icons identify the file type. For example, Setup files appear as a small computer, and Excel documents show a small spreadsheet. Thumbnail programs turn your picture icons into small representations of the picture itself. That way, you can know what the picture is just by glancing at the icon, as shown in Figure 5.7.

Figure 5.7
Cerious Software's ThumbsPlus is a popular, well-thought-out thumbnail program that helps you to keep track of all your pictures.

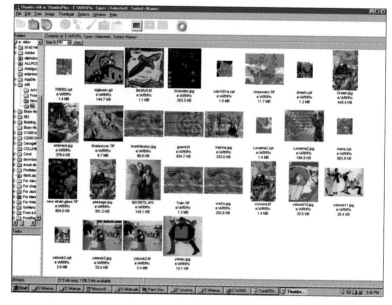

Table 5.1
Categories of software uses and sample programs suitable for those needs.

Software Category	Fast and Easy	Complex and Powerful
Photo Editing	Jasc Paint Shop Pro Adobe PhotoDeluxe* Ulead PhotoExpress STOIK Software Picture Man* PictureWorks HotShots*	Adobe Photoshop Corel PHOTO-PAINT Micrografx Picture Publisher
Fun Projects	InSoft Media's Family Archive Amber Softwork's PictureImage Nouiehed's SlideSmith 2 Fujimiya's Morpher Broderbund's The Print Shop Signature Greetings*	Broderbund Print Shop Deluxe 6 STOIK's PM Stitch Creator (turns scanned photos into stitching patterns)
Special Effects Editing	Adobe Photoshop Corel PHOTO-PAINT Kai's PhotoGoo Ulead Cool 360 STOIK Software Picture Man Cyberware Sinthetics 3D Photo 4.1	Auto FX PhotoGraphic Edges Photo/Graphic Patterns XAOS Tools plug-in collections
Word Processing	Corel WordPerfect Microsoft Word	Micro Vision Word Express DC Al Coda Editor Pro
Desktop Publishing	Microsoft Publisher Pressworks Draw Poster Software's Draw It! Broderbund The Print Shop Broderbund Press Writer*	Adobe Pagemaker Adobe InDesign Creative Stars Page Focus Pro Micro Vision Word Express
Digital Art	Corel PhotoPaint XAOS Tools Paint Alchemy (Photoshop plug-in)	MetaCreations Painter Right Hemisphere Deep Paint (Photoshop plug-in)
OCR	NewSoft OCR* Presto! Page Manager* Caere OmniPage* Cognitive Technology Cuneiform	Presto Page Genie Presto! Page Manager GmbH Archivista
Family Fun	Broderbund Print Master Adobe PhotoDeluxe Ulead PhotoExpress Ulead PhotoImpact	Broderbund Print Shop Deluxe 6 G & A Imaging PhotoRecall Deluxe
Faxing and Copying	KlickSoftCopyShop 2000 JetSoft Art-Copy	
Business Applications	Cam Development Business Card Designer Plus	EZX Corp. E-Z Forms Maker Electrasoft 32-bit Fax
Web Graphic Design	TriVista 3D Image Scene CyberView Image American Online AOLPRESS Adobe PageMill Sausage Software Hot Dog Pro Gameni Production's GIF Movie Gear Steve Jackson Web Media Publisher Pro Diji's Album Editor Ulead's Web Razor	G & A Imaging PhotoRecall Deluxe TriVista Ultimate Online Photo Gallery Microsoft Front Page Macromedia Dream Weaver
Thumbnail and Archive	Jasc Media Center Paint Shop Pro "Browse" Feature Cerious Software's ThumbsPlus	Ulead PhotoExplorer O'Neil Software Digital Photo Librarian GmbH Archivista

CHAPTER 5

Downloading Software from the Web

The World Wide Web allows small companies and even individuals with great ideas to hawk their wares based on the quality of their product alone. Even without big marketing budgets, the Web allows the word to spread on good software simply by merit alone.

And since every software entrepreneur needs exposure, and every one of them seems to have determined that the Web is *the* place to obtain it, most make a working demo of their products available for you to try out for free. Each of these entrepreneurs hopes that if you try the product, you will buy it. Software companies will often give you the keys to their most valuable products in hopes of piquing your interest. The idea of giving something away is far less onerous than the thought of missing a huge potential consumer base, which is what the Web represents.

So, if you have the patience and computer capacity required to download large files, you can try out dozens of full-featured programs that could end up transforming your scanner into the most important feature of your PC. After you have your scanner up and running, you simply need an Internet connection to gain access to just about any kind of scanner software tool. Here's how to find those tools.

To use them, you must have an Internet connection, a Web browser, and a basic understanding of what occurs when you access a Web site. We'll discuss how to locate and download files, "unpack" and install programs after you download them, determine the limitations of the programs that you download, and, finally, uninstall the programs that you decide not to keep.

Before Downloading Software…

We need to kick off with a few "buyer beware" caveats: a heads-up about viruses and the need to be able to uninstall the software, if you decide you don't want it.

Surf-Protected

The Web sites we discuss in this chapter are well traveled, and the software recommended has been tried and tested; nonetheless, it's always a good idea to have antivirus software up and running before you make a habit of downloading. Protect yourself with one of the many commercially available antivirus programs that can be found at any software store. You can also freely download trial versions of Symantec or McAfee anti-virus products from the Web.

Know Your Way Back

Gracefully uninstalling a program isn't always easy. Most programs that you're likely to come across in the collections of freebies that we'll be talking about include an automatic uninstall feature. This can be important, because some programs leave little unwelcome reminders of their existence after you remove them. They will duplicate or replace shared files used by other programs on your computer or leave information in your Registry database that simply increases your computer's bootup time, even after they are uninstalled. For this reason, you may want to install a program that monitors all the new programs that you load on and allows for a thorough, clean uninstall process.

What This Section Covers

The following are the skills that you'll need to make use of Internet resources:

▶ **Locating programs that you may want to try**—Before you go to the trouble to download a program, let alone install it, you'd like to know as much as you can about it. You want to carefully evaluate the terms of use. Is it truly free or free for only a few weeks? Is the program fully functional or has some important feature been disabled? Most importantly, is this program right for you?

▶ **Downloading the program itself**—Most often, a downloaded program will consist of a single *executable* or *zipped* file. You'll determine where on your hard drive the file should be stored and how to retrieve it later when you want to install it.

▶ **Installing the program**—*Downloading* the file isn't the same as *installing* it. Most often, installation requires only the click of a mouse. However, when you install a program, new files are being written to your hard disk and, in some cases, important *system files* are being added, updated, or even replaced. It's not entirely clear where they are going or what their purpose is. So, it's good to know enough about that process to make sure it's reversible, and that it doesn't end up causing harm.

▶ **Types of files**—Roughly speaking, files on your computer can be classified as follows—program files, which provide instructions for programs to carry out their work; data files, which contain information used by the programs; and system files, which provide the backbone of your computer's operations.

▶ **Uninstalling the program**—If you decide that a program isn't right for you, don't just let it sit on your computer, taking up space. Get rid of it.

CHAPTER 5

Downloadable Software Types

You should know a little bit about the different types of downloadable software you may run across on the Internet:

Freeware

▶ Freeware programs do not require that you pay for them, ever. Freeware programs range from screensaver creation tools and font collections on up to full operating systems like Linux. Often, freeware programs perform simple tasks in a painless, uncomplicated manner with a simplicity neglected by larger companies. For example, freeware personal information managers can be organized and uncluttered, while similar products released by larger companies can have so many features that the user is often confused.

▶ Most often, basic freeware graphics programs usually do one or two things well. They could, for example, be good at recoloring photographs or turning your photo into a hyperlink that you can post on your Web site. Basic freeware programs are usually small and utilitarian.

▶ Some simple, convenient freeware programs are created and distributed by the programmer simply for the satisfaction of making something that works and that could potentially become known worldwide. Other freeware is distributed for the purpose of creating an awareness of commercially available products.

Trialware

▶ Often called evaluation versions of software, trialware is downloadable software that you can try out for a limited time. After the trial period, you must uninstall the program or purchase it.

▶ Software companies and developers are increasingly moving their products to this model so that consumers can install their product, begin using it, and decide whether they want to purchase it. This concept of test driving software has fueled the growth of many products and enables you to shop packages before committing to a specific one. Generally, the trialware that you are invited to download will have almost all the features of the version you'd buy in the store. Sometimes, the trialware version will exclude "extra" features, such as clip art and template collections, but for the most part, you'll get the real thing.

Commercial Software

▶ Commercial software products can also be purchased and downloaded from many Web sites. Commercial products require you to purchase the software online (usually using a credit card), and then you will download the software to your computer. Many software developers allow you to download the trial version of the software for free and then provide you with the option to purchase the commercial version on their Web site.

CAUTION

Unless you've obtained permission or a license agreement with the software owner, you are not allowed to sell or market a free program. Selling your favorite shareware program without permission from the author is never allowed, even if you can't find anything in the program directly prohibiting it.

Where's the Manual?

Trialware and freeware often come with documentation built into the software's help system or separate electronic documentation. Occasionally, little or no documentation is provided and you are on your own to figure things out for yourself. The need for comprehensive and printed instructions is one big incentive to buy the program outright. Also, if you call technical support and ask for assistance, you probably will be asked for your product serial number or registration ID. Since you are a trial user, you have no such thing, and many software companies will not provide tech support for unregistered users (people who haven't paid for the product yet).

To locate written documentation that may have come with the software, open the folder where the product is installed, and look for any files that end with a .doc, .txt, or .pdf file extension. If there is no set of documentation readily apparent, the software usually has a built-in Help system which covers all of the major features of the product. To access the Help system, click the Help menu, usually located in the upper-right corner of the menu bar.

NOTE

The Adobe corporation has developed the "portable document format," which can be read on just about any computer, Mac or PC. These documents (identified by their .PDF extension) are created by a popular program called Adobe Acrobat and are independent of any word processing or desktop publishing program. Computers that do not have Word, WordPerfect, or any similar software can still read Adobe Acrobat files. Anyone with a computer can read a PDF file simply by downloading a free, ever-available Adobe Acrobat Reader (get it at **http://www.adobe.com**). PDF files can be created from just about any program, such as Word, Pagemaker, or Ventura Publisher, and allow the author of the document to save the file in a universally available format that is cross platform.

Often, software manufacturers include electronic versions of their manuals, saved in PDF format, with the trial versions of their software. You can read the manual, print it out, and refer to it easily when using the software product.

How the Trial Period Is Enforced

So, what's to prevent someone from continuing to use a trialware program indefinitely and never pay anything for it?

Software manufacturers often institute a *trial period* for programs that you download. These can last anywhere from 15 to 60 days, most often somewhere in the middle. After this trial period, you are supposed to buy the program or uninstall it.

Trial periods can be enforced in a number of ways:

▶ The program simply stops working.

▶ Certain important features of the program stop working.

▶ The software comes with the Save feature disabled. You can create something with the software but cannot save it to disk. Nor can you print it or copy the creation to the Windows Clipboard for use in another program.

▶ You receive messages on your screen reminding you that the trial period is over—and asking why you haven't sent your check.

▶ Pictures of the programmer's wife and children are posted on the screen, appealing to your sense of moral fairness (I'm not kidding).

Finding Good Software on the Web

This section explores some Web sites so that you can see what software is available, learn how to find out as much as you can about a program before downloading it, and learn how to download a file to your computer.

Generally, you can download from two types of sites:

▶ **Company sites.** Companies such as Adobe, Jasc, and MetaCreations encourage you to download trialware right from their own sites.

▶ **Shareware collection sites.** These are the sites that we explore in this book. Each of these sites has grouped together thousands of programs and categorized them into a searchable database. You are free to browse and see what's available or to type a keyword to locate a specific program.

Recommended Sites

The following list has sites that I recommend for looking up software. Each site has thousands of files organized in a searchable database. These sites are easy to navigate, have a very complete selection of graphics utilities for scanners, and keep their files very current.

Here are the sites that I recommend:

▶ **TheFreeSite.com (www.thefreesite.com/).** This site has a little of everything that's free, including many personal and private collections of simple, helpful programs of all types. The Graphics section emphasizes collections of graphics by digital artists who want to share their work with the world.

▶ **ZDNet (www.zdnet.com/swlib/).** This is the most complete site for downloading trialware and freeware programs. Every trialware program I refer to in this book is available here.

▶ **CNET Download.com (www.download.com/).** Another huge site with thousands of shareware programs, this site is very well laid out, comprehensive, and provides particularly creative searching tools.

▶ **TUCOWS (www.tucows.com).** This compressive trialware site is easy to search and has lots of Mac programs as well.

Downloading a File

Let's go to ZDNet's site (see Figure 5.8) and look up and download Jasc's Paint Shop Pro. This program really is a must-have for anyone with a scanner. It is a simple yet powerful graphics editing program with many professional features. It's also convenient and easy to use. Paint Shop Pro can be downloaded from its manufacturer's Web site (**www.jasc.com**) or from any number of shareware collection sites. We'll go to ZDNet's shareware site at **www.zdnet.com/swlib/**. While we are here finding Paint Shop Pro, let's discuss how to search for and find any file available and what you can learn about a program before you decide whether to download it.

Figure 5.8
ZDNet's superb software download site.

CHAPTER 5

Exploring a Download Site

When you arrive at the site, you'll see a rectangle near the top-center part of the screen labeled Search For Downloads. A text box appears for you to type in a keyword. As explained earlier, keywords can be specific or general, depending on the type of search you have in mind. With this type of Search feature, when you type a keyword and click Go!, a list of files will appear, each of which links to a program that can be downloaded.

Choosing Keywords

You can choose keywords in a few different ways, each of which is demonstrated next so that you can see how typing in different keywords yields unique search results.

First, type "editing photos" with the quotation marks in the Search For Downloads text box. Capitalization does not matter. Click the Go! button or press Enter. A list of files will appear (see Figure 5.9). If you scroll down, you'll see several entries. Look at each line. Each is the title of a program that matches the criteria set by your keyword. Notice that each has a short description of the downloadable program right underneath its title.

Figure 5.9
Typing a keyword in ZDNet's software search engine.

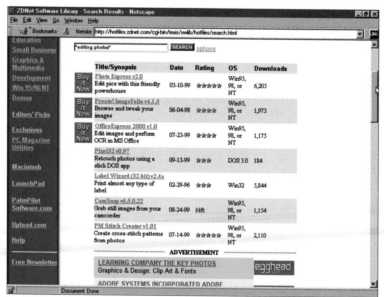

General Keywords

▶ Before we get into the specifics of downloading a file, let's use a different keyword. You'll note in these examples that I'm moving from general searches to more specific ones.

▶ Using keywords that search for a more general listing of files, such as "graphic design," "OCR," or "scanning utilities," gives you a big picture of what's available, indicating the size and features of each type of program in your chosen category. By using a general keyword, your results will be more numerous and have a wider variety of entries. As you can see in your search results, your keyword choice returned dozens of programs, even ones that are only remotely concerned with editing photos. This type of keyword search lends itself to exploration, "seeing what's out there," to give you a feel for what types of programs you can download.

Specific Keywords

▶ Using keywords that contain a portion of a specific product name (such as "Paint Shop" or "Paint Pro") will return a shorter list of files. The specific program you are looking for will appear nearer the top of the list. Finally, if your keywords are the full name of a specific product (such as Photoshop or Paint Shop Pro), your results will be largely limited to files that pertain to that product. Using quotes not only ensures that the entry with that specific product name will appear in the list but that it will appear closer to the top.

▶ For our example, type Paint Shop Pro, and you'll see may versions of this program. If your computer is running Windows 95 or 98, download the version with the highest number by selecting the 32-bit version. If your computer uses Windows 3.1, select the 16-bit version of Paint Shop Pro, the highest number available for that operating system.

Now that you know how that you can locate a file by using various types of keywords, let's get back to downloading Paint Shop Pro.

Here are some suggested keywords you can use with the Web site links previously provided. These keywords will give you access to many programs that will increase your scanner's functionality. (Scan the description for the word TWAIN, which indicates that the software directly works with your scanner, as shown in Figure 5.10.)

CHAPTER 5

Figure 5.10
Look through a product
description for the word
TWAIN or some other
indication that the
product supports
scanners.

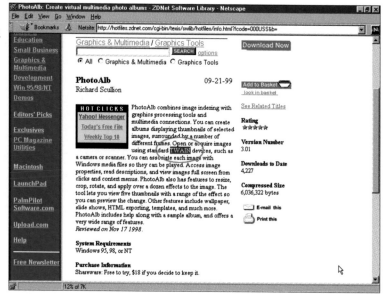

▶ Scanning utilities

▶ Scanning

▶ Graphics

▶ OCR

▶ Fax

▶ Create screen savers

▶ Desktop publishing

▶ Word processing

▶ Editing photos

▶ Web design

TIP

Using quotation marks around a search phrase ensures that the entire phrase
will be used in the search, rather than each individual word. For example,
searching for "scanning utilities" results in a list of scanning utility programs.
Searching for scanning utilities (no quotes) results in a list of all scanning
programs and all utility programs. Not all software search engines treat quotes
the same way. Some will still give you a list of all programs that use either
word, while reserving the top of the list for programs that use the entire
phrase. You may use Boolean values to search with as well–for example,
Graphics NOT Web returns every instance of the word "graphics" that does
not also include the word Web.

Viewing the Product Description

Clicking the name of the program takes you to the download page. To find out more about a program, click its name, and you'll see a page with detailed information and a direct link to begin downloading. As you can see, Paint Shop Pro is one of the keyword results. Click the Paint Shop Pro line, and the information page appears.

The information page enables you to read more about the program. Note especially the terms of use and the price of the program, should you decide to buy it. How long is the trial period? How much space does it take up on your hard drive? You'll also want to know the size of the file that you'll be downloading, which determines how long your modem will be tied up while transferring the file to your computer.

It's a good idea to read product descriptions thoroughly, to determine whether a program is going to be useful to you. Just because it's free doesn't necessarily mean you have to try it. Don't lose sight of what specifically you want to use these programs for. If you spend a little time scrolling through a list of free downloads, it's easy to become convinced you need a little of everything. Try not to dissipate your energies on software that you are pretty sure you are never going to use, even if it is "free."

CAUTION

When evaluating a program to download, look at the system requirements. If you need 32MB of RAM for a program, and you don't have that much RAM, then don't waste your time downloading it. If the system requirements say you need Windows 98, 95, or NT, and you have Windows 3.1, then look through the list for a specific Windows 3.1 version of the program (it will say "16-bit version").

Begin Downloading

At this point, you could click Download and begin downloading the program, or you could take advantage of ZDNet's Download Basket, which allows you to collect up to ten programs and download them later at your convenience. (It's a bit like going to a supermarket and filling up a shopping cart rather than having to march through the checkout counter with each item.)

Keeping Track of Your Download

Let's move the file from its Web location to your computer, choosing a destination folder that you can locate easily later. The number of regular computer users who spend half a day asking themselves, "Where did I put that file?" is amazing. I'm going to make sure you are not one of them.

1. Click the Download Now (or Buy It Now) button, and you'll see a screen telling you that the file will momentarily begin downloading. Your browser points out that you are downloading a file from the Internet and asks you for instructions on handling the download (see Figure 5.11). Choose Save it to disk and click OK.

Figure 5.11
Before downloading, choose the Save it to disk option.

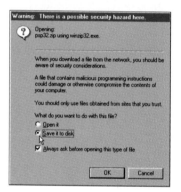

2. A Save As dialog box appears, asking you to specify a location for saving the file. After the file is downloaded, you'll have to locate this file on your hard drive and execute it, which will install the program. I recommend creating a special folder for these executable installation files, something such as "downloaded programs," or anything you can remember easily. You don't have to save this file in a folder that already exists. Just make sure you can find it later, whatever you do.

3. After you specify or create a folder for storing this executable file, click OK, and another Download File dialog box will appear. A blue progress bar fills from left to right, indicating the download progress. Remember, some of these files are huge, containing entire programs. Your computer could be busy downloading for quite some time, depending on how fast your Internet connection is.

4. After the file is downloaded, you'll see a Download Complete notification. The file is now on your computer in the folder you specified. You can then log off, open the folder, and double-click the file to install the program.

What Did I Just Download?

After you download it, the program is not yet installed. It is an *executable installation file.* To install, double-click the file with your mouse. This "executes" installation, and setting up the program will begin.

Installing the Program

Here are some general tips to supplement the onscreen instructions you'll receive when installing most programs.

Automatic vs. Customized Installation

You may be asked to specify a Typical (Automatic) or Custom installation (see Figure 5.12). Choosing Custom installation will give you at least some of the following options:

Figure 5.12
Many programs allow you to choose between Typical and Custom installation.

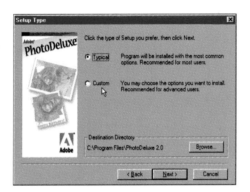

▶ You are asked to verify a location for the program. Normally, a program installs itself in its own folder within the Program Files folder. The only reason you may want to change this location is if you have a new hard drive that has more room, and you want to specify that the program be installed on this newer, less-cluttered, and perhaps faster drive. Or perhaps you want to have a special folder for installing shareware programs, helping you to keep track of those that you may want to uninstall later.

▶ You may be asked whether you want to install all the program features or just some of them. If you are just experimenting with the basic features at this time, you may not need all the tutorial files, special effect filters, and other such options.

▶ You'll be told how large the program will be after it's installed on your computer. Please note that the size of the actual program will be far larger than the compressed, downloaded file. Make sure you have the disk space to support this program. If you are cutting it close, abort installation and erase some files to make more hard drive room.

Where You'll Find the Program

The software designer wants to make sure you never forget about this program. It's in the interest of the software publisher to make sure you always see the startup icon right in front of you. Here's where startup options are usually installed:

▶ The installation program will offer to create a new program group in your Start menu. If your Start menu is already a bit crowded, adding more program groups may cause you to have to scroll to see them all. This can be a bit inconvenient, especially considering that, at the moment, you are merely "checking out" software and don't want to overwhelm your Start menu and desktop with programs that you may not even keep. Thus, consider creating a single program group in your Start menu for all of your "tryout" programs, leaving the rest of your menu intact. Windows 98 automatically creates Downloaded Program Files folder (inside the Windows folder), which is good for this purpose.

▶ Some programs may offer to start the program for you automatically every time you turn on your computer. This may make sense for screen savers and calendars, but be careful about allowing a program you have no experience with to become a constant presence on your computer.

▶ The installation program may ask to put a startup icon on your desktop. The startup icon can be convenient. Avoid desktop clutter, however. Having too many icons defeats the purpose of the desktop convenience.

Once the program is installed, you may be asked to reboot your computer. Please do so. Some features may not be enabled or could *crash your computer* if you do not reboot as directed.

You can then start the program by opening its folder in its program group, or by clicking its icon on the desktop, if one was created.

Now that you've learned how to download and install freeware and trialware, in Chapter 6, you'll start putting all the pieces together and take the first steps toward using your scanner effectively.

6

Scanning Successfully

In this chapter, we'll discuss how to get a great scan. You'll learn which settings you can adjust before you scan the picture and which editing tasks are best left for later. You'll discover that determining what you want to do with your scan beforehand will save you work and grief down the road. We'll also talk about tips for scanning magazine and newsprint, to avoid some of the telltale *artifacts* that cause such images to look dull and unconvincing. Finally, we'll talk about how to scan 3D objects.

During the discussion of these topics, you'll learn your way around the basic scanner interface, become familiar with the various controls, and understand the basic principles for scanning for the Web, scanning to retrieve text (OCR), and scanning for high-quality printing. We'll also talk a bit about oversized documents, such as what to do if you have a 10×20-inch picture that you want to scan. Most scanners only support 8.5×11-inch media. You'll learn how to "stitch" two images together, ending up with one big picture as a result.

Thinking Ahead

What you intend to do with your picture will determine your scanning settings. This section provides a list of some guidelines to keep in mind. These recommendations, for the most part, refer to scanned resolution (dpi). Later in this chapter, we'll discuss how to proportionally resize an image before scanning, while maintaining the desired dpi. In each of the following recommendations, scanning in True Color mode (or Millions of Colors, the highest setting) is the best choice, unless otherwise noted.

▶ Pictures to be printed on regular 8×11-inch paper can be scanned at between 90 to 150 dpi.

▶ Images to be printed on high-quality inkjet paper using the printer's highest-quality print mode can be scanned at 150 to 200 dpi.

CHAPTER 6

▶ Images to be printed on a photograph printer can be scanned at 300 dpi.

▶ Images that are to be resized after scanning (made larger) should be scanned at a higher dpi proportional to the intended resizing amount. For example, if a 3×5-inch photograph is going to be printed at 6×10 inches on inkjet paper, scan at twice the dpi you normally would. Instead of 150 dpi, use 300 dpi.

▶ Images scanned for extracting text (OCR) should be scanned at 300 dpi, in 2-bit color mode (sometimes called Line Art mode). Some scanning software provides one-touch OCR scanning, applying a built-in text scanning setting that frees you from having to worry about OCR scan settings.

▶ Grayscale images (images composed of shades of gray) can be scanned in Grayscale mode rather than True Color mode. You don't need to include color information if your image only has shades of gray. The file size will be smaller, and the image will look just as nice.

▶ Drawings composed of black lines (as in Figure 6.1), without any shading, can be scanned at the same resolution your printer delivers. For example, if your printer prints at 600 dpi, you may scan a line-art drawing at 600 dpi. Make sure that you scan in 2-bit, or Line Art mode. Your scan will have no color information, because it doesn't need any. If the drawing was done in a color other than black, you can still scan as line art, but the resulting scanned image will be black.

Figure 6.1
A line-art drawing can be scanned at the full resolution of the printer.

▶ Images ultimately destined to be printed at a commercial print house should be scanned according to the printer's recommendations. Make sure you check with the printer before scanning.

▶ Pictures scanned for the Web or for e-mailing should be less than 200K in size. In fact, scans bound for the Web should be as small as possible, while still maintaining a decent appearance. You may scan your image at 72 dpi, and you shouldn't ever need to scan higher than that for Web or online viewing. Shrink your image to approximately 3×5 inches by 72 dpi for *landscape* orientation, (or 5×3 inches by 72 dpi for *portrait* orientation). See the following note and Figure 6.2 for a description of these orientations.

NOTE

Landscape orientation refers to an image that is wider than it is tall. *Portrait orientation* refers to an image that is taller than it is wide. When a scanner interface provides a way for you to type new dimension numbers (resizing the picture by measurements, not by resolution), make sure that when you adjust one dimension, the other dimension automatically adjusts proportionally. Do this by selecting "Maintain Aspect Ratio" or otherwise "lock" the vertical and horizontal measurements together while resizing.

Figure 6.2
Examples of portrait and landscape orientations.

How Scanning Interfaces Work

Before you actually get started scanning, read this section to familiarize yourself with the basic scanning software interfaces. This section discusses features common to all or most software interfaces and looks at two specific interfaces. Then, it walks you through the steps of an actual scan.

The following are the two basic types of scanner interfaces. Which one you use depends on whether you rely on the software package included with the scanner you bought or if you shop around for a different one, perhaps by downloading one from the Web.

CHAPTER 6

▶ **Low user control**—One type of scanner interface asks you simple, plain-language questions about the picture you are scanning and makes all the technical scanning decisions based on your answers. You are none the wiser about the workings of the scanner settings. For example, if you answer that the picture you are scanning is a black-and-white photo, the scanner interface adjusts the color bit setting to Greyscale. Adobe PhotoDeluxe and Broderbund's Print Shop Deluxe 6 provide such a user-friendly interface (see Figure 6.3).

Figure 6.3
The Adobe PhotoDeluxe scanning interface asks you questions in "plain English."

▶ **High user control**—The most common type of scanner interface lets you adjust settings numerically, giving you lots of flexibility.

Common Scanner Interface Features

This section first describes features (or tools) that are common to most scanning interfaces that you're likely to encounter. Then, it takes a close look at two scanner interface examples so that you'll be able to recognize and refer to the various tools.

> **NOTE**
> Each scanner brand's interface will look different from the rest. While the basic features will be similar, the position of the tools, where the image appears, and how each option is presented will vary from brand to brand.

Every scanner interface will give you tools to perform the following tasks:

▶ **Preview your image**—A quick scan that confirms that the image is in position.

▶ **Choose the color depth of your scan**—The choices are as follows:

—**16.7 million colors** (sometimes called Millions of Colors, 24-bit color, or High Quality Photograph)

—**256 colors** (sometimes called 8-bit color or Normal Color Photograph)

—**Grayscale** (sometimes referred to as Black and White Photograph)

—**Line drawing** (sometimes called 2-bit color)

—**Text** (a special setting just for extracting text that you can edit in a word processing program)

▶ **Set the resolution of your image**—Determines the image's dots per square inch, or dpi. Most often, you can scan an image at a dpi of 72 to 150. See Chapter 2 for more information.

▶ **Reduce the area of the image you want to scan (*crop*)**—Cropping your image enables you to avoid scanning more of an image than you really need. For example, if an image has several buildings, and you want to scan only one of them, you can draw a rectangle around that one building with a Crop tool, and the scanner will scan only what's inside the rectangle.

▶ **Determine to which graphics program the scanner should send the image after scanning it**—After scanning, the image will open in a program you designate. You may have special image editing software that you always use to "touch up" photos after scanning. Most scanning interfaces will let you specify where the image should open right after scanning.

Scanner Interface Example 1

Figure 6.4 shows the scanning interface that comes with the HP PrecisionScan LT interface (for the HP4100 scanner). This interface is what appears when you select Acquire or Import from a graphics program, such as Paint Shop Pro, when using this scanner. Even if you don't own this specific scanner, this interface is a good example of what you're likely to see packaged with most low- and mid-priced scanners. After opening the interface, here's what you'll notice:

Figure 6.4
The Hewlett-Packard
4100 scanner interface.

CHAPTER 6

▶ **Preview**—As previously mentioned, you must first preview the image. In this interface, you click the Start a new scan button, which activates the Preview feature. Depending on CPU and scanner speed, the prescanned image can take anywhere from 10 seconds to four minutes to appear onscreen.

NOTE

Your final scan will look much better than the Preview. The image Preview is meant only to give you an idea of what your image will look like. After you scan your image and it opens in a graphics editing program, you'll marvel at how much better it looks than the Preview.

▶ **Color depth**—Select the output type. The Change Output Type dialog box (see Figure 6.5) presents your color depth choices.

Figure 6.5
Setting the output type determines the color depth of your scan.

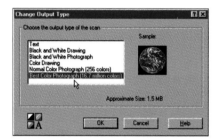

▶ **Cropping**—Choose the selection border. You can draw a rectangle around the area in the previewed image you want to scan. In other interfaces, this usually is called a Crop tool. Otherwise, your scanner will scan the entire image. This saves both scan time and disk space on your computer if you know you need only a small section of the previewed image.

NOTE

Remember that you can always crop an image after you scan it. All graphics programs let you crop a picture. Unless you're very sure that you won't need the entire image, you may want to scan the whole picture and crop later. However, the smaller an image is, the less room it takes on your hard drive. So, if you are quite certain you won't need the rest of the image, go ahead and crop now, and save the disk space.

▶ **Zoom**—Look closely at a small portion of your image to check details, using the magnifying glass shown in Figure 6.6, which is a Zoom tool. When you click the magnifying glass over part of an image, that section fills the entire screen. Note that the Zoom tool (in any scanner interface, not just this one) doesn't change the scanned image area, but simply lets you examine a particular area close-up. To scan an image segment rather than the entire image, use the Crop or Selection Border tool.

Figure 6.6
The Zoom tool lets you view a portion of your image close-up but does not affect the scanned area.

▶ **Set resolution**—Set the custom resolution settings. The scanner interface often determines what it deems is the best resolution for you, but you can override this choice by choosing your own resolution settings.

CHAPTER 6

Scanner Interface Example 2

The Visioneer scanner interface uses different dialog boxes and terminology than the HP scanners, but the purpose of the tools is still pretty much the same. You'll be able to generate a preview, set the color depth, resolution, and cropping, and determine the program that opens the resulting scanned image. The following list looks closely at how the Visioneer PaperPort interface prepares your document for scanning:

▶ If you own a Visioneer scanner, then the Visioneer Scan Manager, shown in Figure 6.7, will appear whenever you access your scanner. Depending on your model of scanner, the options may not be exactly the same as those displayed here.

Figure 6.7
The Visioneer Scan Manager.

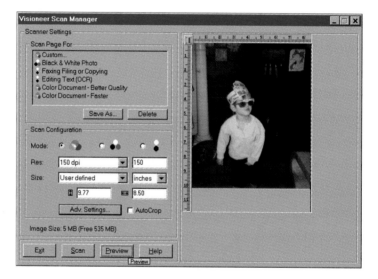

▶ At the bottom of the Scan Manager is a Preview button. Click this, and after a minute or so, a prescanned representation of your image will appear.

▶ At the top of the Scan Manager are the automatic settings. Click one option (for example Black & White Photo or Color Document-Better Quality), and you are ready to scan. In Figure 6.8, Editing Text (OCR) is selected. Notice how the numbers in the Scan Configuration panel show a setting of 300 dpi and the inches are set to full-page (8.5×11 inches). These are the preset OCR settings determined to be the best for this scanner.

Figure 6.8
The Visioneer Scan
Manager configures
special OCR settings
when OCR is selected.

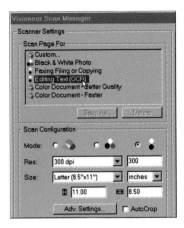

▶ The Scan Configuration panel (see Figure 6.9) enables you to dial in
your own settings. The three radio buttons to the right of the word
Mode let you choose either 24-bit, 8-bit, or 2-bit scan modes. Below
that, you can type your own resolution and size settings. If you plan
to resize your image before you scan, first see the following Tip.

TIP

Resizing an image before you scan presents the same problems as doing so
after you scan. Chapter 2, "How Scanners Work," in the section
"Understanding Resolution," discusses the inaccuracies and pixel distortion
that occurs when you resize an image. If you are planning to make your image
larger, it's much better to increase the resolution of your scan, as indicated in
the preceding section, rather than to use a resize option. However, it's fine to
shrink an image before scanning, using the prescan resize settings. If you are
scanning a full-page picture and you notice that the file size is far too large for
what you require, shrink the image, maintaining the same resolution you
determine is best for your final output. The file size will decrease as you
shrink the image. The scan time will be shorter, and manipulating your image
in a graphics program will take less time, since adjustments are being made to
a smaller document (less CPU-intensive, which means the operations will
take less time).

When resizing, make sure the changes are made proportionally. When you
make a horizontal adjustment, look at the vertical number as well. Did it
change? It should. Most scanner interfaces adjust the image proportionally
when you type either a vertical or horizontal measurement change, because if
an adjustment is made to only one dimension, the image appears distorted.

CHAPTER 6

Figure 6.9
The Scan Configuration panel lets you specify size and resolution settings.

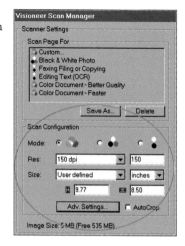

Making Global Color Adjustments

Near the bottom of the Scan Manager is the Advanced Settings button. Clicking this button opens the Advanced Settings dialog box (see Figure 6.10), which includes brightness/contrast and gamma controls. Most scanner interfaces offer something similar, such as the ability to adjust how intense and bright the colors (brightness/contrast) of your scan are and how shadowy the dark areas of your image should appear (gamma). You must consider carefully the wisdom of making these adjustments, as explained next.

Figure 6.10
The Advanced Settings dialog box lets you make broad adjustments to your image before you scan it.

CAUTION

You should make color adjustments before you scan only if you have identified that your monitor or scanner has a *bias,* meaning that images that you scan tend to appear overly dark (increase the brightness), not distinct enough (increase the contrast), or a bit too dark in the shadows (increase the gamma number). This is all trial and error. Scan an image and then print it. If the printed version just looks "off," and each time you print, the same bias appears (too dark, too light, or whatever), then make these prescan adjustments in the Advanced Settings dialog box.

The key is to think of prescan color adjustments as "global" settings. These are the settings that will apply to *all* of your scans. The purpose is to adjust for the idiosyncrasies of your scanner, monitor, or printer, to correct problems you see in all or most of your scans.

Editing Individual Scans

For individual scans that need treatment, use a photo editing program to fine-tune the colors for that single image. Photo editing programs provide more sophisticated and finely honed tools for color correcting. You'll get instantaneous feedback on your results, whereas if you make prescan adjustments, the cloudy interface makes it hard to judge your settings.

TIP

Here, then, is the rule: Use *prescan* color adjustment tools (brightness/contrast, gamma correction, hue/saturation/brightness, and RGB adjustments) to make global adjustments affecting *all* of your scanned images. To make changes to *individual* scans, use the tools found in your chosen photo editing software package.

CHAPTER 6

Saving Scans As Thumbnails

One final Visioneer PaperPort feature we should peruse is the *thumbnail image view* (see Figure 6.11). It's the best way for a scanner interface to save your scans for easy browsing later.

Figure 6.11
Visioneer PaperPort lets you view all of your scanned images. The bottom row of icons are applications. Drag an image thumbnail to any application to open it there.

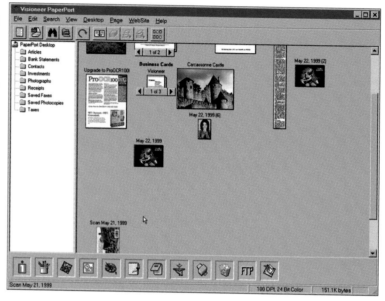

Thumbnails allow you to open images quickly in any graphics program that you have on your computer. After an image is scanned, it isn't automatically saved to your hard drive. The scanner interface deals with your scanned image in one of two ways:

▶ Sends the scan automatically to an image editor you have designated beforehand (you could then switch to that program, edit the image if you so desire, and save it to disk).

▶ Saves the scanned image in a thumbnail form. You can then view all of your scans row by row. Visioneer PaperPort creates a row of icons at the bottom of the screen, each of which represents a program that you can open your scans with, if you want to edit them. You simply click and drag the thumbnail to the icon representing the program you want to edit with. The scanned image opens in that program, ready to edit. You can then save the image to disk in any file format you desire.

Another company's product, Presto! PageManager, has this same type of
thumbnail interface, automatically storing images that you scan and
lining them up as thumbnails (see Figure 6.12). You can then drag any
thumbnail to the graphics editing program of your choice, where it will
open automatically. The program even prevents you from dragging an
image onto a program that cannot support the file type. You can scan,
perform OCR, and even do basic photo editing all within the program.
When working with numerous scans, it's very helpful to have a
thumbnail interface to help you keep track of all your hard work.

Figure 6.12
The Presto!
PageManager stores
your scans as
thumbnails.

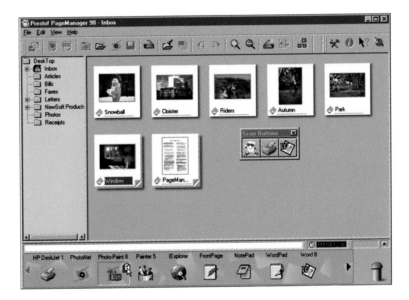

NOTE
Some of the newer scanner programs won't present you with the settings
discussed here. They simply ask you plain-English questions, such as
"Are you scanning a magazine or newspaper?" or "Is this image going to be
e-mailed or put on a Web site?" The software makes calibration and color
adjustments based on your answers. If you own a software package that makes
such choices, and you are happy with your scans, you may not need to bother
with any of the adjustments discussed here. However, if you want flexibility
and the ability to fine-tune your scanner settings to adjust for problems, then
the information in the following section may be helpful to you.

CHAPTER 6

Advanced Scanning Options

This section looks at some advanced scanning options, such as the settings that you can adjust for shadowy or overexposed photos, or to scan tricky materials, such as magazines, newspapers, and books with particularly grainy paper.

Adjusting Color Hue and Tone

Figure 6.13 shows the Microtek Scan Wizard. This is another example of a different scanner interface. If you own a Microtek scanner, this is the interface you'll see when you access your scanner. Again, note the Preview button in the upper-left corner, which provides you with a quick prescan, providing a visual reference for what your final scan will look like.

Figure 6.13
The Microtek Scan Wizard interface.

On the bottom half of the control panel (in this image, the control panel is labeled Untitled Job1), you'll see controls for adjusting Brightness and Contrast, which were discussed earlier, as well as sliders for adjusting Shadow, Highlight, Midtone, and Exposure.

Just like other prescan color calibration tools, applying these tools often can be too subjective, because the preview image that you use to adjust your settings by is not high-quality. You don't really know what you're getting until after the scan, when the image is opened in a photo editing program. So, again, it's best to think of these settings more as *calibration controls* to be used to offset a color bias you discover through your own scanning and printing. For example, you e-mail an image to a friend, and he responds, "Gee, that picture you sent me was very washed out." You then decrease the Highlight setting. Another example: You print a few images and find that they are all a bit shadowy. You then decrease the Shadow setting, making a global adjustment for all future scans.

Descreening Scans

So, what are the Descreen and Filter tools for? Descreen improves the quality of newspaper and magazine scans. Newspaper and magazine scans have a characteristic "paper grain" pattern across the entire image. Removing this grain is a chore, and sometimes the Descreen filter helps. (See the following Note.)

NOTE

The best tools for treating newspaper and magazine scans are Photoshop's Dust and Scratches tool and Despeckle tool. After scanning, open the photo in Photoshop. (Remember, some scanners come with limited editions of Photoshop, which would include the tools discussed here.) Then, select Filter>Noise>Dust and Scratches. Try a Radius setting of 1 Pixel, and a Threshold of 27 Levels. Open the Filter menu again, and choose Noise>Despeckle. Other photo editing programs, such as Jasc's Paint Shop Pro, Broderbund's The Print Shop Deluxe, Corel's PhotoPaint, and Adobe's PhotoDeluxe, have similar tools. For more details and related topics, see Chapter 9, "Special Effects Photo Editing."

Scanning the Image

Now that you understand how some of the scanning interface controls work, let's scan a document:

1. Open the scanner interface, using the software of your choice.

2. Select an image and place it face down on the scanning bed, lining it up with the positioning arrow, and gently replace the scanner cover. At this point, remember that some interfaces may walk you through the scanning steps question by question and not require you to select paramaters or make adjustments on your own.

NOTE

If the picture has been placed backward or upside-down, you need not reposition it. After the scan, the software can flip or rotate the image without any loss of quality.

3.   Click the Preview button (or something similar) and wait for a preview of the scan to appear onscreen.

4.   Determine whether the picture is positioned properly. Are the edges straight? If not, place the edge of the image flush against the edge of the scanner bed to facilitate positioning.

5.   If the picture was repositioned, preview it again to ensure proper placement.

6.   Once an image is previewed, every scanner interface will display the size of the image. You'll see the number in inches, the dpi, and the amount of hard drive space the image will require.

Cropping and Color Adjustments

After positioning the image, you crop your image and adjust for image imperfections, if need be, as follows:

1.   Determine whether you want to scan the entire image or just a portion of it. If only a portion of the image is needed, use the Crop tool to draw a rectangle around the part you want to scan. After you crop, notice the new size at which the figures are displayed. Reducing the size of the scanned area dramatically decreases the image size in bytes. Scanning only a portion of the image takes less time and does not demand so much CPU power and RAM from your computer.

2.   Determine the color mode for your scan. If you are not scanning a full-color photograph, perhaps you can scan at a lower color depth. Drawings, text, cartoons, and black-and-white photos need not be scanned in Full Color mode (16.7 million colors). For color depth recommendations, see the previous section, "Making Global Color Adjustments." If you choose a lower color mode (less than 16.7 million colors), your image will consume far less disk space and take far less time to scan.

3.   If needed, make any advanced color-correction adjustments or descreen adjustments, keeping in mind the caveats regarding the types of adjustments that are best applied later, after the scan.

Setting Resolution and Making the Final Scan

Before making the final scan, look at the resolution. Make sure you don't scan too much or too little. Remember your needs. Then, you can click the Scan button with your mouse and decide where to save the scan on your hard drive.

1. Type or select a scan resolution. For scan resolution guidelines, use the recommendations in the previous section. Remember that reducing resolution doesn't necessarily mean that the image will print smaller or appear smaller onscreen. The dimensions of your image are not directly related to resolution. For example, you can scan at a low resolution and still print your image full-size. Just change to a lower resolution when you print.

2. Press the Scan button and wait for your image to appear.

3. The image may appear in the scanner interface area or perhaps a photo editing program will automatically open and the scan will appear there. As part of the scanner interface setup process, you may have designated an editor for your scan (see Figure 6.14), or perhaps you have a program that "takes care of everything" for you.

Figure 6.14
The Hewlett-Packard 4100 scanning interface lets you select a program in which to automatically receive your scans.

4. At this point, your scan is done, and you still must save your image to your hard disk. Your scanner interface may have already saved your pictures as thumbnails, which you can later edit in a photo editing program. But if your image simply opens in a program, you must save it; otherwise, your work will be lost.

CHAPTER 6

Scanning Objects

Scanners are not just for paper. You can scan other objects: your keys, a comb, or any object that fits reasonably well on a scanning bed. Figure 6.15 shows a calculator being scanned. Notice the objects surrounding the calculator. Why are they there? To block light from leaving or entering the scanning area, because when an object with height is scanned, some of the light from the scanner lamp dissipates and the image is not as sharp. Figure 6.16 shows two images. The image on the left shows the results of scanning the calculator without blocking light. The image on the right had the light blocked before scanning. Placing objects such as magazines next to the object being scanned will block light loss as the lamp passes under the scanning bed.

Figure 6.15
Scanning a 3D object, such as this calculator, is perfectly acceptable.

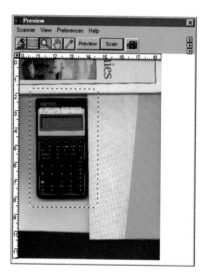

Figure 6.16
The duller image resulted from a scan without blocking the light first.

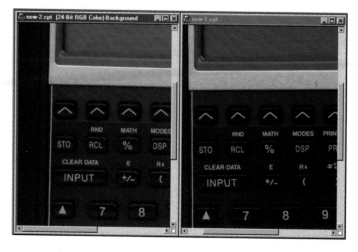

Scanning Oversized Documents

Suppose that you want to scan a poster or some document larger than 8.5×11 inches, which is the largest document capacity of most scanners. You can do it. Just scan small portions of the document, one at a time, and then "stitch" the pieces together to create a single, seamless picture. The resulting file may be huge, so before you take on such a project, make sure you have adequate RAM and hard drive space.

The work of "lining up" the image segments can be tedious and complex, but fortunately, software is available to help you do this. Pana Vue's Visual Stitcher can be downloaded from www.hotfiles.com and actually lines up the image sections top to bottom, side by side, forming a new picture as a result. To use Visual Stitcher, do the following:

1. Scan your picture segments. Make each segment the same dimensions. Scan even image segments from left to right, and then top to bottom.

2. Number your segments as you save them, moving from left to right, and then top to bottom.

3. Open Visual Stitcher and select File>New Project.

4. Click the Images tab, and begin adding your image segments, using the Add button at the bottom of the Images tab. Image marker flags appear, showing where the next image segment will line up with each (see Figure 6.17).

5. After adding your final image segment, select Actions>Execute. Visual Stitcher will now stitch together a complete image, as shown in Figure 6.18.

Figure 6.17
Visual Stitcher fits image segments together and combines them into one complete image

CHAPTER 6

Figure 6.18

A complete Visual Stitcher image.

Other image stitching programs are available. For example, Corel PHOTO-PAINT has a Stitch function that is similar to Visual Stitcher. The trick lies in scanning segments that are identical in size , which makes it easy for the stitching program to line up all edges exactly.

Now that you know how to set up and scan an image, Chapter 7 will discuss your choices for saving the images. Not all image formats are created equal, and each image use has an ideal file format for saving. You'll learn all about that next.

7

Saving
Your Scans

Everything in computing involves choices, and the simple act of saving an image is no exception. It requires a little thought, and a bit of planning.

When you save a scanned photo, you need to ask yourself what you are going to do with it later. Edit it with a photo editing program? Use it as part of a product brochure or desktop publishing project? Post it on the Web or print it out professionally at great expense? Your answers to these questions determine how you save your file.

There are many graphic file *types,* and most serve a good purpose. In this chapter, you'll learn a bit about naming files. We'll spend most of the time exploring the main image file types. You'll learn the uses of, and the options associated with, each type, as required.

NOTE
The two file types largely associated with Web viewing, GIF and JPEG, are covered in detail in Chapter 13, "Graphics and Web Design."

How We'll Proceed

After you scan or edit an image, you need to save it. From your scanning or editing program, if you select File>Save As and then click the Save as type drop-down menu, you'll see more than a dozen available file types. Which do you choose?

Before we look at individual file types, we need to consider the following questions:

▶ Is size important? Do you want the image to take up very little disk space?

▶ Is the image destined for the Web?

▶ Will you need to print this picture professionally, at a third-party print shop?

▶ Will the image be part of a desktop publishing project, mixed with text and other images?

▶ Do you plan to crop part of this picture, to remove the subject matter from its background?

▶ Do you want to save additional channel or masking information with this image?

▶ Does this picture require 16 million colors, or can you reduce it safely to 256 colors or grayscale?

▶ Will you need to share this image with a Macintosh user?

▶ Will this file require features specific to the photo editing program you are using right now?

First, let's consider what to name your file. Then, we'll discuss file extensions, how it is that a file always opens in a particular program when you click on it, and the most important graphics file types you are likely to encounter. You'll also learn about the various saving options you'll see in any photo editing program.

Naming Your File

A filename is your key to retrieving the file later. You need a way to identify what you are looking for. When did you scan that image and why? Name a file in a way that brings to mind important facts about it. A good filename can jog your memory and save you from searching your computer for something that should have been easy to find. You can name a file by any of the following categories:

▶ Topic

▶ Date

▶ Customer or client

▶ Subject matter

▶ Project name

What matters is that you name the file something distinct and quickly recognizable, with a pattern that will make sense to you later.

Here are three additional points to remember regarding file naming:

▶ Web filenames are case-sensitive, meaning upper- and lowercase letters are often not read by programs as being the same. If you are creating a file for the Web and include capital letters in the name, it's best to use the same capitalization when referring to that file in a hyperlink. So, when naming files for use on the Internet, be consistent in the capitalization conventions that you use.

▶ If you are using Windows 95, 98, or Windows NT, you can name your picture anything you like, up to 256 letters. Don't use symbols, such as "&" or "*." You may use spaces in between characters and mix upper- and lowercase letters, if you like. But if you are sharing this image with someone who has Windows 3.1 or posting your image on the Web, your long filename may not survive the transition. The picture you named "The day we all went to the beach.tif" may show up on your Web site as "theday~1.tif," or "The_day_we_all_went_to_the_beach.tif." In such cases, try something such as "beach.tif" instead.

▶ Filenames have two components: the name itself and the file extension. The following section presents a brief discussion of filename extensions.

Filename Extensions

The name of the file can be almost anything you wish: for example, "my favorite museum." However, when you save a file, a period is automatically placed at the end of the filename and three characters are placed right after that period (see Figure 7.1). Every time you save a file, you are also saving it as a specific file *type*. This file type is specified by those added three letters at the end, called the *file extension*.

Figure 7.1
A filename has a name, followed by a period, followed by an extension.

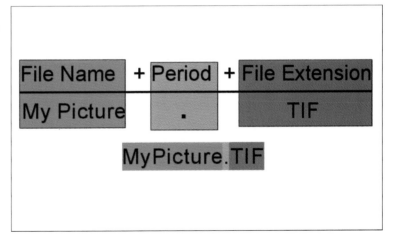

A file extension identifies to the computer the type of file at hand. When the file's icon is clicked, your scanned file will open automatically in its native application, the program associated by Windows to work with that type of file. The file extension helps identify the purpose of the file as well. PCs have system files, program files, and data files.

Here are two examples:

▶ If you've selected TIFF as your saved file type, then a scanned photo called "my favorite museum" really is saved as "my favorite museum.tif," identifying the file as a TIFF.

▶ Likewise, if you've selected JPEG as your file type, then the image "my favorite museum" will be saved as "my favorite museum.jpg."

NOTE

When viewing a list of files in Windows Explorer, for example, you may not see the file extension. Windows gives you the option to view or not view the additional period and three letters. If file extensions are not visible, you can change this preference by opening Windows Explorer and selecting View>Folder Options. Then, select the View tab and remove the check next to Hide file extensions for known file types, as shown in Figure 7.2.

Figure 7.2
To see file extensions, remove the check next to "Hide file extensions for known file types" in the Folder Options dialog box.

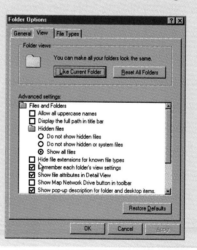

Working with Graphic File Types

Table 7.1 lists the most popular graphics file types and the important characteristics of each. We'll spend some time learning why it's important to be familiar with the benefits of at least a few of these file types. If some terminology is unfamiliar, don't worry. Features such as compression type, saving clipping path, and alpha channels are discussed later in this chapter.

CHAPTER 7

Table 7.1
Popular Graphics File Formats.

File Type Name (Abbreviated name)	File Extension	Clearest Benefits	Saved Alpha and Path Clipping Information	Compression	Color Bit Depth
Tagged Image File Format (TIFF)	.tif	Cross-platform (PC/MAC). Suitable for high-end printing. Can save in CMYK color.	Saves alpha channel information	Lossless (LZW) compression	8-, 16-, 24-, and 32-bit depth
Joint Photographic Experts Group (JPEG)	.jpg	Viewable on the Web. Highly compressed file format.	No alpha channel or clipping information saved	Highly compressible, lossy compression	24-bit depth
Graphics Interchange Format (GIF)	.gif	Viewable on the Web. Saves transparency data. Can create animations.	No alpha channel or clipping information saved	Lossless (LZW) compression	8-bit depth
Portable Network Graphics (PNG)	.png	Viewable on some newer Web browsers. Saves transparency data. Downloads faster than GIFs.	Saves alpha channel information	Variety of compression schemes	8- and 24-bit depth
Targa (TGA)	.tga	Familiar file type for video production. Many DOS-based graphics programs can open TGA files.	Saves alpha channel information	No significant file compression	Grayscale, 8-, 16-, and 24-bit depth
PICT	.pict	Popular Macintosh format for shuffling graphics between applications. Very compressible.	Saves alpha channel information	Highly compressible file compression	Grayscale, 2-, 8-, 16-, and 32-bit depth

Continued on page 114

Table 7.1 continued from page 113

Z-Soft Paintbrush (PCX)	.pcx	Read by almost all PC applications. Very small file size.	No alpha channel or clipping information saved	Lossless compression	Grayscale, 8- and 24-bit depth
Encapsulated PostScript (EPS)	.eps	Saves page layout information. Saves curve, fill, line, text, and bitmap placement data. Saves CMYK color.	Alpha channel and clipping information saved	Variety of compression schemes	Saves vector information and image placement, not bitmap color depth
Adobe Acrobat (PDF)	.pdf	Universally readable cross-platform with free viewer. Virtually any type of graphic or text file can be saved as a PDF.	Saves page layout platform, not image info	Lossy compression	Page layout platform, not image info
Windows Bitmap (BMP)	.bmp	Every Windows-based computer can work with BMP files.	Does not save alpha channel or clipping information	Lossless compression; file size is comparatively large	8- and 24-bit depth

Why File Types Are Important

TIFF and JPEG files are two examples of graphics editing files. Each file type takes a specific approach to recording vital information about the image. When your computer tries to open a graphics file, it first reads the file type and, based on that observation, starts to locate important image information specific to that type.

The program will need to know the following facts about any image it tries to open:

▶ What is the image's size and resolution?

▶ Is this picture a series of lines and shapes or is it rows of dots of color?

▶ What is the image's color space, or color model?

▶ How many colors does this image use and what type of palette?

▶ Is text saved with the picture?

▶ Is an alpha channel or clipping path saved with the picture?

▶ Is the image compressed, so that it takes up less hard drive space?

▶ How will this image be printed?

▶ Are any user comments embedded in the file that need to be reported?

TIP

If you post an image online, you can attach a small bit of file information that identifies the image as your own, called a watermark. It is a digitally stored number, registered by you, traceable by you, and traceable to you. A watermark can also appear as a slightly visible "ghost" image in the background of your picture, or it can be detectable only electronically. Watermarks act as a digital name stamp, which would deter others from downloading your pictures and claiming them as their own. You can download watermarking technology from www.digimarc.com and check out their more advanced image protection options while you're at it.

The Development of Graphics File Types

Most of the file types that are standard throughout the industry first became popular because the software company that developed them grew to be very influential. Here are some examples of different file types:

▶ **TIFF**—Created by the Aldus Corporation while developing the desktop publishing program PageMaker. As PageMaker, later purchased by Adobe, became an industry standard, so did the TIFF file format.

▶ **PCX**—Developed years ago by the Z-Soft Corporation. It caught on because of its ability to display 16.7 million colors and retain a small file size.

▶ **BMP**—Developed by Microsoft to be read on any and all Windows-based computers. It's the universal Windows graphics file.

▶ **GIF**—Developed in 1986 by Unisys and licensed by CompuServe for Internet use. It grew to universal acceptance along with the CompuServe brand name. Thus, to this day, GIF files are one of the very few graphic file types viewable on the Web.

▶ **TGA**—Developed with video graphics professionals in mind, for use with the Truevision video board. It survives today because it is one of the few high-end graphics file types that can be opened by DOS-based graphics programs.

Other file types were created to be deliberately universal and were immediately adopted as standards. Here are two examples:

▶ **JPEG**—Developed by the Joint Photographic Experts Group (hence, the name) to accommodate the need for a highly compressible, full-color file type that could be viewed on the Web.

▶ **PNG**—Developed as a license-free alternative to the GIF file type. It is relatively new and has yet to catch on widely as a replacement or supplement to GIF files.

Saving a File As a Particular Type

All graphics programs can work with the major, common file types. Before we examine the benefits of each, let's go through the following steps on how to save a file as a particular type:

1. From the graphics program you are working in, select File>Save As.

2. Click the Save as file type drop-down arrow to see the menu of choices.

3. Scroll down and click a file type from the list. You'll notice that next to the name of each type is its three-letter extension. For example, next to CompuServe Graphic Interchange is its extension, .gif. Next to Windows Meta File is its file extension, .wmf. The file type you choose will appear in the drop-down menu as it closes.

4. Click OK, and your picture will be saved as that type of file. Later, when your picture opens, it will still look the same, but its digital information will be stored and organized according to that file type's rules.

NOTE

Any program that recognizes the file type you choose can open your file. You don't always have to open your picture in the same program. That's the beauty of universal, standardized graphics file types.

CHAPTER 7

CAUTION

Regarding file types, there are two problems that can occur later, when you try to open that image.

Occasionally, certain graphics programs won't recognize a file type, even one that's fairly popular. For example, Fractal Design's Painter 5 will not open PCX files. Also, optical character recognition (OCR) programs are quite picky about the file types they can work with, which means that when you save an image for text recognition, pay close attention to your OCR program's suggested file type.

Sometimes, when opening an image, your Open menu's Files of type box will be set to look for only a specific file type. If your saved file type is different than the type that your Open menu is looking for, the filename of your image won't appear with the filenames listed in the main box. To make your file appear in this box, simply select the All Files option in the Files of type drop-down list (see Figure 7.3). Then, you'll see every compatible file type appear in the list.

Figure 7.3
To see all the files in the Open dialog box, make sure All Files is selected in the Files of type drop-down menu.

The significance of file size and resolution is covered in chapters 1 and 3, so let's look at some of the other types of file information saved with your image.

Bitmap and Vector Images

The two broad image categories are *vector* and *bitmap,* and all scanned pictures fall into the category of bitmaps. Nonetheless, at some point, you may incorporate drawings or shape elements with your scans, which are vector images, so it helps to know the difference between the two image categories.

Bitmaps

Bitmaps, as discussed in the early chapters of this book, are images composed of many rows and columns of colored dots (or pixels). These rows and columns are aligned in such a way that they blend together to simulate the shades and intricacies of your original photograph. You cannot enlarge a bitmap image without introducing inaccurate information and making the picture appear somewhat blurry.

All the image types we examined, such as TIFF, JPEG, GIF, and so forth, fall under the category of bitmap images. They differ in the way that they present size and color information to the software program that opens the picture file type, but they all consist of rows and columns of pixels.

Vector Images

The other category, vector images, consists of images with precisely calculated shapes and lines. The colors that fill these shapes are either solid color blocks or mathematically calculated blends from one color to another. Because of this precision, text created in vector drawings looks very accurate, clean, and sharp. Furthermore, vector images can be resized without limit and still retain their crispness. You can double or triple the size of a vector drawing and not lose quality. The best-known vector drawing programs are CorelDRAW, Adobe Illustrator, and Deneba Canvas. Figure 7.4 shows a bitmap text sample resized and the same text sample created as a vector image.

Figure 7.4
A bitmap text sample resized is not as clean as the same text rendered in a vector image program.

This text was resized

This text was resized

Bitmap   Vector

It's very common to bring a bitmap image into a vector program, to "get the best of both worlds." That way, you can enjoy the precision of perfectly rendered shapes and text, with the realism of a photograph. For example, as shown in Figure 7.5, you can import a TIFF (the photographic backdrop behind the saxophone player) into CorelDRAW, mixing the sharp shapes and clarity of a vector image with the photographic realism of a bitmap.

Figure 7.5
A CorelDRAW project
that includes an
imported TIFF file.

Color Models

When an image is saved, it needs to be accurately reproduced at a later time. The image may be printed, posted on the Web, or opened in another program on a different computer. In any case, you want each shade of color to appear as it did on your screen originally, whether the final results are seen on paper, on film, or online. Toward this end, a saved image includes not only color value, but also a reference to a *color model,* or *color space.* This color model provides the image with the ability to accurately describe each hue it contains.

Color models assign a number to each color. In an electronic image, each hue exists in numerical relationship to all other colors used in that image. Each hue has its own number, no matter how similar it is to its neighboring hues. The distinction between all colors in an image, no matter how subtle, is vitally important to the image's integrity.

NOTE

The first attempt to create a color model that could be applied by visual technology was developed in the 1920s by CIE, the Commision Internationale de l'Eclairage. It describes every humanly perceptible color along a three-dimensional axis. One value describes the luminance (brightness) of a color, while the other two values describe the actual chroma, or perceived color values. Today's color models, or color spaces, are derived from this original effort. They all provide a numerical continuum along which any hue can be described and recorded by your image and later reproduced accurately. When you save your image as a particular file type, the color model information is saved along with it.

Thus, when you are adjusting the colors in your image—moving the Saturation slider a little to the left or the Hue slider to the right just a bit—you are assigning a specific color number to that portion of your image. These specific measurements make it easier to print, upload, or publish your images with accurate color values.

RGB and CMYK

Each color model accurately represents an image according to the hardware system used to reproduce those colors. For example, the technology used to create colors on a computer monitor is not the same as the technology used to print colors on paper; thus, each of those two media requires its own color model.

The two main color models are RGB and CMYK—RGB is used for monitors and scanners, while CMYK is used for printers.

The RGB Color Model

The *RGB (Red, Green, Blue)* color model works with technology that creates colors by *transmitting light*. Examples are computer monitors, scanners, and televisions. A computer monitor, for example, displays colors when beams of light hit red, green, and blue phosphors. The combinations of these light projections create the 16.7 million colors that a computer monitor is capable of displaying. Similarly, a scanner's CCD elements (See Chapter 2, "How Scanners Work.") create colors by emitting specific voltages of electricity when hit by the scanner bed lamp reflected off the surface of the scanned image. These elements are red, green, and blue. In both technologies, colors are created by adding colored light to colored light. The secondary colors (those colors created by combining the primaries red, green, and blue) are brighter than the primaries (see Figure 7.6). This is the RGB color space, and it is additive in nature. In *additive* color models, adding equal intensities of red, green, and blue results in white.

Figure 7.6
Combining colors in
the RGB model creates
brighter hues.

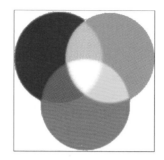

The CMYK Color Model

The *CMYK* color model is intended for colors that are created by *reflecting* light, which applies to inks used by printers. Printers create colors by combining cyan, magenta, yellow and black ("K" stands for "key color") inks. Ink creates the colors we see by absorbing and reflecting light, not by transmitting it. Ink is a passive element. It sits on a page. It does not create light. For example, magenta ink looks magenta not because it actively transmits magenta light, but rather because it absorbs green light and thus reflects red and blue (which looks like magenta to us).

When inks are combined, darker colors result. This is the opposite of what occurs when colors are combined on your monitor or scanner. Thus, the color model used by printers, which combines cyan, yellow, and magenta inks to obtain all colors, is called a *subtractive* color model. When your printer combines ink, the results are darker hues (see Figure 7.7).

Figure 7.7
Combining colors in
the CMYK model
creates darker hues.

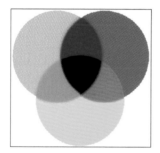

NOTE

Black ink is needed to round out the cyan, yellow, and magenta inks used in the CMYK model (the K, referring to the black ink, is called the key color). In theory, black should not be required, because the CMY colors, combined in equal amounts, should create black, being a subtractive color model. In reality, though, those three inks combined equally will create a smudgy, dull, dark brown. Black is used not only to create a rich true black but also to deepen other hues. That's why most commercial printers today have four ink cartridges: cyan, magenta, yellow, and black.

You may have already discovered that the colors you see on your monitor don't look the same when you print them. The reason is that the RGB and CMYK color models do not coincide exactly. When creating or editing an image displayed on your monitor (which uses the RGB color model), it's important to know what you'll be missing when you print.

For this purpose, some photo editing programs provide a Gamut Warning feature. *Gamut* is a label that refers to all the *legal* colors displayed on your screen ("legal," in this sense, refers to their ability to be printed on your printer). A Gamut Warning is a method for indicating which colors cannot be printed. When displaying a Gamut Warning, Corel PHOTO-PAINT replaces all illegal colors with a lime-green, although you must have set up a Corel Color Profile to use this option. When choosing a color, Adobe Photoshop displays an exclamation point in the Color dialog box every time you click or select an illegal color. To select the nearest legal color, click the exclamation point.

File Compression

Graphics files contain huge amounts of data, and many file types deploy ways to minimize the image's hard drive space consumption. The science of trying to squeeze a big picture into a tiny file is referred to as compression. File types such as JPEG, TIFF, and PCX use complex algorithms to shrink an image and still maintain quality. When you save scanned images with file compression, you'll encounter two types: lossy and lossless compression.

Lossless Compression

TIFF and GIF files are examples of file types that deploy lossless compression. They shrink a file to as small a size as possible without sacrificing image quality and without tossing out real image data. Lossless compression uses algorithms to conserve space, rearrange file segments, and otherwise squeeze image bits together without a loss of quality. Be aware, though, that when you convert an image to the .GIF format, you are reducing its colors to 256. Some images, especially photographs, will not look right as a result.

Lossy Compression

The JPEG file type is the chief example of a lossy compression scheme. When you save an image as a JPEG file, you choose how compressed your image should be, understanding that more compression results in a loss of image quality. The JPEG file type, and other lossy compression schemes, actually throws away image data, never to be retrieved again. Lossy compression schemes can shrink your files to a fraction of their original size, but at the price of quality. You must determine for yourself the tradeoff. For more information on JPEG images, refer to Chapter 13, "Graphics and Web Design."

Saving Alpha Channels

Chapter 8, "Basic Photo Enhancements," discusses ways to select only a portion of your image for editing. Making specific selections in your picture enables you to separate the background from the main subject matter of your picture, for example, or one object from another. You can then perform adjustments and special effects only on the selected portion.

Alpha channels enable you to save those selections for later use. Suppose that you've spent hours creating a perfect selection around a human form in your image. It would be nice to save that selection for later, in case you decide more editing is necessary. This is important, because in many photo editing programs, a selection is blended right back into the background as soon as you click outside of it. Most photo editing programs, however, let you save your selection as an alpha channel. Later, simply load that channel, and the "marching ants" that mark off your selection will reload just where you had them last.

If you intend to use this selection after you save the image, you must make sure you save your picture in an image format that supports alpha channels. Examples are TIFF, PICT for the Macintosh, and most proprietary image types, such as PSP, PSD, and CPT.

NOTE

Alpha channels also allow you to save your selections (masked areas) with variable levels of transparency. This is an improvement over creating a standard selection (or mask). When working with a standard mask, only a portion of your image is selected.

With alpha channels, you can create a blended mask, in which areas of your image are partially protected from edits. That means if you apply a color around the mask, a little of the color will show behind it. This variable transparency technique allows you to create such special effects as "glowing" outlines around an object and mist that gradually seeps into the foreground of an image. To retain your alpha channel, make sure you save your image in an "alpha-channel-aware" file type, as previously described.

CHAPTER 7

Common File Types

Now that you know a bit more about the significance of file types, as well as how to save your file, we'll discuss the main file types and their important uses.

Joint Photographic Experts Group (JPEG)

JPEG files, which have a .jpg file extension, have these important features:

▶ JPEGs can compress to a tiny percentage of the image's original size. If your image is 1.2MB after you scan it, it can shrink to about 200K if you save it as a JPEG, about one-sixth the size of the original.

▶ JPEG files are universally recognized on the Web. JPEGs, GIFs, and the new PNG files are the only file types you should employ when creating Web images.

▶ Even though JPEG files are small, they can still display 16.7 million colors and are good for saving full-color photographs.

JPEG images are so small because they use a *compression scheme*. JPEG file compression can cause a loss of image quality (the pictures have a fuzzy look to them) if too much compression is used.

Fortunately, when you save your picture as a JPEG, you can choose how much compression to use. The more you compress your picture, the less room it takes up on your hard drive, which is nice. However, if you compress too much, the image starts to look sort of ragged. Figure 7.8 shows the Corel PHOTO-PAINT JPEG Save Options dialog box. You can set your compression amount while previewing how the picture will look when you save it. This prevents you from compressing to the point of quality loss.

Figure 7.8
The Corel PHOTO-PAINT JPEG Save dialog box lets you view the effect your chosen compression level will have on the image's quality.

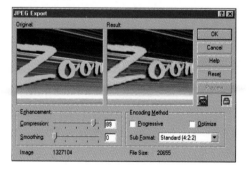

CAUTION
When you open a JPEG image and edit it, make sure you save it with the same compression factor as it had previously. Do not add more compression when resaving the image.

NOTE
Saving a file as one type and then saving it as another is perfectly fine. For example, you can save a file as a TIFF and then later save it as a JPEG.

Graphics Interchange Format (GIF)

Due to their intelligent compression scheme, GIF images are very small in file size. GIF images can contain a maximum of 256 colors. This is one of the image formats used on the Web. GIFs are ideal for the Web for several reasons, listed here:

▶ When you save an image as a GIF, you are allowed to select one color in your image that will be replaced by a *transparency*. Thereafter, that color will appear transparent, with no color at all. That means that if you chose white, for example, as your background color, any white in that GIF will not display at all (the Web browser color will show through, as shown in Figure 7.9).

Figure 7.9
You can specify that a GIF file not display its background color when viewed in a Web browser.

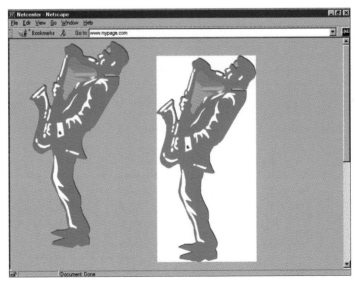

▶ Whereas some images will not show up at all on your Web site until they have fully loaded, GIFs start appearing as soon as they begin to load. That way, visitors can *at least see something* while the rest of the page loads.

▶ GIF files can be viewed on Macintosh, UNIXs and Linux computers.

▶ GIF files can also be combined and sequenced to form an animation. In fact, creating animated GIFs is one of the easiest and most effective ways to spruce up your Web site.

Keep in mind, though, that GIFs display only 256 colors and are best for displaying drawings with large areas of solid, flat color. Full-color photos saved as GIFs can have a characteristic "blotchy," grainy appearance. Transitions from one color to another are not smooth. You'll especially notice this effect with skin tones, where blending between subtle color tones is needed for realism.

Portable Network Graphics (PNG)

The PNG file type was developed as an improvement on the GIF file type. It is used for compressing graphics on the Web. It has these advantages over the GIF file type:

▶ It supports 24-bit, 16.7 million colors, suitable for full-color photos.

▶ You may save an alpha channel with a PNG file. This alpha channel can be used to define varying degrees of transparency. Images can appear as blends with nearly opaque to fully transparent sections.

▶ When viewed on the Web, the image can appear to be loading, not from top to bottom, but gradually appearing evenly (called interlacing). While loading, the whole picture gradually comes into view.

▶ You can select varying degrees of compression, depending on the image's color mode and viewing needs.

Please note that most older browser versions may not support PNG images. You cannot create animations from PNG files, as you can with GIFs.

Tagged Image File Format (TIFF)

The TIFF format is the most widely used file type for storing large, full-color, professional images for both PCs and Macs and has a .tif file extension. If you have an image that you may want to print professionally someday (perhaps for a product brochure or a wedding invitation), consider storing the image as a TIFF file. TIFF files can be saved in CMYK format, which is required for professional printing. TIFFs can also save masking and channel information, features important to sophisticated photo editing programs (more on those later). TIFF files can be compressed when they are saved onto your hard drive, but not to the dramatic, space-saving degree that JPEG images can be shrunk. However, TIFFs suffer no quality loss when they are compressed.

Encapsulated PostScript (EPS)

An EPS file is not a simple file *type,* but rather it is a *language* that describes the image objects on a page. This includes the placement of pictures, text, and file characteristics, such as color separation and clipping path. PostScript is called a *page descriptor language.* It originally was used to allow illustrators to save and print complex curves, lines, and text across many platforms. However, it was discovered that PostScript could be used to save data about bitmaps as well, not just curves and lines (vector images). So, an EPS file takes full advantage of PostScript's ability to isolate (encapsulate) and save specific parameters about any bitmap images on the page.

EPS files often have several components, such as text, vector graphics, and bitmaps, so you normally won't edit an EPS file in a photo editing program, because such programs are used for editing bitmaps. Still, you may need to open an EPS file in a photo editing program for identification purposes, as well as to position a graphic correctly on the page. For this reason, EPS files include a preview. The preview displayed onscreen when you open an EPS file in a photo editing program is not the entire EPS file, but a representation for placement purposes only. The preview contributes to the overall size of the file; thus the size of the preview, and its quality, are kept on the low side. Remember this when viewing an EPS file in a photo editing program and it appears to be subquality.

Adobe Acrobat (PDF)

Developed by the Adobe Corporation, the PDF format is a single-solution method for creating documents that can be viewed on PCs (Windows-based, UNIX, and DOS) and Macs. Adobe Acrobat can convert any file—any combination of text and graphics—into a universally readable document. With Adobe Acrobat, creating a PDF file is as easy as printing. As far as reading or viewing a PDF file, anyone can download the free PDF viewer from Adobe's Web site (**www.adobe.com**) and from many other locations. To create PDF files, you must purchase the full Adobe Acrobat program, which runs between $200 and $400.

Proprietary File Types

The previous section covered file types that can be opened in most common photo editing programs and imported into almost all word processing and desktop publishing programs. Beyond these near-universal file types are the *proprietary* formats. The purpose of proprietary formats is to complete your work with the full features of a particular program, such as Photoshop or Paint Shop Pro. You would then *publish* your work (make it available to the world) in a universal format, such as TIFF for paper publication and JPEG for Web posting.

▶ **Corel PHOTO-PAINT (CPT)**—CPT is the proprietary file format for Corel PHOTO-PAINT. CPT files cannot be opened in any application other than PHOTO-PAINT. To save complete object, clipping, channel, color management, and layering information in a PHOTO-PAINT image, the image must be saved as a CPT file. PHOTO-PAINT can open PSD files with layering information intact.

▶ **Photoshop (PSD)**—PSD is the proprietary file format for Photoshop. For all printer registration, image history, layer, color profile, and clipping information to be saved, you should save your work in Photoshop projects as PSD files. PSD files can open in other applications, as well, such as Jasc's Paint Shop Pro 6, MetaCreation's Painter, and Corel's PHOTO-PAINT.

▶ **Paint Shop Pro (PSP)**—PSP is the proprietary image file format for Paint Shop Pro. If you've created layers in a Paint Shop Pro image or saved or promoted selections, then you should save your work as a PSP file. No other application supports PSP files. Paint Shop Pro can open PSP files with layering information intact.

▶ **MetaCreation's Painter (RIF)**—RIF is the proprietary file type for MetaCreation's Painter. Painter's unique Floater Layer, Wet Layer, and Opacity Layer settings can be saved only in the RIF file format. Except for other MetaCreation's programs, such as Poser, Bryce 3D, and Ray Dream Studio, no other image editors open RIF files. Painter can open PSD files with layering information intact.

There are many other image file formats that we did not look at here, but the discussion in this chapter should cover all the bases for creating flexible and professional scanned images that do not take up tons of room on your hard drive. In a nutshell, the following is all the information you really need to have at your fingertips:

▶ To save files for the Web, use GIFs for drawings and tiny photographs in which detail is not that important. No other image format is directly supported on the Web. Use JPEGs for high-quality photos.

▶ To save images that you may use professionally at some point and thus want no loss of quality, use the TIFF format.

▶ For day-to-day scanning and editing of images, without losing quality each time that you open and resave the picture, use PCX or TIFF. OCR programs for extracting text work well with the PCX file format.

You now know how to save your scans in the right *file type* for your needs. Your choice depends on your plans for your saved pictures. In the next chapter, we'll discuss how to edit your scans, spruce them up, and bring out the best in color and image quality.

8

Basic Photo Enhancements

In this chapter, you'll learn a lot about photo editing. You'll discover tools for treating damaged photos, getting rid of "red eye"and adjusting the overall color of a photo, as well as sharpening pictures and removing dust and scratches. We'll also make a calendar and a photo montage.

We'll be jumping back and forth among different software packages in this chapter so that you can see the advantages and disadvantages of the various approaches that a particular type of program may take. For example, one program may allow you to adjust the amount of Red Eye Reduction to the exact degree you choose, whereas another program may perform the task for you, giving you no choice in the matter. We'll look at expensive, full-featured programs, such as Adobe Photoshop, and programs you can use as trialware, such as STOIK's PictureMan and Jasc's Paint Shop Pro. We'll also look at Adobe PhotoDeluxe Business Edition, because it basically leads you by the hand through various tasks. We'll do a few chores with Broderbund's The Print Shop Deluxe 10, because it does almost anything that a novice scanner user is likely to need.

Restoring a Shadowy Image

Let's start with a very common occurrence: a scanned photo that loses detail in the shadows, because the dark areas are just too dark.

Color Correction with Photoshop

The best tool for restoring color to a shadowy image is Adobe Photoshop. You can download a trial version of the program, but it will be Save-disabled, meaning you can't save your work to disk. However, some scanner packages include Adobe Photoshop LE (Limited Edition), which has all the features we'll be discussing in this book. We'll also restore color to the shadows by using Stoik's PictureMan, which is available as trialware on the Web.

Figure 8.1 shows on the left a creative photo of a woman with half her face in a shadow. The photo itself looked great, but after the scan, it somehow lost something. This loss of detail in the shadows could be caused by a scanner without a good color range, a video card that's unable to deliver true color values to your screen, or even a monitor that just doesn't display details well at the outer edges of the color range. Either way, you can fix the photo so that it looks good to you, as was done to the photo on the right in Figure 8.1.

Figure 8.1
A photograph with too much shadow (left) and after being corrected in Photoshop (right).

To bring more color to a shadowy image in Photoshop, do the following:

1. Open the image in Photoshop, and select Image>Adjust>Levels. The Levels dialog box appears (see Figure 8.2), which is divided into two halves: The Input Levels graph shows you where most of the color in the image is found. The way that the graph in Figure 8.2 is bunched toward the middle indicates that this photo contains very little bright color. We want Photoshop to redefine the color curve in this picture, by pulling more subtle color differences out of the poor color range that this picture has to offer.

Figure 8.2
The Levels dialog box in Photoshop.

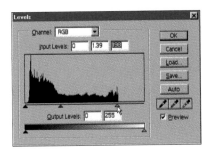

2. Position the Levels dialog box so that you can see your image. You'll want to see the effects your changes have on the picture.

3. Locate the Input Levels slider (a small triangle located below the graph) on the far right and drag it toward the middle. Click Preview so that you can see the tonal range change in your picture. This action redefines the high-end range of color for this picture.

4. Locate the middle Input Levels slider, the tiny triangle positioned between the right and left triangle sliders. Drag it toward the left. While dragging, watch your image. At a certain point, the color definition will be optimum and dragging further to the left will just cause the image to appear too bright and washed out. Manipulate the slider to get the balance just right.

5. Save your image. If you have doubts about your changes, save the picture under another name, thus preserving the original.

Color Correction with PictureMan

You can perform a similar treatment on a shadowy photo by using STOIK's PictureMan, a program available as trialware on the Web (www.hotfiles.com). Like many beginner-friendly photo editing programs, instead of giving you sliders to manipulate, PictureMan lets you choose among several preset effects. To restore brighter colors to a shadowy image in PictureMan, do the following:

1. In PictureMan, open the image you want to restore colors to.

2. Click Retouch, near the bottom of the toolbar on the left side of the screen. Notice that the tool options on the upper toolbar change, revealing ten photo editing tools.

CHAPTER 8

3. Click Smart tune. The Smart tune parameters dialog box appears, as shown in Figure 8.3.

Figure 8.3

PictureMan's Smart tune parameters dialog box.

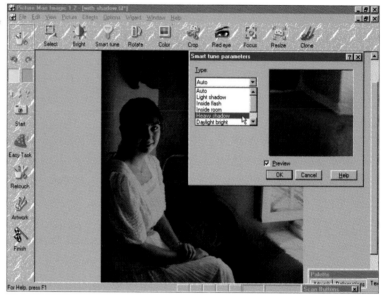

4. Click the Type drop-down arrow and select Heavy shadow from the options that appear.

5. Make sure the Preview box is checked, so that you can see your changes in the preview area provided. To see other areas not visible in the preview box, drag your mouse inside the preview area, which causes the picture to move, showing additional image segments.

6. Click OK, and the effect will be rendered in your picture. If you like the change, save the image.

You may notice that the difference between Photoshop and other, less professional-oriented software is the precision of the tools. Whereas Photoshop allows you to be very specific about what color ranges to restore and alter, PictureMan provides a handful of preset choices. Depending on your photo and the degree of restoration needed, the more beginner-friendly programs may or may not be adequate for your needs.

Correcting Overexposure with Paint Shop Pro 5 or 6

If an image looks washed out and too bright, and its detail is hidden by an overly light exposure, you can increase saturation to restore color and increase the image's midrange value. Saturation measures the colors in a picture, and how deeply saturated the image is with a particular color. An image that has zero saturation is composed only of shades of gray and white.

Increasing saturation is not always the best approach to restoring color. Its overuse can create unrealistically bold hues and reduce subtlies of color range. But in cases where a photograph appears to have a white layer of mist across it, increasing saturation can be helpful. Increasing saturation works best if you use it in conjunction with other adjustments, such as increasing midtones and shadows.

Figure 8.4 shows a before and after image with too much exposure. In Paint Shop Pro 5 or 6, you can treat this image by doing the following:

Figure 8.4
An overexposed image.

The same image corrected with Paint Shop Pro.

1. Open your image in Paint Shop Pro and select the Color menu.

2. Click Adjust, and pick Highlight/Midtone/Shadow from the options that appear.

3. Using the sliders, change the Midtone to approximately 24, and change the Shadow setting to 15. Click OK to confirm the adjustment.

4. From the Color menu, select Adjust>Hue/Saturation/Lightness.

5. Raise the Saturation level to about 20. Click OK to confirm the adjustment. The colors in your image should be more vivid and lively.

6. If you like the change, save your picture.

Adding Detail to Grainy Paper Photos

Aged photos, pictures printed on grainy paper, magazines, and newsprint often create scans that look dull and grainy. Figure 8.5 shows the before and after photo that has been corrected after being scanned from a grainy source. Here's how to treat this problem in Photoshop:

Figure 8.5
A grainy, dull photo (left) corrected with various Photoshop tools (right).

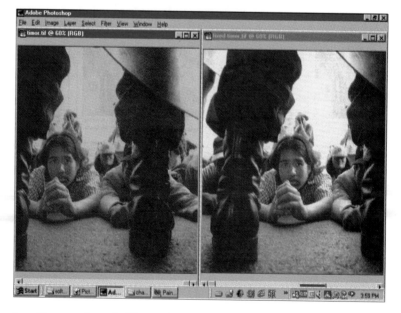

1. Open a photo in Photoshop and select Filter>Noise>Despeckle.

2. Select Filter>Noise>Dust and Scratches.

3. Select Image>Adjust>Hue/Saturation. Increase the Saturation level to 22.

4. Choose Image>Adjust>Color Balance (Figure 8.6). The Color Balance dialog box offers three color ranges to adjust: Highlights, Midtones, and Shadows. You can adjust three Color Balance settings for each range: the balance between the picture's Cyan and Red levels, between the Magenta and Green levels, and between the Blue and Yellow levels.

Figure 8.6
The Photoshop Color
Balance dialog box.

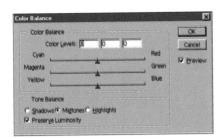

5. In the Tone Balance panel of the Color Balance dialog box, select Shadows and make any adjustments necessary to each slider. Then, do the same for Midtones and Highlights, in turn. You won't need to adjust each slider. Only certain color range adjustments will be effective—not every single one.

6. When adjusting these sliders, follow these guidelines:

    —Watch for image detail and clarity. Make color adjustments that bring out hidden color depth in the picture's objects.

    —Restore flesh tones. Watch the highlights on people's faces. Don't make adjustments that cause skin color to look blotchy or artificially orange or yellow.

    —Avoid causing a *color cast* while adjusting a slider. That means avoid giving the entire image an overall "green shine" or "red hue," for example, that washes over everything else.

    —Restore depth, which is the most important benefit these adjustments can bring to an image. In this example, the boots are in front, the folded hands are one layer back, the main subject's face is two layers back, the rows of people follow, and the journalist with the camera is in the back. Your color range adjustments should make each object in the photo appear to be in its own space, which in turn should give the photo more depth.

6. After making your final adjustments, select OK to confirm your changes.

7. If you like the results, save your photo.

CHAPTER 8

Removing Red Eye

Red eye occurs when the flash of a camera causes a photo subject's eyes to appear to glow red rather than display their natural color. It is caused by the flash bouncing off the retina of the eye. Photo editing programs remove red eye from your picture by drawing a boundary around the eye segment that is glowing red and replacing it with a color that you determine is more similar to the subject's real eye color. There's nothing very elegant about this, and the results quite often look more artificial than the red eye itself. Few characteristics give you more of an appreciation for the human face than when trying to change the way someone's eyes look. Most often, you'll find you've created a monster.

Correcting Red Eye with Paint Shop Pro

Scanning images is great, but usually you'll want to touch up photographs to get them looking perfect for a Web page. For example, many times photos capture "red eye," which occurs when someone stares directly into a camera as the flash goes off. With a print photograph, your options for fixing this phenomenon are limited, but once that photo is digitized, Paint Shop Pro gives you a lot more flexibility.

Figure 8.7 shows a sample picture that includes a bad case of red eye. This photo was taken with a standard 35mm camera and scanned into Paint Shop Pro.

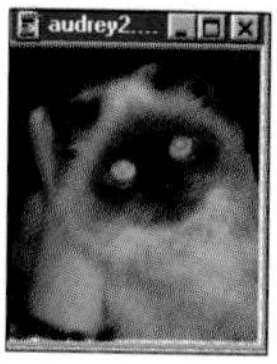

Fig. 8.7
Audrey was caught staring straight into the camera.

To correct the red eye in this picture, zoom in on the eyes and select the Magic Wand tool. This tool lets you select multiple shades of color on an image, which is extremely useful when you are editing photographs and images. Often many different shades are used together to make up a larger image, and selecting this collection of shades manually can be difficult.

Figure 8.8 shows an up-close zoom on the cat picture with the Magic Wand tool selected.

Fig. 8.8
The Magic Wand makes image editing a breeze!

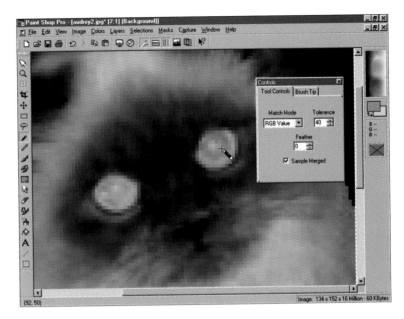

Now I am going to use the magic wand to select all of the red/orange color material in the eye. In the Control Palette, you have several settings for the Magic Wand, including Tolerance and feathering.

▶ **Tolerance**—The Tolerance setting tells Paint Shop Pro to select similar colors besides the one you click on. If you look carefully at figure 8.10, you'll notice that the eye is made up of several shades of orange, not just one. By changing the tolerance setting in the Control Palette, you are telling Paint Shop Pro to select all of the Orange colors that make up the eye, not just the one color clicked on. For this example, I'm using a Tolerance of 40, which means that PSP will select forty similar shades of Orange/Red when I use the Magic Wand. I can do this because all the colors around the eye are not even close to orange in color, so they won't be selected.

▶ **Feather**—The Feather setting tells PSP how many pixels outside of your color to select. Think of this setting as a buffer around the area you want to select. It's not useful here, because I only want to change the red eye, not the whites of the eye or any other parts of the image. So, for this example my Feather value is set to 0.

Once my Magic Wand settings are selected, I am going to click anywhere within the eye. Paint Shop Pro now selects the entire section of the eye for which we are going to change color using the Magic Wand settings. Figure 8.9 shows one of the eyes selected.

Fig. 8.9
We are recolorizing the selected area of the eye.

The Selected Area

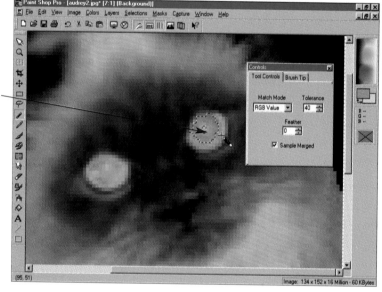

Once the proper area is selected, to change the color of the eye, I am going to use the PSP Color Adjuster. Choose Color>Adjust>Red/Green/Blue from the menu bar. Figure 8.10 shows the Red/Green/Blue dialog box that appears.

Fig. 8.10
Only the selected part of the image will be affected.

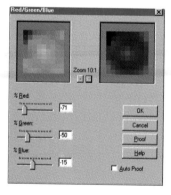

This dialog box lets you re-mix the amounts of Red, Green, and Blue for the selected part of the photo. Since the original eye had too much red, I am using the color bars to remove most of that color. The left side of this dialog box shows the original selected area, and the right side shows a preview of how your settings will affect that area.

For this example, I want to darken the entire eye to make it look more realistic. I selected –71% Red, –50% Green, and –15% Blue. Once I find the right mix and match of color percentages, I make my changes by clicking on the OK button. Paint Shop Pro changes only the area selected with Magic Wand. After repeating the same steps again for the other eye, figure 8.11 shows the final image, much improved and more realistic.

Fig. 8.11
Now this photo is ready to be used!

Sharpening an Image

The Sharpen tool is the first order of treatment for a blurry image. People turn to it first because it's easily applied and it actually sometimes works. Not all types of image blurring will respond to a Sharpen tool, and new users sometimes overapply it in hopes of getting a little more crispness from their pictures.

Avoid Oversharpening

In Figure 8.12, the image on the right shows scanned text that came out a bit on the blurry side. After applying Paint Shop Pro's Sharpen command four times, the text looked much crisper (the image on the left) and would make for more accurate text extraction using OCR.

Figure 8.12
A blurry text scan (right) treated with Paint Shop Pro's Sharpen tool (four passes).

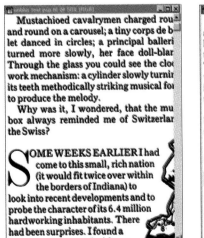
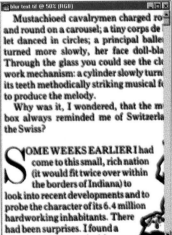

CHAPTER 8

That's an example of a success story, whereas Figure 8.13 shows an image that has been oversharpened. Note the characteristic "frosty" white halo effect around the edges of the image objects. You'll know that an image is not going to respond to the Sharpen tool if you start to see this unpleasant effect. Just click the Undo button a few times, and try something else.

Figure 8.13
An "oversharpened" image. Note the frosty halo over many objects.

The Unsharp Mask Tool

In the Image menu of Paint Shop Pro, two degrees of sharpening can be applied to an image: Sharpen, or Sharpen More. Another, more precise tool is also available, called Unsharp Mask (Figure 8.14). The term is borrowed from the film editing world, and this tool neither unsharpens your image nor creates a mask. This filter selects pixels according to lightness value and increases the contrast between them. This leads to more pronounced edges, hence a sharper image. You also determine the size of the area to be sampled (Radius). Sampling a smaller radius for sharpening creates crisper lines. The Clipping Value smoothes out the jagged edges that can appear when sharpening tools are used.

Figure 8.14
Paint Shop Pro's Unsharp Mask tool.

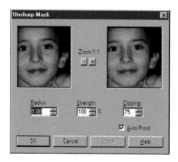

Cropping

Cropping refers to creating a rectangular box around a portion of your image and trimming the picture down to only what is inside that rectangle. Cropping does not resample (create a smaller version of the entire image); it simply cuts off the edges, leaving only the contents of the cropping rectangle. Figure 8.15 shows a picture before (left) and after (right) applying cropping in Paint Shop Pro. Circled in the image is the cropping symbol. Many photo editing programs use this symbol to signify the cropping tool.

Figure 8.15
An image before and after cropping. Note the cropping tool symbol, circled in this figure.

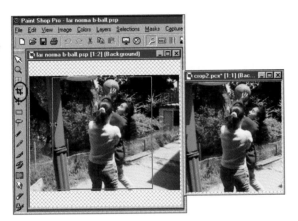

Programs such as Ulead's Photo Assistant provide automatic cropping. The main subject matter of the image is identified, and when the Auto Crop button is clicked, the picture is trimmed appropriately.

Correcting Imperfections with Clone Tools

The best way to remove tears and folds from your scanned picture is by using the Clone tool. Most photo editing programs have a Clone tool, and we'll use Paint Shop Pro's tool as our example.

Working with the Clone Tool

First, let's discuss how Clone tools work. The Clone tool lets you sample one area of your image and "dab" it somewhere else, similar to the way a paintbrush works. Use the Clone tool to sample an object in one section of your image and paint it into another area.

First, you'd right-click on an area you want to copy *from*. Then you'd paint over a different area with the clone tool (hold down the left mouse button and drag). The area around the image where you right-clicked would appear beneath your brush strokes as you paint with the Clone tool.

The Clone tool is good for extending the water of a beach a few feet forward over the shore, for example, by sampling and brushing waves over the existing sand (Figure 8.16).

Figure 8.16
The Clone tool applying strokes that extend water onto a shoreline.

Fixing Bends and Tears with the Clone Tool

The Clone tool is also good for removing imperfections from an image. You simply need a similar, if not identical, portion of the picture that is not damaged. That's the area you sample from. The following steps show how this works:

1. Open an image with an imperfection in Paint Shop Pro and select the Clone tool.

2. If the Clone tool's Controls palette is not visible (the Controls palette displays brush size and shape options), select View>Toolbars, and place a check next to Control Palette, which causes it to appear (see Figure 8.17).

NOTE

In Paint Shop Pro 6, the Control Palette is referred to as the Tool Options Window

Figure 8.17
The Paint Shop Pro
Clone tool and the
Controls palette, which
adjusts brush size and
softness.

3. Zoom in on the imperfection and look closely at the area surrounding
    it. Try to identify areas around the imperfection that look almost
    identical in coloring and subject (see Figure 8.18).

Figure 8.18
An image with a tear,
being treated with the
Clone tool.

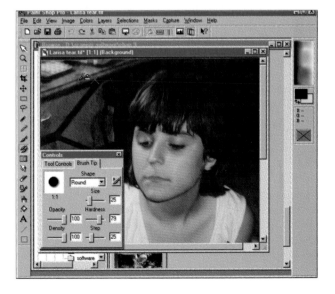

4. Looking at the Brush Tip tab of the Controls palette, locate the Size
    data box. Type a number between 4 and 20, depending on how large
    your image is. Sometimes, because the areas you want to cover with
    the cloned sample need an almost identical area to sample from, you

can only sample a tiny part of your image. That means you need a small brush size to sample with. When you paint with your clone, if the brushstrokes look out of place and not similar enough, try using a smaller brush size.

5. Make your Hardness setting around 40. A softer brush blends the clone more naturally into the surrounding image where you make your strokes.

6. Right-click the area where you want to take your sample from. In the example shown in Figure 8.19, the tear in the picture occurs over the desk and the panel on the side of the desk. When stroking over the tear right on the desktop, first right-click a similar, undamaged portion of desktop to obtain a sample. When painting over the panel area, right-click an undamaged area of the panel to get a usable sample.

7. Now that your Clone brush has a sample to paint with, place brushstrokes over the damaged area. Your brush is actually painting with another section of your image. If you imagine your brushstrokes occurring over the area where you sampled from, you'll have a good idea what your new cloned area will look like.

Figure 8.19
Cloning strokes from an area of the desk that does not have a tear in it.

8. Go back and resample (right-click) areas that look like they would believably cover up the imperfection. After resampling, just paint over the damaged area until the results look smooth. You can resample as often as you like.

9. After cloning, use the Retouch brush (select Retouch from the Tool Palate, and on the Control Panel, choose Smudge) to blend areas around where the imperfection used to be. This helps get rid of jagged areas where you placed cloned strokes.

10. Save your image, and if you are not sure whether the results look much better, save the file under a different name, reopen the original, and try again.

Creating a Calendar

Many family-project-oriented photo programs let you quickly create calendars with photos of your choice. Figure 8.20 shows a calendar created in Adobe PhotoDeluxe. The program prompts you with questions about what you want to make and creates the calendar before your very eyes.

Figure 8.20
A calendar created with
Adobe PhotoDeluxe.

You can create a monthly or yearly calendar, determine when the calendar should begin, and choose from various layout and style options. Then, you add background photos and a main feature photo for each calendar page. PhotoDeluxe chooses the calendar's font, font size, and color scheme, based on your style and layout choices. If you want to change any element—perhaps select a new font type or replace one of the drawings—double-click it, and the calendar element appears in an editing window, ready for you to adjust or make a new selection.

Broderbund's The Print Shop Deluxe Calendar Creator (see Figure 8.21) and Microsoft Publisher work with you in the same step-by-step fashion. Each initially creates a calendar based on your answers to the program's questions and then allows you to personalize and edit the final results.

Figure 8.21
A calendar created with
The Print Shop Deluxe.

Now that you've had some exposure to photo editing, in the next chapter, we'll explore what you can do with special effects and your photos. You'll learn about combining different types of images with your photos for unique projects, and changing the appearance of your photo in ways you may never have thought possible.

9

Special Effects Photo Editing

In this chapter, we'll create special effects with your pictures. You'll see that you can do a lot more with images than simply scan and reproduce them. Your pictures can display your own creative, personal touch. They'll become works of digital art. You'll learn how to apply warping and mirroring effects to your pictures, dramatically altering the image perspective to create a sense of distance, and other special effects. Your pictures will have more of a personal stamp.

You'll also explore how to alter color as a special effect, how to turn the background of a picture into a black-and-white image while accenting the colors of the main subject, and how to apply a drop shadow to a small segment of your picture.

Types of Photo Effects

There are roughly three types of special photo effects:

▶ **Color effects**—These effects make changes to the color range, either to the entire image or to a section you specify.

▶ **Deformation effects**—These effects distort image pixels, pulling, shearing, embossing, and bulging your picture, as well as giving your picture a "textured" look.

▶ **Cut-and-paste effects**—To create these effects, you select a segment of your image and move it somewhere else, perhaps leaving a hole in your picture to be filled with a new color or design or perhaps pasting the segment you cut in an entirely different picture.

As we get started, you'll see examples of each type of effect and how each can be applied with photo editing tools discussed in previous chapters— all with programs you can download from the Web as trialware. You'll also learn to create photo compositions that combine all kinds of effects, using the same types of tools.

CHAPTER 9

Before We Get Started

I'd like to share a few words about restraint, keeping in mind a few standards about what tends to look pleasing to the eye. I also want to encourage you not to overwrite your original scans; instead, save your special effects work as a separate file. That way, if your creation goes awry, you can always return to the original and try again.

Also, I need to reiterate a few system requirements for special effects photo editing. Few things are more boring and tedious than watching that Windows hourglass go around and around. I'll mention briefly how much computer firepower is required to have this much fun.

NOTE

The purpose of this chapter is to acquaint you with a broad array of image effect tools, providing only a handful of step-by-step instructions specific to particular programs. No matter what program you end up using for your scans, you'll find a high degree of uniformity in how tools are applied. In this chapter, I'll emphasize general instructions that will, by and large, be helpful to you regardless of your chosen software effects package. After you choose a software package and are happy with it, you may want to purchase a book that is specific for that product.

Creative Restraint

Special photo effects are a great creative tool, and to achieve results that someone may find interesting, here are a few aesthetic "rules of the game" that you may want to keep in mind. You'll soon find that, in the world of photo effects editing, the sky is not the limit–nor are the stars. You can pretty much do whatever you want. But rules of color and contrast, organic shapes, and basic geometry still apply, even if your imagination takes you to Orion and back.

▶ Rules of color still matter. It's a good idea to use complementary colors (for instance, orange and blue, purple and yellow). Don't use every color in the world just because you can.

▶ Make your people look like people. Everyone who buys a graphics editing program can't wait to put their least favorite uncle on the top of Mount Everest or change that bemused smile on the Mona Lisa. But there's still a lot to be said for the human form. No matter how creative you get, you'll probably find it quite satisfying to keep arms, legs, and facial features recognizable as such.

▶ Watch the way you position objects in your pictures. Too much linearity is boring. Not enough organization, and people get confused ("What am I looking at here?"). So, make geometry work with you, not against you.

▶ Even as you discover the myriad tools at your disposal, think about a unifying theme. Most artwork, no matter how abstract, is still either a landscape or a portrait. Which is yours?

Finding Your Way Back

One thing that truly unleashes lots of creativity is the knowledge that you'll always have your original photo to go back to. Anything you can do can also be undone, as long as you don't erase your original scan by overwriting it with your edited photo. Refer to Chapter 7, "Saving Your Scans," for tips on keeping edited photos separate from your scanned originals.

Additionally, remember what Ctrl+Z is for. In almost every case, you can undo your most recent edit if you change your mind about something. In fact, most photo editing programs provide *multiple undo,* allowing you to undo several of your most recent changes. That way, you can go crazy experimenting, and then compare "before" and "after" images before finalizing and saving your changes. When choosing a photo editing tool, investigate how to turn on the program's multiple undo feature, usually found in the Options or Preferences menu. Keep in mind, though, that adding multiple undo will increase the program's memory requirements. Most often, a multiple undo of between eight and twelve events is sufficient, unless you have a Pentium 400 computer or better.

I also recommend saving an image under a new name after a substantial edit. For example, when you substantially resize, add a filter to, or recolor an image, save it under a new name, thus preserving the earlier version as well.

System Requirements

Previous chapters discussed system requirements for scanning images and doing basic editing. Special effects editing places an additional burden on your CPU and video card. Even the less expensive special effects photo editing programs discussed here can take up to five minutes to render a complex effect, unless you have a Pentium 300 MHz computer with 64MB of RAM. Of course, when it comes to improving how quickly special effects render, the more computer power you have, the faster you'll see results. Some special effects, such as changing coloration and adding gradients, are not going to tax your system too much.

Special effects rendering also moves much faster if you have a video card with 16MB of RAM.

CHAPTER 9

Color Effects

Here are a few examples of special coloration effects. Note that color is the only feature we'll be altering in the following photographs.

Basic Color Effects Editing

Figure 9.1 shows a closeup photo of a cat and the same image, altered with Photoshop's Gradient tool. The Gradient tool fills your image with a two-color blend, moving along a color gradient from the background color to the foreground color. Drawing a long line with the Gradient tool creates a more gradual gradient from one color to the next. A short line creates an abrupt transition between the two colors.

Figure 9.1
A photo of a cat's face (left) and the same photo treated with Photoshop's Gradient tool.

It's easy to accomplish this. Here's how:

1. Open the photo in Photoshop.
2. Click the color squares at the bottom of the toolbox and select two contrasting colors, perhaps lavender and yellow, for example.
3. In the Merge drop-down menu, select Color.
4. Select the Gradient tool and drag diagonally from the top left of the image down to the bottom right.

You'll notice that the image *content* of your photo is fully intact, but the gradient you applied changed the *coloration*. If you like the effect, save your image under a different name.

Color Combinations and Selection Tools

Figure 9.2 shows a different kind of coloration effect. Achieving this effect will be our first real chore, using a masking or selection tool. We'll also explore how to use a Transparency tool (in this case, Corel PHOTO-PAINT's Transparency tool).

Figure 9.2
A photo with a color subject and a black-and-white background.

This image is a combination of two photos, one black and white and the other color. The image of the young bridesmaid was cut from the original photo and pasted into the black-and-white picture. The bridesmaid's feet were made transparent, giving her more of a ghostly appearance. Let's talk briefly about removing the bridesmaid from the original picture and pasting her into the black-and-white photo. You'll need to learn a little bit about selecting, or masking, part of an image.

Selecting a Portion of Your Image

When you select or mask part of an image, you are setting aside a portion of a picture for cutting, copying, or editing. The trick is to evenly select only the image portion you want, keeping your selection free of little bits of white around the edge. Roughly two types of selecting or masking tools exist, each of which is good for different types of tasks:

▶ **Shape Carving**—Cut out your selection, dragging your mouse around the edges of the shape or subject, bit by bit. You'll need to use the Zoom tool to magnify the image and make sure you are truly sticking to the edges of your subject matter. Figure 9.3 shows a selection in progress in Adobe PhotoDeluxe.

Figure 9.3
Gradually carving a selection in Adobe PhotoDeluxe.

CHAPTER 9

Shape Carving tools are great for cutting out simple shapes, such as rectangles and ovals. Many types of Shape Carving tools are available. Micrografx Picture Publisher has a Smart Mask that automatically trims away excess bits of background that you do not want with your selection. Most photo editing programs have an Irregular Shape selection tool of one kind or another, allowing you to closely carve out intricate edges.

▶ **Magic Wand**—Sometimes, a shape is too intricate to carve away from its background. Magic Wand tools create a selection by examining differences in color between the foreground and background. Click an area of nearly solid color in your image. All nearby pixels of similar color will be added to your mask.

The Magic Wand tool is great for selecting a complex image against a solid-color background. You don't have to carve anything, which means that if you have a photograph of a car sitting on a green lawn and you want to select the car for a project, you don't select the car: select the lawn, and all pixels that are green and nearly green will be selected. When you use a Magic Wand tool, several mouse clicks usually are required to select the entire area you want for your selection. Magic Wand tools allow you to "build" your selection, clicking areas of similar color throughout your image, adding to the masked area each time.

Setting Magic Wand Tolerance

When selecting colors for your mask, Magic Wand tools let you determine how "picky" the mask should be. When you click a blue section, do you want only areas of that exact hue of blue to be selected or areas that are somewhat similar? You can specify that your Magic Wand tool select only the exact color you start your selection with. Suppose you first click a shade of bright red. The next time you click, the tool will add only pixels that are a similar hue of red. Or you can make the tool add all colors that are on the same end of the spectrum as your original choice. So, for example, if you first click red, multiple later clicks adds all shades of red-orange and yellow-orange.

You determine how "picky" your Magic Wand tool is by selecting a Tolerance level (see Figure 9.4).

Figure 9.4
The Tolerance control in Photoshop.

Here's how Tolerance works:

▶ Set a high Tolerance number (15 or higher) and each time you click your image, the Magic Wand tool will add all similar shades of color to your selection.

▶ Set a low Tolerance number (generally, below 15, depending on the variety of hues found in your image) and only very similar shades of your original color selection will be added with each mouse click.

Working with Your Selection

After creating a selection by any means, you can do one of the following:

▶ Edit the area you've selected.

▶ Cut the area you've selected to the Windows Clipboard and paste it elsewhere for editing.

▶ Invert the selection. Now, everything other than the area you selected will be editable. The selection is reversed.

The image with the bridesmaid against the gray background was created as follows:

1. The bridesmaid was cut away from the original image by using a Magic Wand tool, as shown in Figure 9.5. The checkerboard pattern is used by many graphics programs to indicate that an image has no background. If the bridesmaid is cut and pasted into another image, the host image will be the only background behind her.

Figure 9.5
The bridesmaid object was cut away from the background. The checkerboard pattern indicates the absence of a background.

2. The host image (the cityscape buildings) was desaturated of all color. It is called the *host* image because it *receives* the picture of the bridesmaid. In almost any photo editing program, you can remove color by selecting Hue/Saturation/Brightness from the Colors>Adjust menu and decreasing the Saturation to 0. Your image editing program may also have a feature to convert a color image to Grayscale, which would have the same effect.

CHAPTER 9

3.   After desaturating the color from the background image, return to the bridesmaid image and cut it to the Windows Clipboard.

4.   Return to the gray image and paste the bridesmaid. Position the color image anywhere you like. See the following tip, "Free-Floating Selections."

TIP

The procedure just described works best in programs such as Photoshop or Paint Shop Pro, in which selections that you paste from the Clipboard can be moved around and treated independently even after you paste them.

▶   Corel PHOTO-PAINT calls free-floating, editable image segments *objects.*

▶   Paint Shop Pro and Photoshop call them *layers.*

In some photo editing programs, an object is locked in place as soon as you paste it. It just becomes part of the background. That means you cannot edit the object you just pasted independent of the background. This is a severe limitation. Before choosing a photo editing tool, make sure that it supports *multiple object editing.* You don't need to spend lots of money to obtain this feature. Paint Shop Pro 6 and Micrografx Picture Publisher let you move your selections around independently.

5.   To make the bridesmaid's lower body appear transparent, you need a tool such as Corel PHOTO-PAINT's Interactive Transparency tool. In Figure 9.6, PHOTO-PAINT's Transparency tool is placed near the middle of the bridesmaid and dragged downward. The length of the arrow determines how gradually the transparency is applied.

Figure 9.6
Applying transparency to an image.

6.   After rendering the transparency, you'll have a colored object against a background. If you save your image in the program's *proprietary format* (as discussed in Chapter 7), you can reopen the project later and move the colored foreground object again. If you save the image in a generic bitmap format, such as TIF or PCX, you won't be able to independently edit the foreground object after saving.

Deformation Effects

Other special photographic effects may fall into the deformation effect category. Let's look at some examples.

In Figure 9.7, the background of the image has been treated by Paint Shop Pro's Ripple effect. The background was selected with the Magic Wand tool, excluding the boy. That way, the photo's main subject matter can be protected from special effects editing.

Figure 9.7
A Ripple effect applied to only the background of an image.

Paint Shop Pro has a whole menu of deformation effects which let you change the physical shape of your image to a circle, pentagon, or cylinder. You can also warp, pinch, and make your image look like it was blown through a wind tunnel. To reach this menu, select Deformations from the Image menu.

CHAPTER 9

Paint Shop Pro 6 has a new deformer called Rotating Mirror. It reproduces the left side of your image, removing what was on the right and setting it off at an angle. In Figure 9.8, a photo of a car was treated with the Rotating Mirror effect. Figure 9.9 shows Paint Shop Pro's Spiky Halo effect applied to the same image. Spiky Halo surrounds the image with frostlike spikes around the edges.

Figure 9.8
A car treated with the Rotating Mirror effect.

Figure 9.9
The same image then treated with the Spiky Halo effect.

With deformation effects, a little goes a long way. If the effect has a menu for reducing the amplitude or strength of the effect, first apply the effect using a low setting and work your way up. You may be happy with a much less dramatic effect than what the menu offers by default.

Creating Frames, Embossing, and Beveling

Other deformation effects are more tasteful. The frame in Figure 9.10 was created by Kai's Actions, a group of Photoshop special effects by MetaCreations. The effects are controlled through Photoshop's Actions menu. This frame was created with a few mouse clicks. Photoshop's Actions did all the work. After sizing the frame to fit the image, they were combined.

Figure 9.10
The frame around this picture was created instantly with a Photoshop special effect.

Other, more traditional deformation effects common to almost every photo editing program are Emboss (shown in Figure 9.11) and Bevel (sometimes called *Buttonize,* shown in Figure 9.12). Most of these effects are applied with a single mouse click from a menu option. They are great for adding texture and variety to an image or if you want to make an image into a clickable "button" on a Web page, thus creating a 3D effect. You can usually adjust the height and width of the extrusion amount and select a color for the embossing or beveling.

CHAPTER 9

Figure 9.11
A photograph treated
with an Emboss effect.

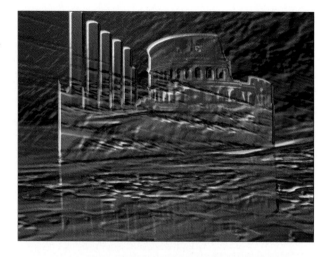

Figure 9.12
A beveled photo.

Cut-and-Paste Effects

Cut-and-paste effects usually involve two images, but what follows is a
cut-and-paste example in which rectangles are cut from a picture, edited,
and pasted into their original location. Each section is first recolored, a
drop shadow is applied, and then the section is returned to the place
from which it was cut.

Cutting Even Selections

Figure 9.13 shows a photo of a sunrise, quite lovely in its own right.

Figure 9.13
A scanned photo of a sunrise, photographed by Jim Wassinger.

But let's have a little fun with it. Figure 9.14 shows the same image after even rectangles were copied and removed, treated individually with coloration, and then given a drop shadow.

Figure 9.14
The photo treated with cut-and-paste special effects.

Each section selected in the sunset photo was colored using a Hue/Saturation/Brightness tool, common to most photo editing programs. A segment was selected and copied (rather than cut). Then, the Hue slider was adjusted differently for each segment. Changing the coloration without changing the image content creates a unified effect while still providing a little variety.

CHAPTER 9

Applying a Drop Shadow to a Selected Area

After coloring each image segment, a drop shadow was applied. Corel PHOTO-PAINT has an efficient, high-quality Drop Shadow tool that was used for this photo. Most drop shadow tools work similarly. We'll discuss the PHOTO-PAINT tool, highlighting how the process works in general.

To apply a drop shadow in Corel PHOTO-PAINT, do the following. Select the object you want to create a shadow for. In the example of the sunrise photo, each of the rectangles was selected one by one. In any event, select Object>Drop Shadow (see Figure 9.15). There are three options that are of great interest:

Figure 9.15
Corel PHOTO-PAINT's
Dropshadow dialog box.

▶ **Feathering**—Controls how gradual the edges of the shadow "drop off." High feathering amounts imply a far-away, diffuse light source. Low feathering implies a close, bright light source.

▶ **Offset**—Implies the light source direction. Should the shadow be projected to the right or left of the image? Above or below? A shadow projected below the image implies that light is shining from above. When casting multiple shadows in one picture, it's important that the shadow offset is the same for each. It looks more natural to imply one light source for an entire image, even if each object casts its own shadow.

▶ **Opacity**—Determines how dark and pronounced the shadow should be. Sometimes a light-gray, subtle shadow can be more dramatic and effective than a large, dark-black one. Higher opacity creates darker shadows.

Cutting and Pasting with Perspective

Let's create a cut-and-paste effect, while simultaneously learning about a superb special effects collection: Kai's Power Tools.

Figure 9.16 shows a "painting" of dozens of cartoon faces. This image was created with MetaCreations' Painter's Image Hose. We'll be spending some time with Painter and other digital painting software later in this book. For now, just keep in mind that Painter's Image Hose lets you load your brush with a series of minipictures. When you generate a brushstroke, you are painting with those pictures. Paint Shop Pro has a similar tool, called Picture Tube, and Right Hemisphere's Deep Paint is an accessory for Photoshop that offers similar digital painting tools.

Figure 9.16
A sea of faces, created with Painter 5's Image Hose brush.

This "world of faces" image was used to create the perspective design shown in Figure 9.17. To make it look like a deep, long runway, the Planar Tiling effect from Kai's Power Tools was used.

CHAPTER 9

Figure 9.17
A study in perspective, created using cutting and pasting.

Applying Perspective with Kai's Power Tools

Kai's Power Tools is not a standalone application but a plugin that can work with MetaCreations' Painter, Photoshop, and PHOTO-PAINT, among other programs. Kai's Power Tools is downloadable as trialware from www.hotfiles.com, and the Planar Tiling effect generated in Figure 9.18 is included in the trialware version.

To create something similar to the image shown in Figure 9.18, do the following:

1. In a photo editing program, open an image suitable to create the Planar Tiling effect. It should have small, repeating patterns.

2. Open Kai's Power Tools in that application. Although it is not a standalone program, Power Tools has its own interface.

3. Select Planar Tiling from the list of effects and click in the Options area.

4. Select Planar Tiling. The image will appear in Kai's interface. Click inside the screen and drag your mouse downward, which brings the Perspective Tile effect upward, filling a little more than half the entire image area.

5. Click OK, and the image will be rendered with the Perspective Tiling effect. The area above the tiling will probably be white.

NOTE

The area above the perspective tiling will be whatever your background color is set to, which most often is white. Some programs automatically fill a "cut" or blank area with the paper color, which again usually is white. What is essential to keep in mind is that the color of the cut area should not be similar to the color of the tiles. Since you'll be using the Magic Wand tool to select the area above the tiles for editing (which is color-sensitive), you don't want to create hardship by allowing the fill color to be something close to the tiles hues.

Filling a Selected Area with an Image

Now let's prepare the background for pasting in an image, and position the image inside the background area.

1. Using a Magic Wand tool, select the area above the tiles. You'll be filling it with a cityscape of some type, as previously shown.

2. Open a cityscape image and consider the wide, long area it will fill. Alter the shape of the cityscape image so that it will conform better to the destination area (see Figure 9.18).

3. As you shrink the image vertically (but not horizontally), the buildings may look a little compressed, but they'll look better as part of the perspective tiling image if you make the shape of the entire cityscape generally match the destination area (the white area selected above the plane tiles).

Figure 9.18
The white, blank area will be filled with the cityscape.

CHAPTER 9

4. Copy the cityscape image to the Windows Clipboard and paste it into the tiling image (make sure the white area above the tiles is still selected).

5. From the Edit>Paste menu, your photo editing program may offer the command Paste Into or Paste Into Selection. This is indeed what we want here, to paste the buildings *into* the selection. Using the simple Paste command simply lays the image over the top of what is already there.

6. After you paste the buildings into the area, use the mouse to reposition the cityscape, to create the realistic illusion of a distant city. Sky, hills, and other structures besides buildings will add to the realism.

7. If you like the effect, save your image.

Remember, saving the picture as a proprietary image format (for example, PSD or RIF) will allow you to edit the building position later. Saving the image as a generic image format (such as TIFF or PCX) automatically locks in the buildings to the background, and no further repositioning can be performed.

Now that you've learned about photo editing and applying special effects to your pictures, let's move on to optical text recognition, or OCR. You'll learn how to scan a document and extract text from it, exporting the text to either a desktop publishing program or a word processing program for further editing.

10

OCR and Working with Text

This chapter discusses optical character recognition (OCR), the technology that enables you to extract text from your scans and use it in a word processing or desktop publishing program. You'll learn basic OCR steps that apply to most programs, as well as some of the various optional features that you can employ to assist you. The chapter wraps up by looking at how to incorporate artistic text into your scanned work without losing text quality.

OCR refers to the process of converting a scanned image of text into true text characters that can be edited individually by a word processing program. Before going forward, let's talk a moment about how your computer works with text.

PCs and Formatted Text

Computers create text from code. When you type in a document, your word processor displays each letter by combining a series of bytes, or characters. Publishing and word processing programs work with a common text language known as ASCII, and from that simple, universal code, the alphabet is built. Bytes are combined to form each letter, number, or symbol you type.

However, when you compose a letter or resume, you demand much more from your computer than the ability to type the alphabet. Bytes of computer code are combined for each and every formatting trick you perform in your document. If you start a paragraph by indenting a word that begins with the letter *A*, the software generates an elaborate code defining the exact size, font type, color style, and paragraph formatting that you specified by typing a keystroke on your keyboard.

But what do you get when you scan a document with text on it? A picture of words. The result is not character codes that your word processor can use but rather a *bitmap,* a series of dots that you see as a letter onscreen. OCR, then, is the process of converting a picture of text into character code that can be edited freely.

OCR in Practical Terms

What we refer to as OCR is usually the entire procedure, from beginning to end, of scanning an image with text, converting it, and opening it in a text program to make sure all is well. However, there are many steps between scanning your image and breezily formatting and editing the resulting text output. The following list briefly describes these intermediate steps:

1. **Obtaining the actual scan**—As mentioned previously, the rules for scanning for text extraction are different from the rules for scanning color photos. This chapter explores the differences in some detail.

2. **Determining the layout positioning**—Technically speaking, an OCR program searches for images of text, converts them to real text, and discards everything else. The following note elaborates on the OCR layout options you may encounter.

NOTE

If you scan an image of a newsletter, hoping that the output will actually resemble what you scanned, you may be disappointed. You'll get text, and that is all (see Figure 10.1). But some OCR programs recognize artistic borders, clip art, and even column formatting, and the programs attempt to deliver the whole document as it was scanned. In these more advanced programs, after you scan, your text will be formatted into columns, just like the newsletter you began with. In the resulting, editable output, the borders and blocks of color may even be in place. Not all OCR programs can deliver layout settings, and among those that do, not all perform the task well. We'll discuss a few good OCR software packages later in this chapter.

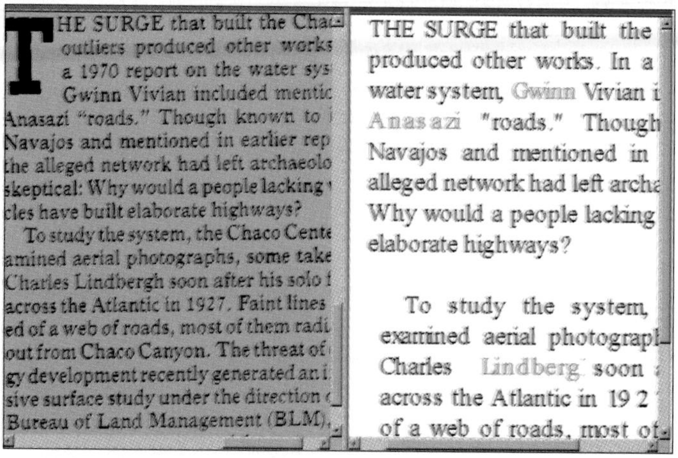

Figure 10.1

Basic OCR simply strips text out of a document. On the left is the scanned newspaper clipping, and on the right is the resulting text after OCR.

THE SURGE that built the Chaco outliers produced other works a 1970 report on the water sys Gwinn Vivian included mentio Anasazi "roads." Though known to Navajos and mentioned in earlier rep the alleged network had left archaeolo skeptical: Why would a people lacking cles have built elaborate highways?

To study the system, the Chaco Cente amined aerial photographs, some take Charles Lindbergh soon after his solo across the Atlantic in 1927. Faint lines ed of a web of roads, most of them radi out from Chaco Canyon. The threat of gy development recently generated an i sive surface study under the direction Bureau of Land Management (BLM),

THE SURGE that built the produced other works. In a water system, Gwinn Vivian i Anasazi "roads." Though Navajos and mentioned in alleged network had left archa Why would a people lacking elaborate highways?

To study the system, examined aerial photograph Charles Lindberg soon across the Atlantic in 19 2 of a web of roads, most of

3. **Recognizing the letters**—A lot is involved when an OCR program reads a bitmap of a letter and identifies it. Think of how many ways the letter *c* is symbolized (see Figure 10.2). OCR programs have tables corresponding to each aspect of a letter's appearance. These tables are like "keys," or legends on a map, that tell you where you can hike or go camping. After reading a scan of a letter, the software compares the image with the data in the table and looks for a match: "Oh, this must be a *c*," is the happy result. Good OCR software employs elaborate *feature recognition,* enabling it to recognize letters by the slightest familiar letter form or shape.

Figure 10.2
The challenge OCR faces when simply trying to read the letter c.

C C C c C C C C

4. **Discarding unrecognizable images**—If the picture of a letter is not clear or not sharp enough to be recognized as a letter by the software, it is discarded and not reported as text.

5. **Converting the data**—After the software makes a few passes and tries to recognize all the letters it can, it converts the results to text character code. It is this code that your desktop publishing or word processing programs work with, formatting and creating editable documents.

NOTE
Keep in mind that all OCR software makes mistakes. "Open" might become OP⊥N≡, and "short" might become _πoΔt. Even with the best of programs, you have to read through the results and make corrections manually. (You can expect about 90 to 97 percent accuracy.) But at least you'll have text to make corrections *to.* Instead of typing everything by hand, you simply read the scanned results and pick out errors, replacing odd symbols with the correct letters, correcting misinterpreted letters, and so forth.

Making OCR Work for You

After scanning a page of text that you really weren't looking forward to retyping, it's quite a relief to view the OCR output page and realize that almost all of the document was recognized and converted correctly. The following are the factors that make for a good OCR session:

▶ **The clarity of your original image**—The old maxim holds true, "garbage in means garbage out." Scanning text from an old newspaper clipping causes more potential problems than does an evenly spaced, typed essay. OCR software works by analyzing light and dark areas of your document. High contrast is good. Nice dark text against crisp white paper is good. Muddy newspaper text against aging yellow paper can lead to errors. Before scanning, make sure the source document has no creases or folds. As much as possible, line up multiple paragraphs and columns evenly.

▶ **Scanning settings**—Documents headed for OCR should be scanned as line art (single-color, 2-bit scanning) at a higher resolution than you'd use for a photograph. Scanning large, widely spaced text (18-point font, for example) can be scanned at 200 dpi. Twelve-point text can be scanned at around 300 dpi, and anything smaller than that should be scanned at 400 dpi.

▶ **Post-scan editing**—Before performing recognition, some OCR software will "clean up" scans for you, but not all OCR programs do this. Here are some judicious edits that you may want to take into your own hands, before attempting text recognition with OCR:

NOTE

Because you scan your document at a higher resolution than you normally would scan a standard photograph, when you first view your OCR scan, the program may automatically resize it to fit your screen. This will be at approximately a 33 percent or 25 percent Zoom level. At such a Zoom level, the text looks unclear. Don't panic. View your document at 100 percent, at least momentarily, and you'll feel better about the results. Then, Zoom back so that you can see the entire scan, and proceed with preparing it for OCR.

▶ **Sharpening**—If you notice that your scan is a bit blurry, use your photo editor's Sharpening tool. You can sharpen multiple times, if each pass appears to help somewhat. The Dust and Scratches tool or Despeckle tool also may help bring clarity to a blurry text scan.

▶ **Straighten the document**—If the scanned document is a bit rotated, straighten it by using your photo editor's Rotate tool. Some beginner-friendly programs have a Straighten feature just for realigning crooked scans (see Figure 10.3).

Figure 10.3
A Straighten feature for aligning crooked scans. Photo by Ariela Ronay-Jinich

▶ **Increase contrast**—The Brightness/Contrast tool can make a marginally readable scan much clearer. Raising the contrast almost always helps. Make that text nice and dark against a bright-white background.

▶ **A good OCR program**—Not all software is created equal, and price is not always the best indicator of value. You need a program that is particularly good at recognizing all kinds of characters and that is not easily flustered by a variety of letter types. If a program came free with your scanner, test it out. Perhaps this free program is good enough. If not, before you spend any money, search the Web for a trialware title that looks good and see how it works.

Now that you have a general idea of how OCR software does its job and know some steps that you can take to make sure text recognition works well for you, let's look at some specific programs, walk through an OCR session, and browse some useful features.

OCR Walk-Through

This section walks through an entire OCR session, with some highlights offered for specific programs. Before we launch in, though, let's talk a bit about the trade-off between convenience and flexibility.

With some OCR programs, you simply put the document to scan on the scanner bed and click Start. A few minutes later, the text is recognized and ready to save as a text file. Figure 10.4 shows the Presto! SmartScan screen, presenting the option to either scan for text only or retain the document's original formatting.

Figure 10.4
The Presto! SmartScan screens automate your OCR choices.

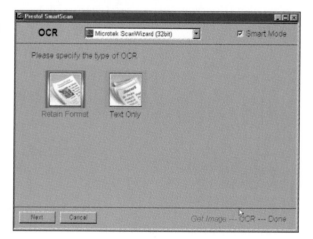

With other OCR programs, you must set up scan parameters first and then, after the scan, tell the OCR program how to divide the text as it appears on the page. After OCR, you must initiate proofreading, spell-checking, and so forth. Figure 10.5 shows OmniPage's OCR Wizard, in which you must choose from four page-layout options before proceeding. In such programs, little is automated. The program waits for your input every step of the way.

Figure 10.5
OmniPage's OCR Wizard leaves much of the decision-making in your hands.

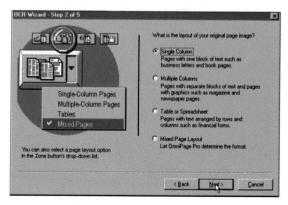

So, one-touch OCR can be very convenient, but what if the program didn't "understand" that you have columns on your page? Can you repeat the OCR and specify for the program to place text into columns? What if the OCR program tried to interpret text on a graphic, and you didn't really want it to do so? Can you tell the program to ignore the pictures?

It can also be irritating to prompt every step in the process. Do you have to specify that the OCR program discard unrecognized data? Wouldn't it be better if it just did it without being told?

My recommendation is this: If you are scanning documents with graphics, borders, or other types of in-line artwork that is positioned close to the text you are trying to scan, look for a program that lets you make OCR adjustments yourself. This is true if you are scanning documents with columns and tables. You want to be able to tell the program "This is a table. Don't bother scanning it." "This is the third column of straight text," and so forth.

However, if you are scanning documents composed almost entirely of text in paragraph or outline form, a simple, more automated OCR program will work well for you.

Using The Visioneer Pro OCR 100

We'll use Visioneer OCR's interface as our guide, while commenting on the features that also are available in many other programs. This program, or one of its more expensive and elaborate cousins, is included with many Visioneer scanners and is pretty typical of what you'll find offered on the market.

Visioneer Pro OCR 100 clearly presents you with the necessary OCR setup choices. By understanding these choices, you'll be more aware of the process and have a better sense of what settings you are likely to need to adjust each time, if any.

Here are the basic OCR steps that we will walk through:

1. Acquiring a scanned file with text, either by scanning or by opening a picture file in your OCR program.

2. Zooming out so that you can see the whole document, not huge letters up close.

3. Specifying document layout structures so that the OCR program knows what to look for (number of columns, what to do with pictures, and so forth).

4. Recognizing and converting text pictures to true text that can be exported.

5. Proofreading and spellchecking the OCR program's output file.

6. Saving the file as a DOC, RTF, or TXT file.

7. Opening the output file in a word processing program to verify satisfactory results.

Each of these steps is explained in more detail in the following sections, using Visioneer Pro OCR 100 to scan, recognize and interpret a document

Obtaining the Page

You can either scan a page or open a previously scanned document from your hard drive. The OCR program will treat them the same.

> **TIP**
>
> Some OCR programs only open 1-bit, black-and-white documents. Some others do not open compressed TIFF files, in which case you should open the TIFF file in the original program you created it with and save it as a 1-bit, black and white PCX file, or grayscale PCX file.
>
> If you scan your document and open it later in an OCR program, save it as a PCX file, because the code is simple, familiar, and understood by almost all graphics programs, new and old.

1. Place a document on the scanning bed and open Visioneer Pro OCR 100. If you've installed it, it should be on the Windows Start menu.

2. Click the drop-down arrow next to Get Page and select Use Scanner (see Figure 10.6).

3. Click Get Page again. Your scanner interface will appear.

Figure 10.6
Click Get Page to activate your scanner in Visioneer Pro OCR 100.

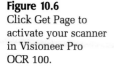

> **TIP**
>
> If you have a previously scanned file that you want to run through OCR, click the arrow next to Get Page and choose Open File. You may skip the following steps that deal with scanning the file and move straight to the Locate option on the Visioneer menu.

Choosing Scanning Settings

Remember that scanning in color not only provides information that most OCR programs cannot use but also creates a huge file that slows down the process unnecessarily. Some OCR programs may simply reject a color file and unceremoniously close the program without explanation. Later in this chapter, however, we'll look at Page Genie, a program that extracts color text, color photos, and other graphics, as well as converts text via OCR. For now, we'll keep it simple.

1. Use the scanner interface to select settings for an OCR scan. Here are settings to keep in mind:

    —If the text is clear and distinct, use Line Art, or 1-bit, single-color scanning.

    —If the text is somewhat gray and not clearly black, you may need to use the 256 Shades of Gray settings.

    —Set the appropriate dpi, using the parameters discussed earlier in this chapter, in the section, "Making OCR Work for You."

2. Preview your document, and resize the scanning area, if necessary, before the final scan.

3. Scan the document. It will open immediately in the Visioneer Pro OCR 100 interface.

Identifying Document Elements

Review your scan, checking for elements that you want to make sure the OCR program accounts for (such as columns or tables) and graphics that you want it to ignore.

1. The scanned document may appear huge, because you scanned it at a high resolution. Click the Zoom Out button in the lower-left corner of the OCR interface. To fit the entire scan onto your screen, you may need to zoom out to between 33 and 25 percent.

2. Click the arrow next to the Locate button (see Figure 10.7). This is where you specify how much attention the program should pay to the scanned document's layout:

Figure 10.7
Set Locate features to identify which structures should be scanned and recognized and which should be ignored.

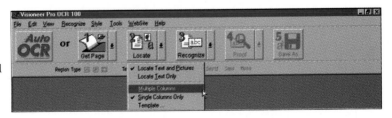

—If your scan includes pictures, and you want the program to scan both the pictures and the text, then select Locate Text and Pictures.

—If you want Visioneer OCR to ignore the pictures, then select Locate Text Only. (Remember that you are not scanning in color, so allow Visioneer to scan the pictures only if you want them in black and white or grayscale).

—Specify whether Visioneer should look for a column-based text layout or should scan text as if it were all one column.

3. Click the Locate button, and the program will interpret the layout of your page. This is a precursor to actually looking for text characters (recognizing and converting them to true text). Right now, the program is only looking at block structures on the page, to format the layout.

Recognizing the Text

Now you'll direct the program to actually recognize and interpret the characters and output the text.

1. Click the drop-down arrow next to Recognize (see Figure 10.8). Specify the quality of the original document. Visioneer applies a slightly different interpretation scheme depending on the quality level you specify. A higher-quality document yields better results.

2. Click the Recognize button, and OCR begins. The program moves through the document, looking for text features that it recognizes, and converting your bitmap letters to actual text. This may take a few minutes and will probably require most of your system resources, thus preventing you from doing much else with your computer during this time. Some programs provide a progress bar to indicate that OCR is going along nicely.

Figure 10.8
Specify the quality of your original document to minimize OCR errors.

Start the actual OCR recognition by clicking the Recognize button. After text recognition is complete, a new document appears in the Visioneer interface. It probably looks somewhat similar to the previous one, although the text is now real text. The characters have been recognized and converted. You are seeing the true text that can be saved as a DOC, RTF, or TXT file and edited in a text editor of your choice at your convenience.

Proofreading and Error Correction

Now that your text has truly become text, you can click each letter, change it, format it, and move it anywhere you like. You can do your proofing now or open it later in a word processing program of some sort.

To allow the program to check your document for spelling errors or to add words to its dictionary that it could not recognize, click Proof. Visioneer will highlight suspect or misspelled words (see Figure 10.9). Allow the program to check each suspected error one at a time; skip this step if you think your word processing program can do this job better, which it probably can. Word processing programs, such as Word 97 or WordPerfect, have much more sophisticated Find/Replace and Spellchecking tools than most OCR programs offer.

CHAPTER 10

Figure 10.9
Click Proof to proofread and spellcheck the document.

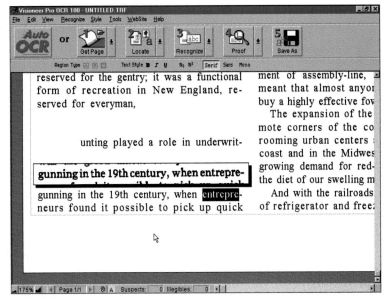

Saving the Document

When you save your text file, you can save it in a format, such as TXT or RTF, that is editable by all kinds of programs (RTF files will retain some formatting, whereas TXT files will not). Or, if the option is available, you can save your file in a proprietary format, such as DOC for Word, or WPF for WordPerfect.

Finally, click Save As and specify the file type and location of your final document. You may want to open the resulting file in Word or another word processing program, just to make sure all is well.

Use AUTO OCR in Future Scans

If the OCR process for your next scan is the same (if the settings just discussed aren't going to change), you can simply click the Auto OCR button (upper-left corner of the Visioneer OCR interface) for that scan. All the steps will proceed without your intervention, except for naming and saving the final output file. After you initially specify the OCR settings, using Auto OCR is how you really save time. Indeed, most OCR programs provide some method for saving your settings, so you won't have to step through each OCR adjustment each time that you convert a document.

Advanced OCR Options

This section looks briefly at some other OCR programs that have particular features of interest. We'll examine programs that let you conveniently scan and keep track of multiple pages, account for elaborate layout options, and retain color images and advanced formatting after you OCR your document.

Scanning Multiple Pages

Presto! PageManager is excellent at managing multiple page scans. Figure 10.10 shows a group of scanned pages saved as a single PageManager project; each page can be recognized as part of the same session. Figure 10.11 shows the same project, expanded to its three pages. To recognize and interpret each page, right-click each page and choose Do OCR. The results appear on the main work screen, ready for you to edit. Simply read the pages after the OCR process and double-click a word to replace it or correct its spelling.

Figure 10.10
A group of scanned pages saved as one project, to be processed as a group.

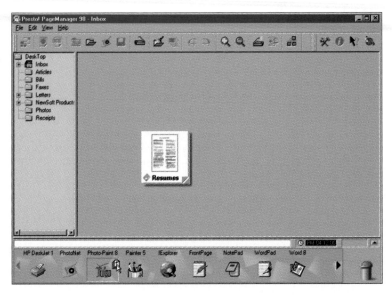

CHAPTER 10

Figure 10.11
The same project expanded to show all of its pages.

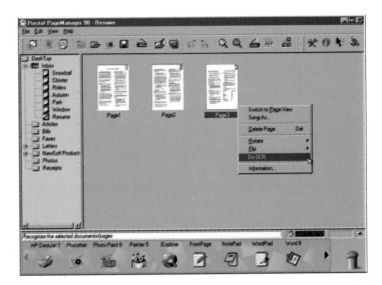

You can also scan multiple pages as part of the same project. Each scan appears in the work screen after you scan it. You can either save the combined pages as a Page Manager project to be processed by OCR later or right-click each page to OCR it on the spot, before saving.

After a page is processed, drag it onto a program's icon at the bottom of the window (see Figure 10.12). Every word processing or desktop publishing program that Page Manager was able to recognize is represented by an icon at the bottom of the screen. Dragging the document to an icon opens the document in that program. Or you can simply save the page as a text file of some sort by selecting File>Save As.

Figure 10.12
Drag your processed documents onto a program's icon to open them in that program.

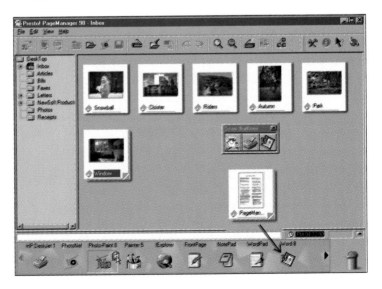

Forcing OCR to Recognize Columns

If your source document includes text in columns, you can force the OCR program to recognize those columns. Figure 10.13 shows the results of a few paragraphs of column text being processed by OCR. The OCR process was able to retain the indents and margins, and spelling errors were few. But sometimes, you need to *manually identify column elements* in your scan before the OCR process begins. To do this, you draw a rectangle around each column, using a Layout tool, so that the OCR program knows to treat them as columns.

Figure 10.13
An OCR-processed document sometimes retains column formatting without too much trouble.

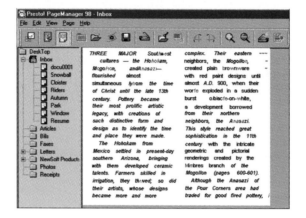

Figure 10.14 shows the OmniPage8 Pro screen after a scan of a document with two columns of text. Notice that even after the OCR process, the mouse can select text across both columns, across a single line, which means OCR did *not* treat the text as column text.

Figure 10.14
The mouse can extend across both columns, showing that OCR did not recognize the text as a column.

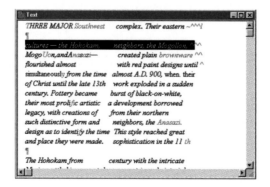

After this text is saved and you open it in a word processing program, your text will flow across the page, not down one column and then up and across to the next column. This represents such a reformatting nightmare that you are better off typing the document from scratch.

Therefore, *before the OCR process,* the program must be directed to treat the text as columns. This is done after the scan, using the mouse to draw a rectangle around each column. Depending on the program you are using, after the scan the mouse may automatically become a selection tool or you may have to select a menu option for identifying columns and other objects. Draw a rectangle around text, and the box you created remains. Draw another rectangle around another section of text, perhaps a column, and that rectangle remains (see Figure 10.15). You may notice the program numbers these rectangles, indicating the order in which OCR will analyze their contents. The numbers, therefore, also indicate the text sequence in the final document.

Figure 10.15
Draw a rectangle around a document element to identify how it should flow.

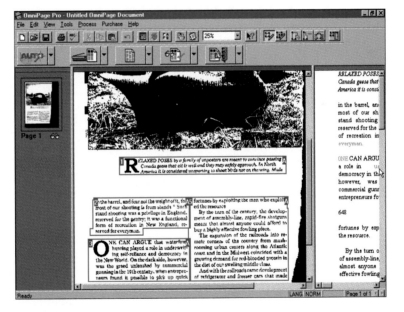

In some programs, you may have to choose a selection tool from the menu (Add New Region, Create Rectangular Selection, Set Layout Zone, for example), but the idea is the same. If you think the OCR program may not pay enough consideration to your page's layout, simply draw rectangles around each section and then perform OCR. The recognition process will abide by your layout rules, and columns will be treated as columns.

Figure 10.16 shows boundaries drawn around each stanza of a poem, assuring that each will be treated separately. This is an important feature for scanning poetry, since layout and spacing is so essential for that medium.

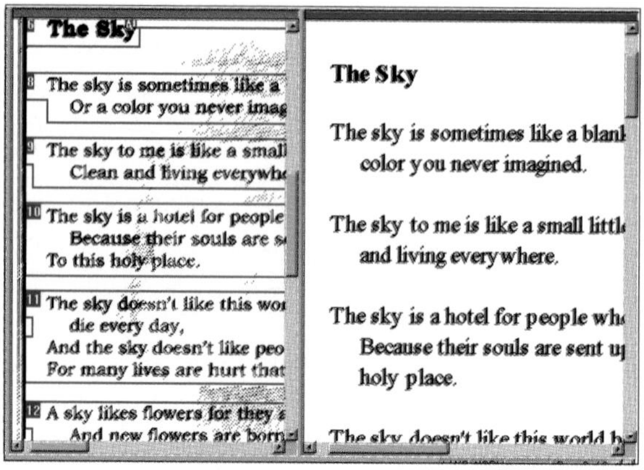

Figure 10.16
The stanzas of a poem are kept accurate during OCR by surrounding each with a layout rectangle.

Working with Complex Layouts

Some page layouts require that attention be paid to each element. Paravision's PageGenie (www.hotfiles.com) allows OCR scanning in color, letting you retain color text and photographs. It does an exceptional job at identifying fonts that are similar to those used in your bitmap scan. This is a great improvement over simply converting all text on the page to the most basic text format and throwing everything else out. Figure 10.17 shows a recipe scanned in PageGenie.

Figure 10.17
A recipe scanned in PageGenie.

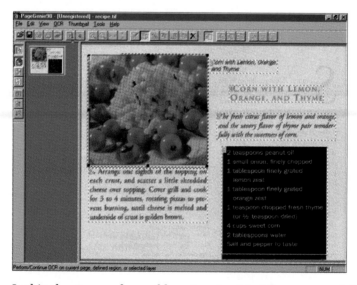

In this chapter, you learned how to extract text from scanned documents and use it in any word processing or desktop publishing program. Next, you'll explore the world of desktop publishing, learning to design various kinds of documents.

11

Desktop Publishing

This chapter focuses largely on desktop publishing software, such as Microsoft Publisher, Adobe PageMaker and Quark. In programs like these, design sense truly counts, including where to place your scanned pictures.

Principles of Desktop Publishing

In the world of desktop publishing, everything on your page is an object (or an element, with the words being used interchangeably here). The borders around your entire page are an object, as are the text blocks that contain the written message you are conveying. All the pictures, separator lines, headlines, charts, and graphs are elements that can be moved, resized, rotated, and recolored as you see fit (see Figure 11.1).

CHAPTER 11

Figure 11.1
Desktop publishing documents are composed of elements. Expression by Ariela Ronay-Jinich.

Balancing Text and Images

In desktop publishing, great attention is devoted to the relationship between pictures and text, achieving a balance between eye-catching, dramatic elements, such as photos and headlines, and elements of substance, such as text blocks and charts. You get to experiment a lot. For example, should the words "wrap around" your pictures, closely hugging the sides, or should the words and photographs flow down across the page in parallel? (See Figure 11.2.) Would the photo look better if it were rotated at an angle or bordered with a thick line?

Figure 11.2
Words wrap around images, when specified. Expression by Ariela Ronay-Jinich.

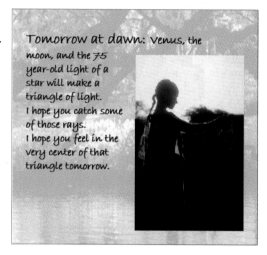

Color Schemes

Color scheme plays an important role in desktop publishing. You can get away with all kinds of borders, tinted photographs, and separator elements, as long as your page has a unified approach to color. Figure 11.3 shows a project page, repeated twice. In each instance, a different color scheme is applied.

Figure 11.3
Different color schemes applied to the same project page. Expression by Ariela Ronay-Jinich.

Text and Graphic Effects

As mentioned earlier, in desktop publishing, text is arranged in blocks, or text boxes. Text doesn't necessarily have to flow neatly from column to column. You can determine where a photograph should interrupt text flow, as well as where the text should restart, such as further down the page or even on the next page (see Figures 11.4a and b). The flow between text frames, and how the words balance out, is a powerful visual tool for desktop publishers.

Figure 11.4
You can determine where a photograph should interrupt text flow in a desktop publishing document. Expression by Ariela Ronay-Jinich

One alternative   A second alternative

In desktop publishing, you can apply a variety of fonts, font sizes, and text colors. Text can be treated unconventionally. Figure 11.5 displays the use of artistic text to convey a sense of flow. The text is faded against the backdrop of a scanned photograph.

Figure 11.5
Artistic text rendered over a photograph.

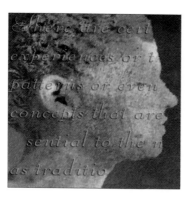

You can apply decorative "drop caps" for the first letter of each paragraph or change the color and font of certain words for dramatic effect. Text need not flow linearly up or down a column. Words can follow a unique pattern or wave set in motion by a photographic element on your page (see Figure 11.6).

Figure 11.6
Text set "in motion" by the photo beneath it.

And what about your scanned pictures? Some desktop publishing programs can recolor them, accommodating a particular color scheme (see Figure 11.7a). Pictures can be rotated to grab the eye, or positioned at the center of an otherwise text-heavy page (see Figure 11.7b). You can also draw a border around a photograph or fade it into the background so that it's barely visible (see Figure 11.7c).

Figure 11.7a
A recolored photograph.

Figure 11.7b
A rotated photograph.

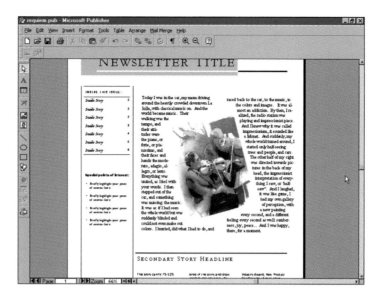

Figure 11.7c
A photograph faded into
the background.

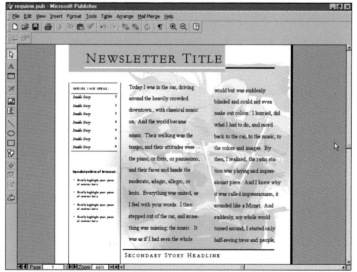

CHAPTER 11

Layering and Transparency

You can create more interesting documents by layering elements. Create a
text block that overlays the edge of a picture, making sure the colors are
distinct enough for legibility. You can take advantage of a frame's
transparency. If an image has an irregular shape, words can wrap around
the image itself, even inside the rectangular bounding box that surrounds
it (see Figure 11.8). The rectangular bounding box that surrounds an
image doesn't block your view of what's underneath, only the image itself

does. You can push your objects up to the edge of the picture without worrying whether part of the rectangular area overlaps, because no one will see the edge of the box anyway. If you apply this extra space, your pages look less boxy.

Figure 11.8
Text wrapping around an irregularly shaped image.

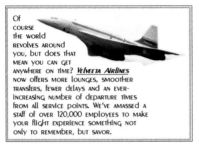

Of course the world revolves around you, but does that mean you can get anywhere on time? *Velveeta Airlines* now offers more lounges, smoother transfers, fewer delays and an ever-increasing number of departure times from all service points. We've amassed a staff of over 120,000 employees to make your flight experience something not only to remember, but savor.

Printing Principles

Desktop publishing documents generally are printed. Although many desktop publishing programs can easily create a Web page from your document, they are designed for the printed page. So, when creating your documents, consider the limitations of your printer, as well as the expense. Printing photographs or pages with huge blocks of color can take lots of ink and CPU power. You may want to limit how densely you populate your page with colorful odds and ends. For Web design, it's still better to use a dedicated Web design program such as Sausage software's Hot Dog Pro, Microsoft Front Page, or Adobe PageMill.

Printing Limitations

If you are commissioned to create a document that will be printed professionally, perhaps a company-wide newsletter, photographs may be out of the question—or at least color photographs. Full-color printing comes with a high price tag. You may be asked to limit your creativity to line drawings and perhaps a dab or two of a single extra color. So, before you spend too much time creating something dramatic, ask about the project limitations first.

Size of the Resulting Print

With desktop publishing, it's not an 8.5×11-inch world anymore. Using legal-sized paper, you can create a six-sided brochure with a single sheet. Printing two sides onto 11×17-inch paper gives you four letter-sized pages to use. If you stitch together several sheets horizontally, you can create a timeline, banner, or activities chart that stretches across an entire table. This means that if you do not use a template when planning your document, you should start by deciding your page size. Then, obtain the right size of paper to accommodate your project and make sure your printer is up to the task. Not all printers can work with extra-large or extra-small paper sizes.

Templates

Desktop publishing tasks are made easier by using *templates.* Templates are predesigned pages with all the elements in place. You simply replace the text and add your own photograph where the "dummy" photograph is positioned. A color scheme is already applied uniformly to all elements, although some templates let you choose from various color schemes. Special effects that are applied to headlines will stay "in place" even after you type your own headline. When you type text into a template, the formatting remains. When you type over the "dummy" text, your message will appear in the same font size, style, and color that the dummy text uses. The template has made all the design decisions for you. All you need to provide is the content.

The key to working with templates is variety. A good desktop publishing program should include templates for creating many types of documents and document styles (see Figure 11.9). For example, you should have at your disposal several styles of business card templates rather than a single template from which to design all business cards.

CHAPTER 11

Figure 11.9
A large variety of templates helps speed up document creation.

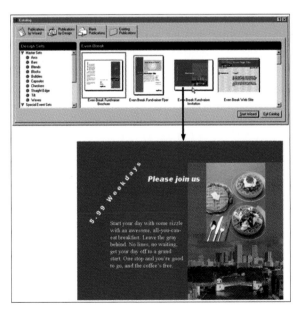

Important Desktop Publishing Features

Although we've been looking at Microsoft Publisher exclusively thus far, many other good desktop publishing programs are available. This section is designed to give you some general guidelines regarding what features you need from any desktop publishing program that you intend to purchase. A desktop publishing program should provide good tools to do the following:

▶ Create fast documents with templates and wizards

▶ Move, resize, and rotate all objects

▶ Overflow text from one frame to another

▶ Create interesting text headlines

▶ Paste or import text from text word processing programs directly into a text frame

▶ Import photographs of various formats (.TIF, .PCX, .JPG, .GIF)

▶ Scan directly into your document

▶ Spell check

▶ Work with transparent layers for overlapping elements

▶ Print oversized documents, such as posters, and small projects, such as envelopes and greeting cards

▶ Prepare documents for professional printing

▶ Add bullets and numbered list

▶ Align objects vertically and horizontally on your page, so that they are even with each other

▶ Create tabs and margins inside text blocks

What You Get When You Pay More

Most desktop publishing programs fall in the $100 range and then suddenly jump up to $500 to $700. This section discusses what you get when you purchase programs such as Adobe PageMaker or QuarkXpress.

PageMaker and Quark Features

Both PageMaker and QuarkXpress have advanced features to do the following:

▶ Produce razor-sharp text

▶ Prepare documents for professional printing in both a PC and Mac environment

▶ Import numerous graphics file types, including EPS and images requiring advanced color control

▶ Update linked graphics quickly and reliably

▶ Create very sharp and distinct lines and shapes via drawing tools

▶ Convert quickly to Adobe PDF files for universal document distribution

▶ Adjust individual letter positions to a very accurate degree, moving even a single character in any direction you see fit

Features Unique to PageMaker

Some features unique to PageMaker enable you to do the following:

▶ Quickly create and update booklets of various chapters

▶ Edit graphics directly with Photoshop effects

▶ Scan directly into PageMaker

▶ Choose from a variety of Pagemaker 6.5 Plus templates

Features Unique to QuarkXpress

Quark is the program of choice for creating professional magazines and books. These unique QuarkXpress features do the following:

▶ Provide a toolbar that lets you instantly adjust kerning for even a single character

▶ Automatically collect and prepare your document for professional printed output

▶ Allow you to intricately customize the use of hyphens, symbols, and other paragraph text options

▶ Allow you to save drawn objects created in Quark as EPS files

▶ Provide the most reliable and universal color proofing tools

CHAPTER 11

A Desktop Publishing Example Using Microsoft Publisher 97

Most of the remainder of this chapter looks at Microsoft Publisher, a great example of an inexpensive and flexible desktop publishing program. A 60-day trialware version of the program is included on the Microsoft Office CD-ROM, and it can be downloaded from Microsoft's Web site. Other programs have similar tools and layout and a common treatment of graphics and scanned photos.

To provide exposure to one of the most professional publishing programs, we'll also take a brief look at Quark Express and see what all that money buys (Quark currently lists at more than $700). Comparable in price and performance is Adobe PageMaker, and we'll spend a few moments exploring what's unique about that program.

Using a Microsoft Publisher Template

This section describes how to make a nice-looking document, including at least one of your scanned photos, with a Microsoft Publisher template. Then, it explores some of the elements used to create a document. We'll identify how these basic documents are made and how they can be altered quickly into something original.

Open the program and the Wizards Catalog opens (see Figure 11.10). This is an extensive menu of templates, predesigned documents that you can quickly put to use by adding your own information. The Wizards Catalog is divided into two halves:

Figure 11.10
The Microsoft Publisher Wizards Catalog.

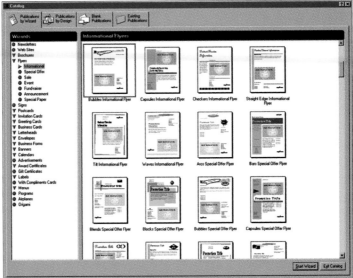

▶ **On the left**—Document types that you can begin working with by clicking them. Clicking a document type may also reveal a list of subcategories for that type. For example, clicking Post Cards reveals a submenu of 15 different *types* of postcard. (Publisher provides more than 100 templates just for postcards).

▶ **On the right**—Thumbnails of document templates. When you click a document type on the left side (for example, Newsletter or Post Card), the right side of the Catalog displays thumbnails of all the documents of that type. Click a thumbnail to open the template in Publisher's main workspace.

> **TIP**
>
> Taking a few minutes to select just the right template will save you time and effort later. Browse through the Wizards Catalog and see how much the program offers.

Creating a Newsletter

Let's create a newsletter. The steps involved in creating a newsletter will expose you to several features that are common to all desktop publishing programs. Initially, Publisher asks you questions about style and appearance and builds the newsletter based on your responses. Then, you can edit the features as needed.

Choosing the Template and Basic Features

1. Click the Newsletter triangle on the left side of the Catalog. On the right side, click Blends Newsletter (see Figure 11.11). This template creates a four-page newsletter highlighted with blended color rectangles. Articles that begin on the first page are automatically continued on later pages.

Figure 11.11
The Newsletter template that features color blends.

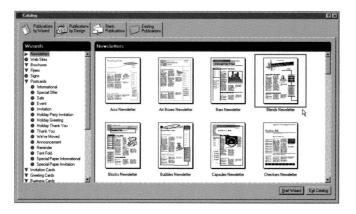

CHAPTER 11

2.   The newsletter opens with the Wizard on the left. You are prompted to choose the newsletter's color scheme, number of columns, printing mode, and contact information preferences. Figure 11.12 shows the Newsletter Color Scheme menu. Click a color scheme, and all colored areas of the newsletter change to reflect your choice.

Figure 11.12
The newsletter opens with the Wizard ready to implement your choices.

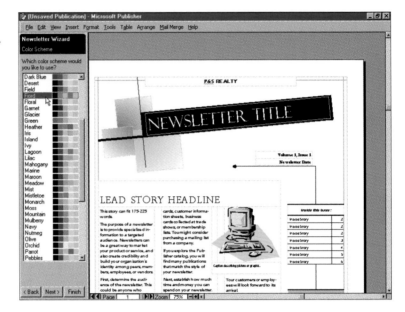

3.   After answering each question, click the Next button at the bottom left of the screen.

4.   After the final question, click Finish.

After the Basics

When the Wizard finishes leading you through the automated beginning steps, you can do the following:

▶   Add content to your newsletter, replacing the placeholder text with real articles and headlines

▶   Add photographs, clip art, tables, and charts

▶   Use the tools on Publisher's toolbox to add shapes, WordArt, and other drawn objects

▶   Move elements around your page, rearranging text blocks, headlines, and photos

▶   Change text font size, style, and color

▶   Resize and recolor your photographs and other artwork

If you want to change your color scheme or overall newsletter design, the Wizard is still available on the left side of the screen to automate those tasks.

Adding Content to the Newsletter

Now, let's get started learning on how to work with the content of your document. After the Wizard sets up the basic newsletter, you're free to edit elements on your own. Let's talk about changing the headings and adding text and pictures to your newsletter.

A First Look at Text and Picture Frames

In desktop publishing programs, all text is in text frames. Text frames are rectangles that can be repositioned and resized on your page. If a text frame is resized so that it cannot hold the text assigned to it, or if you paste a large amount of text into a small text frame, you can create a new frame to hold the overflow (see Figure 11.13). Text can freely pass between these two frames, depending on how they are resized and repositioned. This is how you flow text from one page to the next. Later in this chapter, we'll discuss how to "pour" text from one frame into another.

Figure 11.13
One text frame holds the "overflow" text from the other frame.
Expression by Ariela Ronay-Jinich

Publisher displays the boundaries of text frames and picture frames. These boundaries are not visible in your printed document. Publisher also displays *margin boundaries* and *guides,* which provide visual anchors to line up objects on your page. If you want to see your page without the boundaries or guides visible, press Ctrl+Shift +O. To bring them back, press Ctrl+Shift+O again. You can select Hide/Show Boundaries and Guides from the View menu.

Adding Text to Your Newsletter

A newsletter needs stories, and perhaps you've already written those stories in a word processing program. You'll need to copy them into Publisher, inserting them in the proper locations. To do so, do the following:

1. Determine which story should be the main article for your newsletter and open it in the program you created it in.

2. Copy the story to the Windows Clipboard (choose Edit>Select All, and then Edit>Copy).

3. Return to Microsoft Publisher and click inside the text frame holding the front-page main story (the story under the headline Main Story Headline). When you click in the text frame, all the text appears shaded black (see Figure 11.14).

Figure 11.14
Selected text appears black in a text frame.

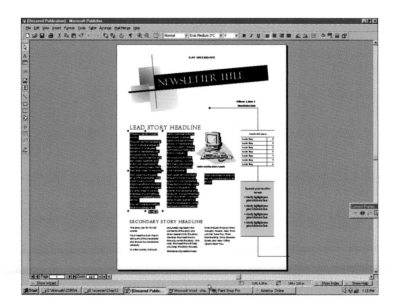

4. From the Edit menu, select Paste. The story you copied to the Windows Clipboard will now appear where Publisher's placeholder text used to be.

The story that you wrote may not be the same length as the text you replaced. Later in this chapter, we'll discuss how to move your text where you want it, resize and reshape the text frames that contain your typed words and paragraphs, and move text frames. For now, simply note that you've *imported* text into Publisher that's now part of this newsletter.

If you haven't typed your story yet, simply click in the Publisher text block that contains the text you want to replace and start typing. Your words will replace Publisher's placeholder text.

Adding text to a Publisher template is the same as adding text to a newsletter: replace the placeholder text either by importing text from Windows Clipboard or by clicking inside the text block and typing. Text blocks are examined in detail later in this chapter.

Importing a Picture

To import a picture into a template that already has a placeholder picture, do the following:

1. In Publisher, click the existing picture that will be replaced.

2. Select Insert>Picture>From File to display the Browse menu.

3. Use the Browse menu to navigate to the folder that contains the photo you want to use. After you are in the folder with your photos, single-click any picture to display it in the Preview area on the right side of the Browse menu.

4. Choose a photo and click OK. The photo appears in the newsletter in the spot where the placeholder picture used to be. The photo will be resized proportionally to fit the area (see Figure 11.15). It might be smaller, but it won't appear skewed. Later, we'll discuss how to reposition and otherwise edit your photos in Publisher.

CHAPTER 11

Figure 11.15
The photo automatically resizes to fit the frame selected at the time of importing.

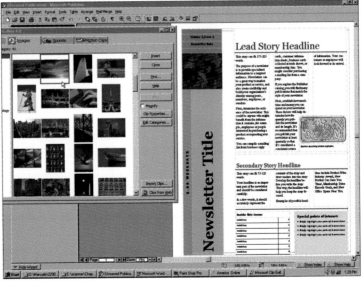

Changing Headlines and Headings

To change the article's heading, click the heading and begin typing. The new text will replace the text that was there, using the same font style and size as the replaced text.

Adding Elements with Publisher's Help

Publisher's Design Gallery enables you to quickly add to your newsletter new headlines, pull-quotes, captions, and other customized elements. This section shows you how it's done.

Replacing Existing Elements

First, you are going to use the Design Gallery to replace the headline (called the *masthead*) for the whole newsletter. Then, you'll discover how easy it is to apply some of Publisher's previously developed design ideas. You'll also replace a photograph in the masthead with a scanned photograph from your own files.

1. Right-click the existing masthead and choose Masthead Creation Wizard from the drop-down menu. A choice of more than 30 masthead selections is displayed (see Figure 11.16).

Figure 11.16
The Design Gallery creates instant page elements, such as mastheads.

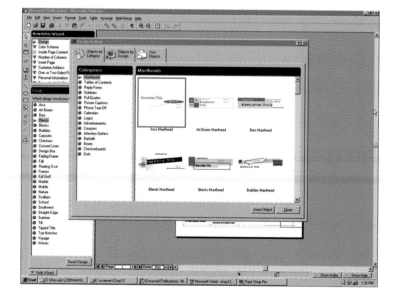

2. Click Fall in the Design list. You'll see the current headline change. The new masthead displays new shapes and lettering and a photograph of leaves in the lower-left part of the screen.

3. Click the photograph. A bounding box selects the entire masthead, and a thin red rectangle surrounds the picture (see Figure 11.17). This shows that all the elements of the masthead are grouped (the main bounding box) and that the picture within the group is selected for editing.

Figure 11.17
A photo selected
within a masthead.

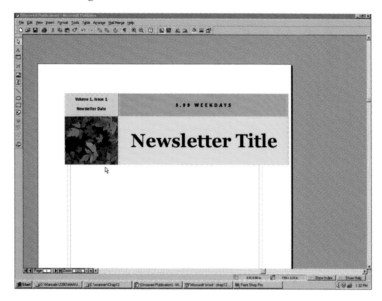

4. Right-click the photograph and select Change Picture>Picture>From File. A Browse menu appears.

5. Locate a photograph. When selected, it replaces the picture of leaves and shrinks to the size and dimensions of the leaves photo.

6. Select a photo and click OK. It will appear in the masthead in place of the leaves photo.

You can also replace any text in the masthead by clicking and typing over it.

Adding an Element

To show how to add an element rather than replace one, we'll add a pull-quote to page 2 of the newsletter. A *pull-quote* is an attention-grabbing sentence or two pulled from your article into its own side box. It is larger and perhaps in a different font. It should be short and pithy and should pull the reader's attention toward the article. By adding the pull-quote, you'll also learn to relocate page elements, moving them wherever you wish. Here's how it's done:

1. Go to page 2 of the newsletter. Clicking the page number at the bottom of the screen opens the Go To Page dialog box. When you select page 2, the newsletter shows both pages 2 and 3 simultaneously. Use the scroll button at the bottom of the screen to center your view of the page.

2. Click the Design Gallery tool, located at the bottom left of the Publisher toolbox. The Design Gallery appears.

3. In the Categories menu, click Pull Quotes. More than 20 pull-quote styles appear on the right side of the page.

4. Double-click a pull-quote style. It will appear on your page .

5. Move the pull-quote to an area with free space on page 2 of your newsletter. Without clicking, position your cursor inside the pull-quote but near the edge. The mouse cursor changes to a Move symbol (see Figure 11.18).

Figure 11.18
To move a frame, position your cursor over its edge. The Move tool will appear.

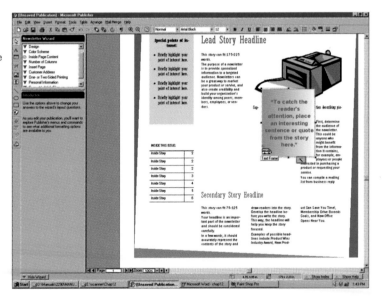

6. When the Move symbol appears, click and drag the pull-quote to a new area on the page.

You've now learned all about making a well-designed desktop publishing document. The next chapter shows what you can do with your scanner to make your home office or small business run more efficiently.

12

Scanning Documents for Business and Other Uses

Much of this book has been devoted to discussing scanning and editing photographs. This chapter focuses on the scanner as a practical tool that enables you to transmit and rearrange words and numbers. With a scanner, nothing on paper has to stay there. After a document is scanned, the data need not look anything similar to how it appeared on paper. And anything you scan can be e-mailed instantly anywhere in the world. A scanner can make all the written material in your life very portable.

The topics discussed in this chapter range from the "pure business" of designing a business card from a scanned logo to scanning chapters from a favorite book of classic literature and printing it double-spaced for easy notetaking. (Appendix A, "Scanning and the Law," discusses the legalities of scanning text and images created by others.)

If you have a small business, various office responsibilities, or important documents that you want to preserve and rearrange, the scanner is your friend. You can use your scanner to send faxes, make copies, develop a logo to use on business cards and letterhead, and scan old documents you want to preserve. In this chapter, you'll learn about those capabilities, as well as how to create an online form from a scanned version. With this form, you can use an electronic database instead of repeatedly filling out the form by hand.

First, you'll discover how to use your scanner to fax from your computer. Then, you'll learn about photocopying and e-mailing from your scanner. We'll discuss how to scan a logo and apply it to all of your business documents. You'll learn how to scan a form, re-creating it electronically with an eye toward "plugging in" data from a database into the form. Finally, we'll talk about scanning documents and rearranging how they look. You can even scan data and set it up to appear as a table in an Excel spreadsheet.

The One-Touch Solution

If you are interested in faxing, copying, and e-mailing documents from your scanner, you may want to buy a scanner that provides "single-button" access to these functions (see Figure 12.1).

Figure 12.1
A scanner with single-button fax, e-mail, and copy features.

However, it's an oversimplification to say that all of these conveniences are yours at a single touch, especially faxing. For starters, the following basic equipment issues exist:

▶ You do not fax from your scanner; you fax from a modem using special software.

▶ You do not photocopy from your scanner; the printer generates the paper copies.

▶ You need a modem and a properly configured e-mail client application to e-mail an image, not just a scanner.

Let's explore scan-and-fax technology first, and then return to using your scanner to photocopy and create e-mail attachments.

Scan-and-Fax Capabilities

Scanning from your computer involves the interplay of various technologies. Adding a scanner into the mix requires an even more elaborate exchange of information, because faxing software must convert the scanned bitmap to fax data that can be understood by another fax machine. This section first discusses faxing from your computer and then explains how you can use scan and fax to your advantage.

Just the Fax

Before you can fax anything, you need the following (these requirements apply even if you own a scanner that boasts "one-touch" scanning-and-faxing):

▶ A fax-compatible modem installed, or perhaps a network server connection to an intranet phone/fax system.

▶ Faxing software configured to work with your modem or network system.

How Your PC Sends a Fax

To help you understand what part of the faxing process involves your scanner, the following steps explain what occurs when you send a fax from your computer:

1. After you create a cover page and specify the document you want to fax, click the Send button from within your fax application.

2. The faxing program converts the document to be faxed into a *proprietary file type,* a type of code that can be read by the modem generating the fax tones.

3. The program sends commands to the modem to dial the fax number and establish a connection.

4. The modem sends tones announcing that a fax will be sent momentarily.

5. The host fax machine must acknowledge that a fax is coming and place itself in a state of readiness.

6. The sender modem reads your document and begins generating fax tones based on the document's content. Regardless of the original document type (simple text, formatted text, or bitmap file), the document must be converted to clearly understood fax tones.

7. The fax is sent, the fax recipient's machine acknowledges that the transmission was successful, and the connection is closed.

Is Faxing That Easy?

Faxing with your PC is not always seamless and effortless. The following are a few things that can go wrong:

▶ Not all modems are capable of generating fax tones, although most are. You would have a hard time purchasing a modem today that is not a fax/modem. However, some older modems and specialized devices simply are not engineered with faxing capacity.

▶ Some modems can transmit text faxes freely (a simple ASCII text message typed as part of the basic fax transmission command) but can't send quality bitmaps and pictures as faxed messages. Faxing software converts your bitmap (which is what a scanned document is) into a *file type* that your modem can interpret and send via fax. However, some modems lack such capability.

▶ An amazing number of fax transmission failures occur simply because of poor phone lines, either "in the wall" on your local side or somewhere else in the link. If you notice a high failure rate of fax transmissions, check whether your phone lines are a bit old and frayed. Request that the phone company perform a line test at your home.

CHAPTER 12

▶ Your modem may not be configured to work with your scanning software. You must take up this issue with your modem or faxing application's technical support documentation or staff.

▶ Faxing software, phone lines, or connections may be unable to handle the large bitmaps you are generating from your scanner. If your faxes are not going through and instead "hang up" in the middle, make sure you are using Line Art or Black and White color modes when scanning.

Transmission Speed

Some faxing programs let you specify *sending urgency levels,* which may mean that only the most urgent faxes are instantly sent. The amount of time required to send a fax depends on three features:

▶ The quality of the phone lines

▶ Modem speed

▶ The size and complexity of any graphics included

NOTE

If you send a lot of faxes, you may find that, when you are getting ready to send the next fax, some of the previous ones haven't been sent yet. Faxing takes time. There's a cover page, the fax itself, and the confirmation process, each adding to the overall time it takes to send even a simple half-page message or two. But what happens when you are suddenly trying to send a fax that is more urgent than the previous faxes in the list (called a queue)? Most faxing software lets you assign *urgency levels.* A higher urgency level will "bump up" a fax to be sent right away, even if others are ahead in the queue.

Faxing and Graphics

Even text-based scans are faxed as bitmaps, because that's what scanners generate. The faxed document generated from your scanner will not consist of simple ASCII text files. The following are some of the issues that may arise with regard to faxing software and its capability to fax graphics:

▶ Some faxing programs provide special options for faxing graphics. For example, if the image you are sending requires high-quality reproduction, some programs enable you to specify "Fine" fax quality on the faxing interface.

▶ Some faxing programs are configured like a printer. You configure your fax machine settings just as you would any other printer (from the application's File menu, select Print Setup, or Printer). From the printer interface, you can specify higher-quality graphics, grayscale, or halftone faxing mode.

▶ If you fax a high-quality graphic, transmission time is increased considerably. If you send a graphic that is too large, your fax software may time out partway through the transmission, meaning that your fax may be incomplete or may not go through at all. If you think that the fax transmissions are choking on your scans, try scanning at a lower resolution.

▶ Your transmission may be hampered by the capabilities of the *receiving* fax machine. If the receiving machine doesn't have a "high quality" or "graphics quality" setting, transmission speed will be affected greatly.

The Scan-and-Fax Phenomenon

If your scanner boasts scan-and-fax capabilities, information is exchanged between your scanner, the faxing software, and the scanned document that you want to send via fax.

When you first installed your scanner, here's what happened:

1. The scanner searched your computer for some sort of faxing application. The scanner interface actually set up a link between its own scanning capabilities and the faxing software it located in your system configuration.

2. The scanning program then arranged to open the fax application and have its own scanned image available for faxing, ready to edit, and then send. This exchange between the two programs occurs whenever you press Send Fax on your scanner or otherwise activate the scan-and-fax feature.

Activating the Scan-and-Fax Application

When you do activate the scan-and-fax feature on your scanner, the following occurs:

1. The scanner scans the document, with settings appropriate for faxing.

> **NOTE**
> Color isn't necessary when faxing. Resolutions higher than 150 dpi invariably just choke the transmission. Scans at 75 dpi are perfectly adequate for text faxes. Scans at 100 to 150 dpi are good for graphics.

2. The scanned document opens in the faxing software program already installed on your computer.

3. The document generated by your scanner is converted to a code that can be read and interpreted by the modem sending the fax.

CHAPTER 12

4. The faxing program then prompts you for contact information and offers to create a cover page for your fax. It may offer to print a hard copy of your scan or save the document to your hard drive first.

5. When you press Send on your fax application interface, the program begins the modem dial-up sequence (discussed previously), and the fax is sent.

Variety in Scan-and-Fax Programs

Scan-and-fax programs vary in the amount of flexibility they offer:

▶ Some let you alter scanner settings for your document, enabling you to exert control over the color mode and resolution. Some simply open the document in the fax program's window, ready for you to press the Send Fax button.

▶ Some prompt you to create a cover page and provide detailed contact information, or to open an Address Book in which frequently faxed names and numbers are stored.

▶ Some prompt you to save the file to your hard drive for later faxing and use, or to print a hard copy. Others simply fax the file and do not prompt any Save options.

NOTE

When you are sending a fax, you should not have your modem connection turned on. The fax software has to be free to direct your modem to dial the fax number and send the document. It can't do this if you are online.

Scan-and-Fax Features to Look For

Immediacy is the reason why having a scanner function as a fax machine is appealing—you can place a document on the scanner bed, press Send, and be done with it. For this to happen, you need the following fax application features:

▶ The ability to save scanner settings, so that you don't have to adjust the scanner interface each time you send a fax. For example, you can have one setting for text transmission, and another setting for graphics-rich documents, in which a higher-quality fax mode is required.

▶ A program that reliably reinitializes and resets your modem each time you fax. For example, if you had just been online, your modem was initialized to send and receive modem data. To send a fax, your modem needs to be reinitialized specifically to send fax tones. The COM port through which your modem sends fax data needs to be accessed and addressed properly. If you ever have trouble sending a fax after being online, it could be because the fax software cannot *hard reset* your modem and obtain clearance to use the modem COM port. You may have to reboot your computer to achieve this.

▶ Software that stores cover page preferences, so that you don't have to configure a cover page every time you send a fax.

▶ An application that stores your most frequent recipients, freeing you from having to type a fax number every time you send a document.

▶ A scanner with a quick warm-up cycle. Some scanners take one to two minutes to adequately heat the scanner bulb. (A warm-up period is required for a clean, uniform scan.) If someone is expecting a fax from you *right now,* it's important to be able to send it immediately.

▶ Software that doesn't automatically queue faxes for later sending, but instead lets you send them right away.

CAUTION

Don't try too many fax programs. This book talks a lot about the value of experimenting with different software packages until you find the one that fits your needs. However, faxing software configures your modem and COM ports to respond to its commands to send a fax. Having two faxing programs on your computer simultaneously could make your modem unresponsive to one program or the other, because the way that one software package obtains access to your modem could interfere with the other program's attempts to do the same thing. You shouldn't have a lot of programs on your computer trying to configure your COM port for their own uses. For the same reason, poorly designed faxing programs can interfere with your ability to connect to the Internet, if you connect via modem. Communication port and modem conflicts can be hard to resolve and usually require eliminating one program or another.

Common Fax Applications

Although faxing with your scanner does require that you have fax software installed, you may not have to go out and buy anything. A standard installation of Windows 95, NT, or 98 includes fax capabilities that work with most commercially available modems.

The benefit of faxing with Window's own fax program is that you don't have to spend any more money. You can fax right from within Word (a scanned photo can be pasted or embedded into Word and faxed as such). You can mix text and graphics freely in your document and print a copy for yourself while faxing, all in a few steps.

CHAPTER 12

A Tour of Microsoft's Fax Wizard

To access Microsoft's Fax Wizard while your document is open in Word, Excel or any other Microsoft Office application, select File>Send To>Fax Recipient. The Fax Wizard opens (see Figure 12.2) and guides you through sending a fax.

Figure 12.2
Fax Wizard's Cover Sheet page.

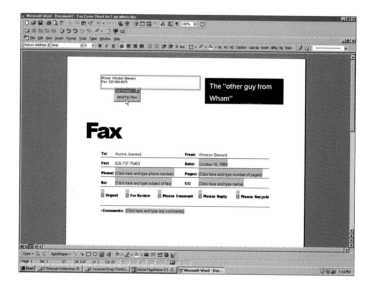

Scan and Fax with Art-Copy

Art-Copy, which is available as trialware online (Go to www.hotfiles.com, and type Art-Copy into the search box), lets you easily fax and make copies of scanned documents. We'll use our tour of Art-Copy to lay out some of the basic principles of scanning and faxing. Then, we'll touch on a few other programs that have a slightly different approach to the process.

As Figure 12.3 shows, the Art-Copy interface is very simple. Digital controls are provided on the interface to set the number of faxes or copies and to adjust the brightness, color mode, and output size.

Figure 12.3
Jetsoft's Art-Copy main screen.

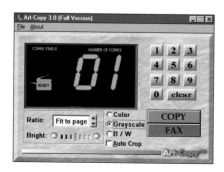

Configuring Art-Copy for Faxing

Before sending your first fax with Art-Copy, you must do the following:

1. Specify a scanner (select File>Select Source). Even if you have only one scanner, you must still select it. This is a one-time-only setup.

2. Specify which fax program you'll be using (select File>Setup and then choose the Output tab). For copying, select a printer. From the Setup menu, choose the *type* of scanner (reflective or transparency, meaning flatbed or film, respectively).

3. On the Option tab of the Art-Copy Settings dialog box (see Figure 12.4), specify whether you want a chance to edit the scanner settings each time or allow each scan to proceed without your input (Show Twain Driver User Interface Before Copy).

Figure 12.4
You can view and edit scanner settings each time you fax or simply go with the defaults.

TIP

Remember that if you decide not to edit a scan, you won't be able to crop the scan area down to the document itself. Unless you first preview the scan and use the Crop feature, the entire scanning area may end up being scanned, black background and all (see Figure 12.5). If your scanning or faxing software is not sophisticated enough to know the difference, you may end up faxing this huge black area as well as your document.

Figure 12.5
If you do not crop your fax area, you may end up faxing a large black background as well as your document.

Faxing with Art-Copy

After the preceding setup steps, you can fax or copy by using the buttons on the Art-Copy front interface. If you directed Art-Copy to display the scanner interface each time you scan and fax, the interface will appear. Preview the scan (see Figure 12.6) and use the Crop feature to narrow down the scan area to the document itself.

Figure 12.6

You can preview the scan before scanning and sending the fax.

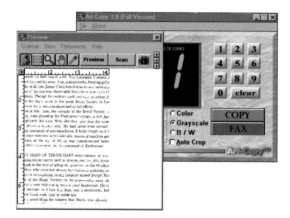

As a precautionary step, when you first set up your scanner and faxing system, save your settings. Next, watch your first few faxes closely, making sure transmission goes smoothly. Then, call the recipient and find out whether the document looked acceptable. After a few tests, you can confidently run the process more automatically.

Scan-and-Photocopy Capability

When a software program configures your scanner to work like a photocopier, it simply generates a grayscale or black-and-white image of the document in the scanner bed and sends it straight to your printer without saving it to your hard drive first. Some scanner/copying programs display the scanner interface first, allowing you to specify either 256-shades-of-gray or black-and-white scanning. Some programs display your printer's interface so that you can determine print quality and quantity settings.

Scan and Photocopy with Copyshop 2000

Klicksoft's Copyshop 2000 is used as the example program in this section because it provides a comprehensive yet simple interface for photocopying from your scanner (Copyshop is available from www.hotfiles.com). Like all similar products, Copyshop 2000 requires that your scanner be properly configured, and it will search your system for a working printer. It sends the scanned data to the printer that you specify, using the default printer and printer settings. If you wish, you can modify Copyshop's printer choices, by selecting File>Print Settings.

The main Copyshop 2000 interface is divided into three panels, as shown in Figure 12.7:

Figure 12.7
The Copyshop 2000
main screen.

Scanner Tab
Copy Tab
Copy Button
Add Text Button

▶ The left panel lets you specify an enlargement value, paper size, and color mode value for the copy and also enables you to mirror or rotate your document. Click the Preview button to open the scanner interface and view a preview of the final output.

▶ The middle panel has two tabs. The Scanner tab displays the document as it appears in the scanner bed. The Copy tab shows how the printed document will look. Changes that you make in color mode, output size, and style are displayed by clicking the Copy tab.

▶ The right panel provides a single-touch Copy button, margin settings, and oversized printing options. Using the buttons at the center of the right panel, you can insert text blocks into your scan, mask out sections from view, and highlight text areas you want to emphasize.

You can also insert Date and Time, Urgent, Confidential, or some other stamped message superimposed on the copies you create. To do this, click the Add Text buttons beneath the Number of Copies digit on the upper right of the screen.

CHAPTER 12

When you click the Copy button, the image is sent to the printer. Copyshop 2000 does not save scanned images to your hard drive. This means if you want to save an electronic copy of the image you copied to paper, you must take an extra step and save the scanned image to your hard drive (File>Save As).

NOTE

If you have a color printer, Copyshop will create color copies of your scan (use the Color Mode tab found beneath the Enlargement Value digit on the left side of the screen). Remember that color copies take significantly longer than grayscale or black-and-white copies, use more memory, and are more apt to tie up your computer while the job is completing.

Other Scan-and-Photocopy Applications

The products discussed in the fax segment of this chapter generate photocopies from your scanner, similar to the process just described. Both Art-Copy and Copyshop scan documents in Line Art mode and send the output straight to your printer, unless you modify your scanner settings before you actually print.

In both Art-Copy and Copyshop, if you don't want to use your default printer settings, select Print Options from the File menu and configure your printer specifically for photocopy use.

Scan-and-E-Mail Capabilities

Fundamentally, three ways exist to e-mail a scanned image to any valid e-mail address:

▶ Use the Send To feature of the graphics or scanner program you are using (select File>Send and choose Mail Recipient from the fly-out menu, as shown in Figure 12.8). However, to do this, Microsoft Outlook or some other e-mail client must be installed on your computer. If configured correctly, almost any Windows 9x application will provide a path to e-mail any open document directly to a proper e-mail address.

Figure 12.8
If an e-mail client is installed, most Windows applications have a Send e-mail feature available.

▶ If your scanner provides a single-touch e-mail button or option, you can scan and e-mail by pressing the button on the front panel. This opens your default e-mail client (such as Outlook, Eudora, CCMail, Lotus, or any other e-mail application). The image will be sent via e-mail as an attached file that can be downloaded by the recipient.

▶ Open Microsoft Outlook or some other e-mail client and attach your scanned file to the e-mail. Recipients can then download the file and view it in their own graphics viewer. When attached to the e-mail document, the image appears as an icon embedded in the file. The recipient also sees the icon and has to double-click the image to open it in its default application.

NOTE

When e-mailing a graphic for others to open and view, send the image in one of the most common graphics file types. When e-mailing an image, size is also an issue, so e-mailing an image as a JPEG file is usually a good choice.

In some Internet applications, such as America Online, you can actually embed a scanned image as a background picture in an e-mail (see Figure 12.9). The recipient will be able to view the image as part of the e-mail message without downloading it first. The recipient must have an e-mail service that supports viewing graphics-embedded messages.

CHAPTER 12

Figure 12.9
America Online lets
you embed a picture
into the background of
an e-mail message.

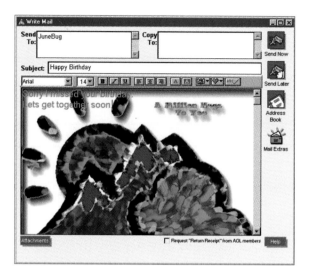

Creating a Scanned Business Logo

To scan a logo that will be used for a business card, letterhead, or even an envelope return address, the key is flexibility and legibility. Because your business logo will be displayed in a variety of formats and sizes, clarity and simplicity of design are also a must.

Most logos have artistic text, which is text saved as a bitmap. Text begins to look jagged and fuzzy the more you resize it, so avoid resizing, by scanning at a higher resolution and reducing and saving your business logo as needed.

▶ One large size, for use in such things as a magazine advertisement or full-color brochure.

▶ One medium size, for use in such things as stationery header or a small newsletter.

▶ One small size, for use in such things as business cards and the return address on envelopes.

Business logos can be created in all kinds of dimensions. In general, always scan your logo (bitmap) at your scanner's highest resolution. Then reduce (resample) your logo based on your needs (see Table 12.1). Providing recommended scanning settings based on horizontal or vertical proportions isn't feasible. Instead, here are some general scanning considerations to keep in mind:

Table 12.1
Resolution
recommendations.

Use	Image Resolution
Business card/ Envelope return addresses	150 dpi
Web site logo	72 dpi
Stationery header	150 dpi
Professionally printed brochure or magazine ad	Photos—300 dpi Lineart—1200 dpi

TIP

After creating a business logo, you can use it in a number of applications. The same image can be used in Excel, Word, a desktop publishing program, or a Web page application. Rather than paste the image into a spreadsheet or letter, for example, you can link it instead. Whenever you change the image, the way it looks in your application will also change. That's because the image is linked, not pasted.

For example, after you scan your small file, you can link this image to a business card file and link the same image to return address information for an envelope. Each project does not require its own logo file. According to its size and resolution requirements, several projects can be linked to the same logo. Don't clutter your hard drive with a bunch of files unnecessarily.

Creating a Business Card

This section looks at a business card creation program called Business Card Designer Plus (available as trialware from www.hotfiles.com). You can quickly create cards and scan your images right there, all designed and ready to go. The interface is clear and easy to use, and it supports a large variety of graphic file types. We'll use this program as an example to show how easy it is to create a good business card.

1. Open Business Card Designer Plus, and the main Card Expert interface appears (see Figure 12.10).
2. Select File>New, and a Template menu appears. Click a template to build your business card from, and it appears in the editing area.

CHAPTER 12

Figure 12.10
The Business Card Designer Plus main screen.

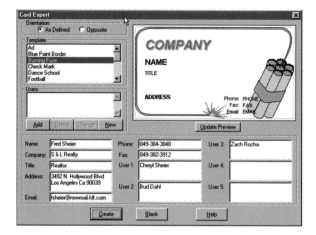

3. Fill in the necessary contact information in the contact information data boxes at the bottom of the Main Interface.

4. Choose a template, and the business card appears in a new window, ready for direct editing. You can move text around, choose a new background, and add new elements, such as your own logo or scanned photograph.

5. Scan directly into Business Card Designer Plus. Resize and relocate the scanned image as needed.

6. Save the card, and the scanned image is saved as well, as part of the file.

7. From the File menu, print your card. The business cards automatically fill the entire page of the printer's default paper size, as many as can fit on one piece of paper (see Figure 12.11).

Figure 12.11
When you print your cards, the program automatically fits as many cards on a page as possible.

Scanned image

Creating Scanned Forms for Automating Text Entry

A particular type of OCR application enables you to create an electronic version of a scanned form. If you have a form that you regularly use, such as a customer survey, invoice, or accounts receivable ledger, you can do two things:

▶ Change the form's appearance—for example, add or subtract the number of data boxes and rows.

▶ Enter data electronically, merging the form with a database.

Your days of manually filling out forms may be over. Simply scan the form and let a form-specific OCR program "recognize" each field. You can then create a database and automatically link each field of your database with your form's fields. That way, forms can be generated electronically for each person you do business with.

To learn how to scan a form and make it an editable electronic document, we'll look at IMSI's FormTool Scan & OCR (available from www.hotfiles.com). It uses an advanced OCR technology to re-create each field of your form as a field that can receive a database entry. Thus, creating the form and the data that goes into it is a one-time-only chore that can be applied any time, according to your business routine.

A quick walk through FormTool Scan & OCR acquaints you with both scanning a form and preparing a form for OCR. This program lets you specify the approximate sizes and shapes of the elements in your paper form. This information stops the OCR program from misreading and misinterpreting form boxes and fields. If you tell the OCR software a bit about your form to begin with, it stands a better chance of clearly recognizing and re-creating the elements accurately.

CHAPTER 12

Here's how FormTool Scan & OCR creates electronic forms from your paper versions:

1. To scan a form, from the Image menu, select Acquire. Your scanner's interface opens, as in the example shown in Figure 12.12.

Figure 12.12
Your scanner interface opens directly in IMSI's FormTool Scan & OCR.

2. Scan with FormTool Scan & OCR's default settings.

3. The image opens in FormTool Scan & OCR, ready for editing (see Figure 12.13). The program has an image editing window that helps you prepare the document for the most accurate OCR possible.

Figure 12.13
FormTool Scan & OCR will scan, interpret, recognize, and re-create your form electronically.

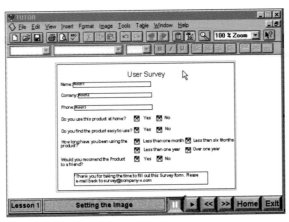

4. Select Image>Recognize Options to specify a size range for all the fields and line borders in your form. If the OCR process has a range of sizes for each of your form elements, errors are kept to a minimum. You can also specify which font and font size the OCR-recognized text should be displayed in.

5. After you specify the OCR settings, select Image>Recognize, and the program will re-create your form electronically.

6. Save the file in the Scan & OCR's own file type so that the program can later add a database to this form.

Importing Scanned Text into a Spreadsheet

Sometimes, you'll want to scan numbers and then import them into a table, such as an Excel spreadsheet. This actually isn't very hard, even if the numbers you want to import are currently in a bit of a jumble.

To import a group of numbers and convert them into an orderly spreadsheet, do the following:

Figure 12.14
Once they are recognized by the OCR program, you can rearrange and align the numbers you've scanned.

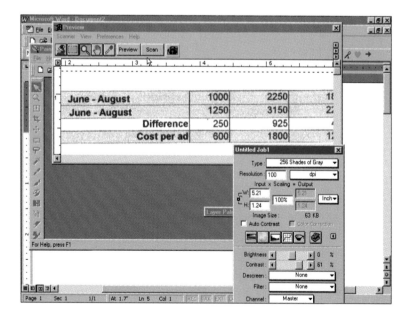

CHAPTER 12

1. Scan the numbers you want to work with.

2. Use an OCR program to convert the scanned numbers into readable data.

3. Open the numbers in Word or Wordpad, or any other text editor.

4. Arrange the numbers in columns and rows, in the manner you want them to appear in your spreadsheet. In Word or Wordpad, you won't have the benefit of built-in row and column borders, but you can still arrange the numbers as such.

5. After each number, press Tab to move the next number one cell to the right. Inserting a tab after a number instructs a spreadsheet to place that number in its own cell. Later, when you copy and paste these numbers into a spreadsheet, it will know to paste each number into a new cell.

6. Copy the numbers to the Windows Clipboard.

7. Open Excel or some other spreadsheet program, and select one cell. You don't need to select as many cells and columns as you are going to use for your numbers. Clicking one cell will do.

8. Select Edit>Paste. The numbers disperse across and down the appropriate number of columns and rows (see Figure 12.15), because when Excel encounters a Tab key command, it moves to a new column, and when it encounters an Enter command, it moves down one row.

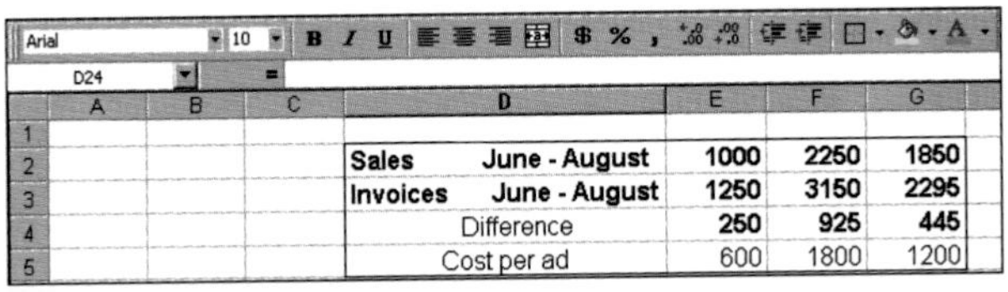

Figure 12.15
The number set appears in a spreadsheet, one number per cell.

Using this method, you can scan any document with numbers and organize them in rows and columns in a spreadsheet without too much fuss.

In this chapter, you learned some ways that your scanner can be a convenient home office or small business tool. You know more about faxing, copying, e-mailing, and creating forms with the aid of your scanner. Next, we'll explore scanning and graphics tips for Web page design and construction.

13

Graphics and Web Design

In this chapter, you'll learn some principles and techniques for adding scanned images to a Web page. This chapter discusses how to create Web-friendly pictures—not how to use HTML to design Web pages.

What are Web-friendly pictures? Pictures that look good in a Web browser and load fast across a typical Internet connection.

The first part of this chapter explains how to make your images load faster online. For Web page creation, this is a central task. A faster-loading page results in a lower frustration level for those who stop by your site, meaning more people are likely to visit your site and can spend more time enjoying your page than waiting for pictures to display onscreen.

The Web-Page Designer's Challenge

For Web-page designers, massaging a photo so that it loads in five seconds and still looks decent is a lifelong quest. A friend who has long owned a graphics business recently remarked that she comes home with a full day's work on a single floppy, compared to "the old days" of carting around huge files that span an entire 100MB Zip disk. In the world of full-color printing, more is better, but in today's Web-centric environment, there's a rush to make every byte count and to make pictures as small as they are clear. This section looks briefly at the tools needed for that task. The following figures are examples of some of the choices every Web-page designer must make. Figure 13.1 shows a 100K JPEG image. This would take nearly a minute to load online with a 56.6Kbps modem.

Figure 13.1
A 24-bit, full-color
JPEG image.

Figure 13.2 shows the same image employing a reduced color palette and a higher compression rate. This image takes approximately 15 seconds to load at the same modem speed. You can see some loss of quality, but not nearly enough to justify waiting four times as long for the image to load.

Figure 13.2
The same image as
in Figure 13.1, but with
an 8-bit, 256-color
palette. The image size
is smaller.

Figure 13.3 shows a small GIF image. Again, there is some quality and size loss, but this picture takes less than five seconds to appear on a Web page. That's because the image uses far fewer colors than the previous pictures. Moreover, because GIF images load progressively, the visitor will be able to see portions of it appear while the page is loading. That's quite an advantage.

Figure 13.3
A simple GIF image,
which loads on a Web
page in less than five
seconds.

The best Web graphic results are obtained by balancing quality with the need for speed.

How We'll Proceed

In Chapter 7, you learned that JPEG and GIF files are the only universally Web-viewable graphic file types. Generally, photographic images should be saved as JPEG files, whereas drawings and line art work well on the Web as GIFs. Within those two distinctions, you have many choices to make. In this chapter, you'll learn how to edit images of those two file types (especially GIFs) more precisely, streamlining your pictures for fast online viewing. You'll learn that although GIF images reduce the number of colors used into an 8-bit (256-color) palette, you can exert detailed control over the colors used in your online image, reducing the colors to a tightly honed 32-color palette, if you so desire. We'll also examine using transparent backgrounds and interlacing with your images to create seamless, better looking graphics on Web pages.

Controlling Color Reduction and Image Palette

This section shows how you can reduce a photograph's color range and size and still keep it sharp. We'll explore different ways to decrease an image's loading time, so that your Web page appears quickly. For example, there are ways to create an image that appears to deploy a full range of colors but actually uses only 64 (or even 32) colors.

Getting an image to load faster is a matter of reducing not only the file size but also the number of colors an image displays. When a Web browser receives a command to load an image for your site, it needs to locate and display all the requested colors that picture calls for and then calculate where those colors appear in the image. Web browsers work with a palette of hues and shades, and the fewer colors your image uses, the faster the Web browser can load it.

CHAPTER 13

We'll also discuss how to specify when a GIF image's background color should be displayed transparently. You can automatically "knock out" the background color of a picture, so that only the main subject matter is visible against the backdrop of the Web page itself. This decreases image loading time and makes for a more seamless, integrated-looking page.

You'll also learn to instruct the Web browser to load your GIF image gradually as data is received, instead of having the browser wait for the entire image to be loaded before displaying anything. If a picture displays a little at a time, your visitors at least see "something" while they are waiting for your page to fully load. This technique is called *interlacing*, a GIF option that is available from almost any photo editing program around today.

Color Reduction Tools

Let's begin by exploring three programs with significant color-reduction tools: Ulead's Web Razor, Paint Shop Pro's GIF converter, and Corel PHOTO-PAINT.

One of the best tools for creating Web-friendly images is Ulead's Web Razor, a collection of Web utilities that includes 3D text rendering and a full-featured photo browser. It deploys a wonderful little program called SmartSaver Pro, which lets you interactively remove colors from your image while monitoring picture quality. (You can download Web Razor from www.hotfiles.com, or Ulead's own Web site, www.ulead.com). The program is downloadable as trialware from the Web. We'll go step by step with SmartSaver Pro to create a fast-loading GIF image, although Web Razor's SmartSaver Pro works similarly with JPEGs, letting you closely monitor the results of your editing.

We'll also look at Corel PHOTO-PAINT's interactive GIF color selection screen. After reading this section, you'll know how to work with complex, full-colored images. You'll be able to reduce these images not only in size, but also to their most essential colors, so that visitors to your Web page will see them with minimal delay.

Web Razor's Color Reduction Tools

In this book, we explore Web Razor's SmartSaver Pro only, not the other programs in the Web Razor collection. Uniquely, SmartSaver Pro displays online file loading time and file size along with every edit you make, letting you know instantly if your efforts are fruitful.

Optimizing an Image

Let's open an image and learn our way around the SmartSaver Pro interface.

Upon opening Web Razor's SmartSaver Pro, you'll see four tabs, as shown in Figure 13.4. The only feature we are covering in this chapter is the Optimizer tab, which reduces color range and applies image compression schemes to your pictures.

Figure 13.4
Ulead Web Razor's SmartSaver Pro, with the Optimizer tab displayed.

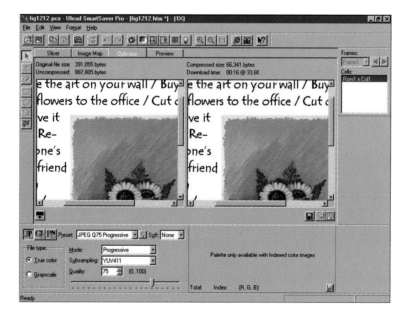

To open an image for editing, click the Optimizer tab and then select File>Open. The image fills two panes. The window on the left displays your picture before editing. The right pane is a preview of each edit you apply. The panel below lets you select file types, colors, and palette corrections.

The key to SmartSaver Pro is the *file size* and *download time* display at the top of each. You are told how large the file is and how long the image takes to appear on a visitor's page when visiting your Web site. Just like the corresponding windows, the information is provided before and after each edit. You'll know immediately whether your edits are having any real effect on streamlining your picture for fast Web viewing.

NOTE

The reported image download time is dependent upon your modem's speed. Set the modem speed used to calculate the reported download time by selecting File>Preferences and choosing a modem speed from the Optimizer tab (see Figure 13.5). The reported download time will be adjusted to the modem speed you set.

Figure 13.5
Change the download time calculations to be based on modem speed.

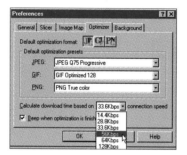

Monitoring Results

With SmartSaver Pro, you can reduce the numbers of colors used to render your image, as well as reduce the file size, allowing SmartSaver Pro to compress your image to conserve space. The trick is to keep an eye on image quality while making each adjustment, looking out for blotchy color transitions, grainy areas, and fuzzy edges around text. Here are some ways to change your view of the picture:

▶ To scroll around and inspect each area of your image, each window provides scroll bars at the bottom and right.

▶ To see your entire image, click the View menu and choose a Zoom option.

▶ To view only the "after" effect of each edit, and allow the edited version of the image to fill the entire screen for closer inspection, click the small black icon at the bottom left of the left window.

Applying GIF Palette Options

To choose a file type for saving your image, click one of the three icons at the bottom left of the screen. Your choices are JPEG, GIF, and PNG. We discuss saving your image as a GIF, because you can exert the most control over the outcome. Saving as a JPEG is quite simple, and we'll briefly return to JPEG files at the end of this section.

To begin working with your image as a GIF file, click the GIF icon at the bottom left of the screen. In the Colors data box, type the number of colors you want your image to use. The lower number of colors, the faster the image will load. Here are some guidelines for choosing the right number of colors for your picture:

▶ No matter how much you tweak and edit your image, most photographs with human faces or reflective surfaces will not look good below 64 colors. Many won't look right below 128 colors.

▶ Pictures with large areas of block color (all red or all blue, for example) can be reduced very effectively. Pictures with simple gradients, such as blends from one shade to another, can be reduced effectively, sometimes to as low as 32 colors. Nonetheless, many drawn GIFs use as few as two or three colors.

▶ Drawn images can be reduced to 16 colors if the drawing is simple enough. However, the 16-color palette used on all PCs is standard, and you cannot choose colors outside that basic palette. Reducing to 32 colors is probably low enough, which reduces the complexity of your image without robbing your image of needed shades or hues. As you type a new number into the Colors data box of the SmartSaver Pro Optimizer screen (the Colors data box only appears when the GIF file type is selected). Watch the image on the right side of the screen. Look for graininess, blotchy transitions between colors, and changes in colors used in the image (see Figure 13.6). Use the scroll bars to inspect the entire image for changes. Make note of the areas most affected by the reduction in colors.

Figure 13.6
Graininess, blotchy color transitions, and changed coloration are all liabilities of reducing the file size and palette.

16 million color .TIF, 200 dpi resolution, 1.2Meg image.

16 million color .JPG saved with moderate compression, 100 dpi, size on disk = 180K.

256 color .JPG saved with moderate compression, 100 dpi size on disk = 120K.

64 color .GIF 72 dpi, size on disk = 80K.

Choosing Palette Emphasis

Each time you reduce colors in the Color data box, you are limiting the number of colors used to create your image by altering the image palette. You can, however, choose which area of the spectrum the palette should emphasize. The palette used for your image doesn't need to be an even distribution of red, green, and blue. SmartSaver Pro examines your image and determines which colors should be in the palette to preserve your picture's appearance.

Maintaining Detail Where Needed

You need not let SmartSaver Pro evenly distribute color range. You can use the Emphasize Area tool to create a rectangle around the section of your image with the most critical detail (see Figure 13.7). SmartSaver Pro then dedicates more of the palette to accurately reproducing that highly detailed area, rather than creating a palette that evenly draws from every section of the image.

Figure 13.7
The Emphasize Area tool lets you pick image segments that require more colors allotted to them.

CHAPTER 13

To use the Emphasize Area tool, do the following:

1. Inspect the image and locate the area most negatively affected by the color reduction you just performed. Look especially around areas that display many colors and high image detail.

2. Click Edit and then click Emphasize Area. The Emphasize Area screen appears.

3. Click the Rectangle tool on the top of the Emphasize Area screen.

4. Use the scroll bars to locate the area of the image most negatively affected by the color reduction, or the area with the most detail in your image.

5. Draw a rectangle around that section.

6. The palette of colors will immediately be redistributed to reflect the colors used in the section you selected. You should notice that the area inside the rectangle now looks clearer, less blotchy, and less grainy.

7. Click OK to close the Emphasize Area screen. Your changes will remain in the image.

NOTE
Changes in the colors used by the palette will not reduce the file size, but they will make the picture load faster.

Image Softness and Transparency

SmartSaver Pro offers a handful of other GIF options for improving online viewing. We'll look at image softness and then learn how to apply transparency to a background color.

Softness

One way to remove graininess from your picture after reducing colors is to increase the softness. Softness can make text look quite blurry, but it can mask color accuracy problems in images with large areas of relatively uniform color. To adjust softness, click the Soft drop-down menu in the GIF screen and choose a number value. Inspect the image to make sure the effect does not blur detail. If blurring occurs, try a smaller number.

Setting Transparency

GIF images allow you to set one color that will appear as transparent when viewed in a Web browser. Effectively eliminating a color from your image reduces upload time and allows the main subject matter of your picture to appear to blend into the background of your page (see Figure 13.8). Almost all graphics programs that have a Save as GIF option let you pick a transparency color. To set a transparency color with SmartSaver Pro, do the following:

Figure 13.8
GIF transparency allows you to select a background color as transparent, meaning it will not be visible at all on your Web page.

1. From the Format menu, click Transparency. The Transparency screen appears, with your image displayed.

2. Use the Eyedropper tool to click the background area of the image. SmartSaver Pro will include areas of similar color in your transparency selection. This is desirable because your "white" or "lavender" background is actually a few different shades of white or lavender.

CHAPTER 13

3. To create a seamlessly transparent background, you want the Transparency tool to select all of those shades. For this reason, SmartSaver Pro allows you to select a range of hues similar to the one you clicked. So, in the Similarity data box, type 3 or 4. This range is usually enough to make sure all of the background is selected.

4. Click OK to close the Transparency screen. When you save your image and load it in a Web page, the color you selected as transparent will not be visible in the image.

JPEG Options

SmartSaver Pro lets you specify a compression type and amount for your JPEG image. To edit and save an image in SmartSaver Pro as a JPEG, do the following:

1. Click the JPEG button at the lower left of the screen. You'll see a Quality data box.

2. Drag the slider to the left for higher compression (faster loading time) and lower quality.

3. Drag the slider to the right for a higher image quality and lower compression amount.

Monitor image size and loading time with the data provided near the top of the SmartSaver Pro screen. Each change you make in compression amount affects these two factors. The Emphasize Area feature is also available with JPEG images. Areas you choose with the Emphasize Area selector will not be as compressed as (and thus will look better than) the rest of the image. This feature allows you to highly compress an image while maintaining a higher quality level in important segments.

SmartSaver Pro also provides a Soft control for smoothing JPEG images that look denigrated because of high compression. Choose a number from the Soft drop-down menu. After applying the Soft features, inspect your image for blurry areas and poorly rendered text. If the results are unsatisfactory, dial in a lower number.

Saving and Viewing Your SmartSaver Pro Image

SmartSaver Pro lets you save your images as GIF or JPEG file types or as part of an HTML document. After editing and saving your picture for online use, take the time to view your image in a real online environment by posting the picture to an online location and viewing it with both the Netscape Navigator and Internet Explorer browsers. There is no replacement for seeing for yourself how fast your Web page loads. SmartSaver Pro's Download Time display is a helpful estimation, but it's worth a few minutes to post your image yourself as a test, to see whether you really got what you wanted from all of your work.

Working with GIFs in Corel PHOTO-PAINT

Corel PHOTO-PAINT has some features in common with Ulead's SmartSaver Pro. PHOTO-PAINT offers a "before and after" split screen for viewing the effects of your changes on image quality (see Figure 13.9), although you cannot view the image size or image loading time while editing the image. You can select portions of the image for emphasis when the program creates a palette.

Figure 13.9
The Corel PHOTO-PAINT 8-bit Convert to Paletted screen.

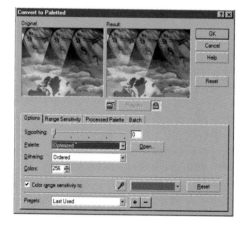

Choosing a Palette

▶ You don't need to start with a GIF image in Corel PHOTO-PAINT, although you'll have to first convert your image to an 8-bit palette type before employing GIF options. To alter an image's palette and reduce the number of colors, from the menu bar, select Image>Convert To>Paletted 8-bit. The Convert To Paletted dialog box appears, as shown in Figure 13.10.

Figure 13.10
The Convert to Paletted dialog box offers many options.

▶ The image appears in a two-paned "before and after" screen. The Options tab is displayed, with default 8-bit settings. PHOTO-PAINT chooses an Optimized 256-color palette that tries to distribute all the image's colors among 256 colors. These 256 colors are selected by PHOTO-PAINT based on their similarity to those in your image.

Understanding Palette Choices

▶ You may use the Palette drop-down menu to experiment with different palettes.

▶ Each palette offers a unique set of advantages and disadvantages for online viewing. Some of the palette choices are the following:

—Palettes optimized for a specific browser (Internet Explorer or Netscape Navigator). After choosing one of these palettes, view your image both in Internet Explorer and Navigator. Make sure your image is at least acceptable in each browser, even if the palette is optimized for one or the other.

—The standard Windows System palette. This option displays the colors used by the Windows OS in the absence of enhancement by a 16-million color video card. Use this palette to see how your image looks in the most unembellished standard Windows graphical environment.

—The Adaptive palette is created by counting the image's colors and using the first 256 colors it comes across. These are your image's colors, before any work is done emphasizing detail within the palette.

—The Uniform palette is simply a range of 256 colors drawn equally from red, green, and blue. This is how your image may look in a "plain," basic 256-color palette.

—Standard VGA is the 16-color palette used by VGA monitors and standard 16-color video cards of yore. Use this palette if your image will be viewed by computers that are six years old or more.

Dithering: Easing the Transition to 256 Colors

▶ When a photograph is converted into a GIF, an image with up to 16 million colors is squeezed into 256 colors (256 onscreen colors are produced by an *8-bit palette*). Some loss of detail will occur. A good graphics program blends those 256 colors into combinations that resemble a full 16-million-color palette. This process of arranging the colors to fool your eye into "seeing" the full spectrum of colors is called *dithering*.

► By default, PHOTO-PAINT converts your image to an 8-bit palette by using the error diffusion type of dithering. This refers to a way of diffusing the errors that occur when the palette tries to locate an exact match for a particular color in your image and cannot find one. The difference between the available color and the desired color is reduced by spreading that color difference across four neighboring pixels.

► Spreading the error across adjacent pixels causes a domino effect, with each set of pixels reflecting the differences in color hues among its neighbors. The error is pushed outwards toward the edge of the image. The result is that the eye sees graduated shades between colors rather than blotches or grainy areas. For this reason, error diffusion is a better dithering method than ordered, which makes your images look grainy.

Choosing Your Colors

To dramatically lower image loading time, reduce the colors used in the palette from 256 to 64 by doing the following:

1. On the Options tab of the Convert to Paletted dialog box, type a new number in the Colors data area.

2. Look at the Result panel and see whether reducing the colors to 64 has made your image look hopelessly ugly.

3. If you see large blotchy areas and a crater-like effect where gradual changes in shades of color should be, then increase the colors to 128.

NOTE

At any time, you can click the Processed Palette tab to see the colors your image will be using. You'll notice, for example, that when you decrease the number of colors in your image from 256 to 64, the number of color swatches displayed on the Processed Palette tab decreases to 64.

If the drop to 64 colors creates a degree of graininess, but not an unsightly amount, then do the following:

1. Click the Color range sensitivity to checkbox.

2. Select the Magic Wand tool to the right of where you clicked.

3. The next place you click with that tool will shift the image's chosen palette dramatically in that direction.

4. Click inside the image (on the left pane) on an area of prominent detail, preferably a bright area.

5.   The palette colors will shift toward the hue selected by the Magic Wand tool. Click the Processed Palette tab to see the color swatches of the current palette, if you like (see Figure 13.11).

Figure 13.11
The Processed Palette tab lets you see the colors your 8-bit image is using.

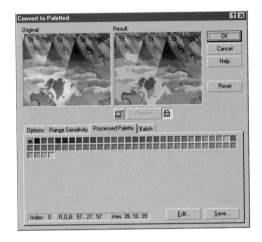

Reduce Graininess

To reduce graininess in your image, drag the Smoothing slider to the right. Smoothing may slightly blur the image, and usually doesn't work well where text is involved. When you clicked in your image with the Magic Wand tool, you set a range of colors to be given more weight in your image than the other colors in the previous palette. To widen or narrow that range of colors, and thus make the palette even more compact, do the following:

1.   Click the Range Sensitivity tab, shown in Figure 13.12. Sliders appear for the purpose of letting you narrow the range of selected colors.

Figure 13.12
Use Range Sensitivity to reduce the number of colors in an image while still maintaining realism.

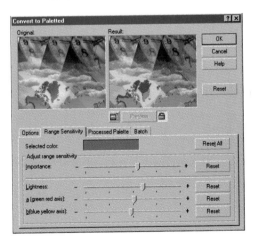

2. To skew the selected color range even more toward the preferred end of the palette, to the exclusion of other colors in the image, drag the Importance slider to the right.

3. To skew the palette range to lighter hues, drag the Lightness slider to the right.

4. Use the green/red and blue/yellow sliders to shift the palette used by the image more toward those hues.

Converting Many Images Simultaneously with PHOTO-PAINT

Since images for the Web are often created in groups, with each image requiring a similar treatment, PHOTO-PAINT provides a batch conversion feature. Click the Batch tab (see Figure 13.13) to specify which images you want to convert and process using the chosen settings previously discussed.

Figure 13.13
Convert many images using the same settings simultaneously, using the batch conversion utility.

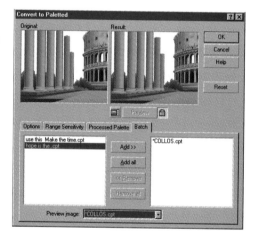

Click OK, and the image (and all images specified in the Batch tab) are converted and processed as specified. The image size will be smaller than previously. Post the image to your Web site to check loading time. You should be pleasantly surprised.

Saving an Image with GIF Options

Now that you've learned about reducing image sizes and the number of colors used, let's talk about GIF saving options, where you can specify a transparency color and interlacing options for your Web-bound GIF file.

Still in PHOTO-PAINT, after converting your image to an 8-bit palette (select Image>Convert To>Paletted 8-bit), you can save a picture as a GIF file.

To save as a GIF file, select File>Save As, and choose GIF from the Save as type drop-down menu. The Gif Export dialog box appears, shown in Figure 13.14.

Figure 13.14
PHOTO-PAINT's Gif Export dialog box.

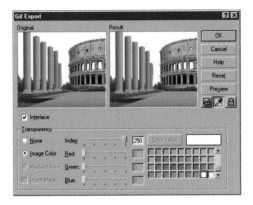

CHAPTER 13

Choosing a Transparency Color

To choose a transparency color, select the Image Color radio button in the Transparency panel of the Gif Export dialog box and then use the Eyedropper tool, found beneath the Preview button, to click the background color of your image.

Instead of using the Eyedropper tool, you can also click a color swatch from the palette squares that appear at the bottom right of the Gif Export dialog box.

Interlacing

An *interlaced* image is one that appears gradually on your Web page as the image is being loaded. A *noninterlaced* image appears only after the entire image has been loaded. Interlacing is an option available for GIF images only. All graphics programs can save GIF files with the interlacing option selected. In PHOTO-PAINT, click the Interlace checkbox, and your GIF file will gradually appear onscreen as the image is being loaded.

In this chapter, you learned both how to reduce your image's size and color values for fast Web viewing and how to create animated GIFs. In the following chapter, we'll discuss how to enjoy your scanner and graphics-related programs with your kids and family.

14

Family Fun

The aim of this chapter is to stir up lots of fun and creativity between your children and their scanned pictures. We'll talk about a program that can create a puzzle from a picture, and one that can read a scanned sheet of music and make a music file that you can play from your computer. We'll discuss how to make a storybook, trace a picture with drawing tools, and do exciting things with maps. Everything in this chapter has a very high "Oh, wow, let ME try!" factor.

Fun can sometimes border on the educational. For example, we'll talk about how to make a booklet, create board games, and keep a nice balance between learning and enjoyment.

This chapter starts with a few tips on making time spent on the computer more of a family time, showing you how to maximize kids' appreciation for all they can learn from scanning. Then, you'll learn some tips for letting kids scan by themselves, requiring minimum supervision on your part, as well as a way to give kids access to their programs without endangering your data.

Your Family and the Computer

Computers can bring a family together or, conversely, speed the creation of isolated worlds cohabiting under the same roof. Here are some tips for steering computer time toward something mutually enjoyable, as well as a few warnings and words to the wise.

▶ **Don't habitually use the computer as a babysitter.** Avoid using the technique "Why don't you go play on the computer for a while?" to get rid of the kids. They will end up resenting the electronic babysitter as deeply as a biological one.

▶ **Let the kids use the mouse.** During family computer time, put your children in front of the keyboard, computer screen, and mousepad. Place yourself to the side. They need to be in charge of what's happening onscreen, exploring and figuring things out for themselves. Allow the kids to experience a little frustration and to resolve it at their own pace, in their own way.

▶ **Set a good example as a patient problem solver.** What children remember most about computer time is how grownups react when something goes wrong. Having fits never fixed a computer or solved a software incompatibility problem. Sitting together and trying systematically to find a step-by-step solution is probably as important a family activity as anything that the computer itself has to offer.

▶ **Steer clear of anxious button pushing.** The almost universal response of children to a slow computer operation is to start pressing keys. This could lead to having to reboot.

▶ **Make deleting files off-limits.** A system file accidentally removed from your computer can eat up several hours of your life. For this reason, just like getting the keys to the family car, learning Delete commands is not the province of children, even smart, precocious ones. Kids can copy their own files, even create folders for their pictures, but deleting should be the domain of grownups.

▶ **Watch out for "mouse potato" behavior.** Make the effort while they are young to direct computer time into good topics for conversation that can be shared with others. People are difficult. Machines do whatever you say. Keep your kids tuned in to the real world.

Why Teach Kids to Scan?

Giving kids "the keys to the computer" is a healthy dose of freedom for everyone. Even young children can be taught the right steps for carrying out systematic tasks, such as scanning, saving a graphics file in a particular folder, and opening a graphics file in a image editing program. Computers can behave unpredictably, so it's quite likely that young children may not be prepared to use the computer entirely free of supervision. But you shouldn't have to do everything for them. A degree of autonomy is a good thing. You can be reading or making supper while keeping an ear out for what's going on in the computer room.

Many children over the age of six can learn these basic steps for scanning:

1. Place the photograph on the scanner bed.
2. Press the Preview button.
3. Zoom in on the desired area.
4. Perform the scan.
5. Save the file.
6. Open the photograph in a kid-safe graphics program and edit it.

However, some principles are still in order. When teaching children to scan, here are some tips to remember:

▶ Each of the preceding tasks has its own rationale. Most children do better when they understand the "why" of a task, not just the "how." Still, it's good not to clutter the air with too many explanations and directions. Keep the scanning instructions informal, clear, and to the point.

▶ Make sure the child can demonstrate each skill. It's perfectly fine to break down a multistep task, such as scanning, into several instruction sessions.

▶ Sometimes, kids appear to grasp complex instructions but are apt to forget them if not demonstrated repeatedly, preferably right after learning the steps. Try to show connections between scanning and skills that kids already possess, such as coloring, cutting, and pasting and drawing.

▶ Take your time letting the kids demonstrate that they "really know" how to scan properly.

NOTE

When teaching kids how to scan, remember that computer skills must be demonstrated, not just passively understood. Your instruction period is not over until they can put the photo on the scanner bed correctly, preview the scan, shrink the scanned area to the desired portion of the image, scan, and then save.

CHAPTER 14

Keeping Kids Away From Important Files

The trick to all of this freedom is to let the kids enjoy these liberating tasks without endangering your important files. If you are going to allow the children to enjoy scanning and photo editing, you still have to protect the rest of your computer from prying eyes and fingers. Fortunately, there are some programs that create a kid-safe desktop, giving children access to programs that you deem safe, and blocking off anything else. The best of these is called KidDesk, by Edmark (available as trialware from www.hotfiles.com, and Edmark's home page, www.edmark.com).

KidDesk creates a decorative, password-protected alternative desktop for as many youngsters as you like. Kids can have full rein over the programs, accessible from their own desktop. They can also decorate and personalize their area. Scanning and graphics programs can be part of this kid-designated area, while preventing them from probing further into your hard drive or other programs.

When you first install KidDesk, you are asked to set up users, establish levels of access, and, most importantly, determine which programs each child should be allowed to access (see Figure 14.1). You can set it up so that children cannot leave the KidDesk area set aside for them. You can also set up a password that accesses the computer's main desktop, if you need to quickly use your programs.

Figure 14.1
With KidDesk, you can determine which programs kids can access.

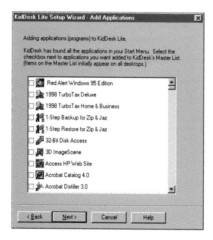

KidDesk provides a fun, personalized area for children to enjoy their own programs. As Figure 14.2 shows, all the kid-safe programs are quite accessible, and nothing else is.

Figure 14.2
KidDesk makes all kid-safe programs accessible at the click of a mouse.

Edmark's KidDesk is just about the only program of its kind that I have seen, and it provides a workable solution for letting kids enjoy their programs while also protecting your files.

Using Subjects to Teach Scanning

Many of the games and activities for children discussed here center on geography, history, and a bit of science. This is a good medium to use for exploring how to make games and activities. Here's why:

▶ Maps are easy to color. Even young kids without fine motor skills can have fun editing maps with graphics programs.

▶ It's easy to paste an image from the kid's own photo albums into a map of the world, combining them in interesting ways. This gives kids a sense of the big world out there.

▶ Pictures and information about historical figures are easy to come by without violating intellectual property laws.

▶ Regarding science, kids can take pictures of items in their own environment and apply them to a study on such things as botany, physiology, or zoology. This can be done with photos, without too many words. Thus, it can still be fun and still feel like a game.

Nonetheless, the activities suggested here really can be applied any way you choose. Historical figures can be replaced with sports or music heroes, or geographical maps can be replaced with simple shapes and objects, if your children are younger or older than the target age implied in these activities.

We'll talk about building simple board games. You can create your own game concept and then employ familiar game rules and procedures such as collecting and trading cards. We'll also talk about manipulating images and combining them with your own scanned family photos. But the suggested games can be enjoyed just as much with homemade flash cards with prime numbers, elements on the periodic table, vampires slain by Buffy, or words that begin with "A" (you have a computer and a scanner, so you might as well use them to their fullest). Which applications you should select depends on what activities interest your children, their ages, and how daring you want to be in working something educational into their computer playtime.

CHAPTER 14

Adjusting for Ages

In some of the activities discussed in this chapter, step-by-step instructions for graphics software applications are provided, as in other chapters in this book. You may be left thinking, "My kids are much too young for that." But the activities involved can still be fun for the very young, even if you have to set the stage for them. For example, the second project we discuss involves filling the states of a U.S. map with scanned photograph "pattern fills." Even young kids can click around the screen, filling areas on the map, although you may have to be involved in the initial setup.

So, when reading these directions, you can determine which steps you need to carry out and which steps you can leave to your kids to work through on their own.

CAUTION

Appendix A, "Scanning and the Law," explores the legal issues about scanned photos and using other people's intellectual property for your documents. For now, with regard to making "home projects" like these games and educational aids, the basic rule is that if you take a picture of something, you can use it for the types of projects described here. You may even use a picture of a public figure. That's part of the risk of being famous. Having you use it on a board game for your own family would be the least of their worries. However, when it comes to using photographs from other sources, you may use only pictures from collections that explicitly say "royalty free" on the box. Scanned photos from magazines, or downloaded from someone's Web site, are not supposed to be reproduced without the owner's permission. When using photographs from electronic encyclopedias, such as Microsoft® Encarta, you may use photos for nondistributive educational use for your own project, as long as you leave the copyright information intact on your document. Don't make copies, sell it, or upload it.

Create a Puzzle from a Picture

B-Jigsaw, by Antony Pranata, turns any bitmap picture into a puzzle that you can fit together piece by piece on your computer screen (see Figure 14.3). Kids can use their own scanned images as puzzles. A clock is provided so that you can rate your proficiency. The program automatically generates easy, intermediate, or difficult puzzles. You can save your ratings and compare your score with others.

Figure 14.3
Create a puzzle with any image by using B-Jigsaw.

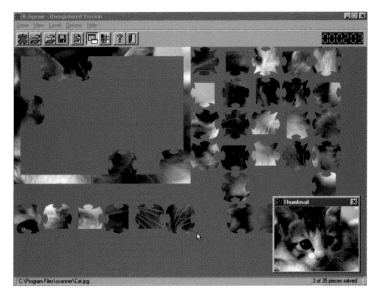

To create a puzzle, simply scan an image and save is as a BMP file. Then open an image in B-Jigsaw, and the puzzle will be generated. If you like, the pieces can be arranged in a grid instead of being scattered. An optional thumbnail of the bitmap can be displayed in the lower-right corner, making it easier to see how the puzzle should be made.

Scan and Listen to Music

SharpEye uses optical character recognition (OCR) on your scanned music sheets, recognizing note values quite accurately, and generates music files that you can play back from your computer (see Figure 14.4). This means that you scan a piece of sheet music and hear what it would sound like, just by running it through SharpEye (available at www.hotfiles.com).

Figure 14.4
SharpEye lets you generate a playable music file from scanned sheet music.

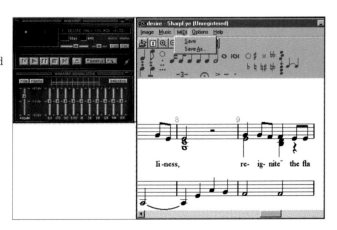

CHAPTER 14

To use SharpEye, scan sheet music in any TWAIN-supporting graphics program, and save your image as a black-and-white TIFF, JPEG, or PCX file. Open the SharpEye program and choose Image>Open. Locate the scanned sheet music. Select Image>Read, and SharpEye begins to extract music notes, assigning a musical value of pitch and time to each recognized note.

Select Save As from the MIDI menu, and SharpEye creates a MIDI file that plays back the sheet music's melody. You can double-click the MIDI file, and the multimedia player configured on your computer will play the sheet music's contents.

Before your expectations for sound quality grow too large, I must point out that MIDI files play simple note compositions generated by your computer's sound card. Most often, the music sounds thin and electronic. You'll recognize the melody, but it won't sound symphonic.

Painting a Photograph Fill

Let's start by learning how to "paint a photograph" with Paint Shop Pro's Flood Fill tool. Your kids can fill their brush with any photograph and click an enclosed area of a picture, and the photograph will fill that entire area, right up to the border. It's creative, fun, and easy. Here's how to do this with a U.S. map, as shown in Figure 14.5:

Figure 14.5
Creating a map with photograph fills.

1. In Paint Shop Pro, open a simple map of the U.S. Avoid maps with topography, cities, and landmarks. The simpler, the better. What we really want for this project is state boundaries (You can download good maps from www.maps.com).

2. Open other images that will serve as the fill patterns with which to click the screen and fill each state.

3. Click the Flood Fill tool, on the lower-left side of the screen.

4. Open the Tool Controls tab of the Flood Fill palette. If this control palette is not visible, select View>Toolbars and check Control Palette.

5. In the Tool Controls tab of the Flood Fill palette, click the Fill Style drop-down arrow and choose Pattern.

6. Click the Flood Fill Options tab and then click the New pattern source drop-down arrow.

7. All currently open pictures will appear in that drop-down menu. Select any of them to be your flood fill pattern.

Now have your child click with the mouse in any state on the map. The pattern you selected will fill that entire state. You can always return to the Pattern menu and change the bitmap used by the Flood Fill tool.

NOTE

I have found that it is nice to have younger kids open several images, such as bodies of water, farms, industrial scenes, and people. The kids can then select a different bitmap for each state and get a sense of variety as they click around the screen.

This same activity can be applied to countries of the world rather than states, or it can be used with your own scanned photographs in conjunction with Paint Shop Pro's drawing tools. The Pattern Fill tool works simply by filling any enclosed area with the loaded image. Kids can really have fun with this one.

NOTE

You can learn lots about this very powerful and inexpensive program Paint Shop Pro from the book, *Paint Shop Pro 6 Power!* (Muska & Lipman 1999; ISBN 0-9662889-2-0).This book teaches you how to edit and adjust scans, pictures, and other types of computer images.

CHAPTER 14

Create a Bookmark

Creating a bookmark is a fast, fun activity to do with a scanned image, as shown in Figure 14.6. You can combine a scanned photo with a bit of artwork and perhaps some drawing around the edges, and even leave room below to keep track of books that the child has read in the last month. Each month, the child can create a new bookmark with a personal photo, marking at the bottom the books that were read for that month. They can look back at the bookmarks and track physical growth and learning at the same time.

Figure 14.6
A bookmark created with a scanned photo in Paint Shop Pro.

The bookmark shown here was created in Paint Shop Pro 6, by layering the clip art Cityscape in front of the main photo. The dimensions are 1080×250 pixels, at 100 dpi. A photograph of a person standing works better with the dimensions of a bookmark. If none is available, try some other sort of vertically oriented subject matter. The clip art was treated with the Bevel effect and was placed on its own layer in front of a statuesque Larisa.

You can use photos relating to favorite books, animal images from favorite classic books, and vertically oriented images such as skyscrapers, trees and pencils.

A Matching Game

Here's another fast, fun educational game: a simple three-photograph "Who Am I?" game in which the information below the photographs relates to one of the people pictured in the photos (see Figure 14.7, for example). This is a study aid and can be fun for kids to create with photos they scan themselves. Although this example uses historical figures, you can create a game similar to this using totally different subject matter. (By the way, the answer to the question is Vincent Van Gogh, but most of you probably knew that, I'm sure).

Figure 14.7
A "Who Am I?" game created with scanned photos.

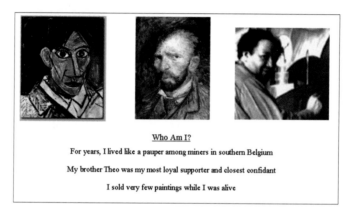

Who Am I?

For years, I lived like a pauper among miners in southern Belgium

My brother Theo was my most loyal supporter and closest confidant

I sold very few paintings while I was alive

Making a T-Shirt Transfer

One big use of scanned photos is to create T-shirt transfers. All the big printer companies produce special T-shirt transfers. They all work pretty much the same. The following is a review of a few of the directions that bear repeating and emphasis:

1. First, purchase a bright white T-shirt, one that will last, and purchase transfers especially designed for T-shirts. Many companies manufacture them.

2. Print out the image onto the transfer. Make sure the image is reversed (Paint Shop Pro has a special "reverse image" setting, or just select Image>Mirror before printing).

3. Properly position the T-shirt as indicated by the T-shirt transfer instructions. Make sure you place the transfer face down over the T-shirt. Use a hard surface, but not an ironing board, which is not hard enough to facilitate a good, clean transfer of the image.

4. Before you begin ironing, fold a corner of the T-shirt transfer toward you. This will be the corner that you'll use as a pull-tab, a way to remove the transfer paper without breaking your fingernails while trying to grab a corner that has been ironed down to stay.

5. Iron the transfer exactly according to the directions. Most T-shirt transfers work best if you leave the iron over an area for 15 seconds or more, pressing hard. Then, move to an adjacent area, holding the iron in place for a long time, rather than moving the iron around as if you were getting out creases.

6. Pay close attention to the directions for how long to iron the transfer, and how many passes to make with the iron before lifting off the transfer paper.

7. Most T-shirt transfers come with washing directions. Follow those. Also, many include initial washing instructions for "locking in" the colors. These directions are designed to increase the life of the transfer colors.

Here are some points to keep in mind when choosing an image for a T-shirt transfer:

▶ Details never show up as clearly as you thought they would. Simple images with an obvious focus are the best.

▶ The T-shirt transfers always look smaller on the T-shirt than you thought they would. A single big picture will look the best.

▶ Bright colors last longer and won't fade so quickly. A darker image will start to become indistinct after a few washings.

CAUTION

Just as the shirt in Figure 14.8 reminds us, if you create text for your T-shirt transfer image, the text must be backward. It will then appear facing the right way when transferred onto your shirt. For a simple way to flip an image with text (or an image without text, for that matter), open the image in Paint Shop Pro and select Image>Mirror.

Figure 14.8
T-shirt transfers with text must be printed with the text backward.

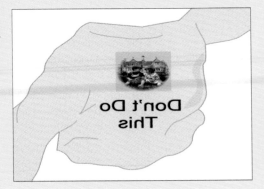

Creating Board Games

Let's create a board game. This can seem a little daunting, so we'll take it step by step. You'll see how much fun it is once we get going.

Here are some components to creating a board game (These will be explored in more detail later in this section):

1. Devise the game's goal, suggested strategy, and rules of play.
2. Create the board theme.
3. Draw the board's layout with a graphics computer program.
4. Print the board pieces.
5. Paste together the board pieces.
6. Glue the printed sheets onto posterboard.
7. Optional: Some board games involve cards that must be printed. These, too, must be designed, pasted onto posterboard, and cut out individually.
8. Optional: Locate a pair of dice, which are usually needed to progress around the board.

You can determine the complexity of the game, depending on your children's attention span, interest level, and age.

Making the Game

Here's how to create an Inventors game, which involves moving around the board, collecting and matching cards of both inventors and their inventions to build complete sets (see Figure 14.9). It's easy to understand and easy to make, as well.

Figure 14.9
A board game created with scanned photos and Microsoft Publisher.

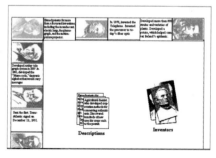

CHAPTER 14

This demonstration uses Microsoft Publisher to create the board, import the pictures used, and make the cards. Publisher is great for this purpose, because the program makes it easy to print a customized project size. If you want your board game to be 24×36 inches, simply set up the page size as you like it, and Publisher will print the entire project across several pages. It's also easy to use Publisher to group many cards on a page and print out many copies of each.

How the Game Works

The Inventors game board is composed of pictures of many inventors, interspersed with written descriptions, as shown being assembled in Publisher in Figure 14.10. The object is to collect the descriptions and pictures of as many inventors as possible. The players have to know which description matches which inventor—that's where the learning and memorizing comes in.

Figure 14.10
Move the image of the inventor inside a game board rectangle.

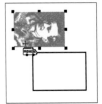

When a player rolls the dice and lands on an inventor or description, she gets to keep that card. Cards can be traded and bargained for, depending on what a player requires in order to obtain as many complete sets as possible. After all the cards are collected and traded, whoever has the most inventor-description pairs wins the game.

The idea of this game can apply to lots of different subjects. You can use scanned photos of a family vacation, matching words with simple photographs of those objects, or any photos of interest.

Dimensions and Size

The size of the board depends on how large you want the photos to be, how much text is required for your written descriptions, and how many rolls of the dice it should take to go around the board. Smaller children might prefer larger pictures, larger text with fewer words, and an easy trip around the board. Bigger kids will, of course, want more of a challenge.

For smaller children, creating a board with twenty-four steps (six steps on all four sides of a rectangle) is just about right. If you create a board with lots of steps, you have to create more cards and more descriptions. I find that a 20×20-inch board can accommodate six 2.5-inch-wide cards, plus a comfortable board margin, while applying the same dimension and number of cards to all four sides.

Creating the Game Board

To create the board and game in Microsoft Publisher, do the following:

1. Scan or otherwise locate pictures in sufficient quantity that can be reproduced on a game board. The pictures should have similar dimensions, making the game board look neater when you are finished. Select File>Page Setup and design a page 20×20 inches, or any size you wish (see Figure 14.11).

Figure 14.11
Use the Page Setup dialog box to create custom-sized documents.

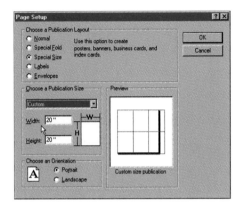

TIP
Overlap your printed pages. Later, when you print, Publisher will print this page on the correct number of pieces of paper, giving you "overlap" room at the edge of the page for easy gluing, as shown in Figure 14.12.

Figure 14.12
The overlapping printing option accommodates combined-page documents.

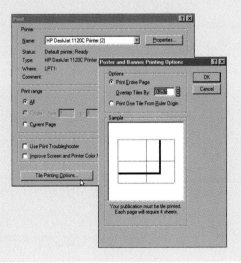

CHAPTER 14

2. After you choose a document size from the Page Setup menu, the entire document will fill your screen.

3. Use the drawing tools to create a rectangle 2.5×2 inches (see Figure 14.13). This size may be varied according to your needs.

Figure 14.13
The single rectangle is the basis of the board game.

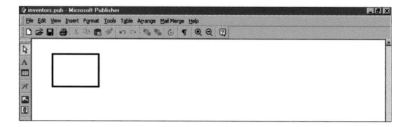

4. Duplicate the rectangle six times (cut and paste), using the Align tool to line up the rectangles evenly, forming one row of the board game.

5. Group this entire row of rectangles and duplicate it. Rotate the copy 90 degrees to form a perpendicular angle of the board. Overlap the rectangles where the two ends meet, so that each side is composed of an even number of rectangles. The rows of rectangles meet at one end, overlapping to create an even number on both sides.

6. Repeat this procedure for the other two sides, creating a square playing board of rectangles, as shown in Figure 14.14.

Figure 14.14
The playing board comprises an entire square.

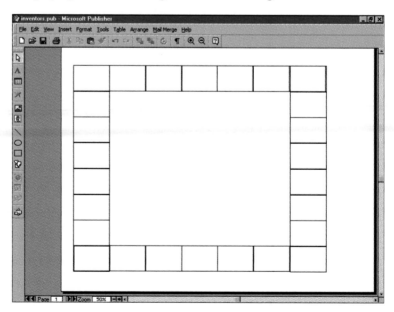

7. Insert the pictures into Publisher. Resize and rotate each picture and place it so that it fits inside a rectangle (see Figure 14.15). Make sure all images face inwards towards the center of the board.

Figure 14.15
Each picture must be resized and rotated to fill the spaces on the board.

8. Make a copy of each inventor picture, since you'll be printing these copies as collector cards.

9. Use the Text tool to create inventor descriptions, and place descriptions around various rectangles on the playing field. Use the Resize and Rotate tools to fit the descriptions in each rectangle.

10. Make a copy of each text description you create, because you'll be printing each of these text descriptions as individual cards (see Figure 14.16).

Figure 14.16
Each text description will become a card.

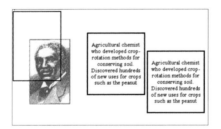

11. Randomly intersperse the inventor descriptions with the pictures, as shown in Figure 14.17, because matching one to the other is part of the goal of the game.

Figure 14.17
Each inventor has a description that matches.

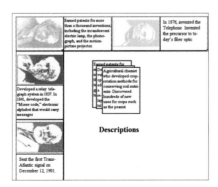

CHAPTER 14

12. Leave some squares blank, for which no card is collected if a player lands on one of them. You may embellish this square with a scanned photo of the family dog or some offspring making a ridiculous face. You may also elaborate on the rule for landing on this square, deeming that the unlucky player must give a card to the person to her right, for example.

Creating the Cards

After the board game is populated with inventors and descriptions, create a blank document where you can place all the pictures and descriptions that will become cards. Having the cards grouped on sheets of paper makes it easier to print them all out at once.

1. On a new page, line up all of your copies of both inventors and descriptions into rows and columns. You'll be printing and cutting these out. (see Figure 14.18).

Figure 14.18
Images arranged for printing and creating cards.

2. You may have to make more than one page to accommodate all of your cards. Set this document aside until you are ready to print and cut out the cards.

Printing, Cutting, and Gluing

Pull yourself away from the computer momentarily and get out the glue and scissors. Then, follow these steps:

1. Print your board, onto either card stock or regular paper that will then be pasted, sheet by sheet, onto poster board. Publisher prints a 20×20-inch document onto four sheets of 8.5×11-inch paper.

2. Glue the board together, using the overlapping area that Publisher provides, making sure that the lines line up for straight, even overlapping.

3. Return to the document with your cards. Print the cards onto card stock.

4. Cut out the cards.

Getting Ready to Play

Now you have to get the board ready for play:

1. Place the cards in the middle of the playing board, to be given to players as they land on the appropriate board square.

2. Create a key for matching inventors with descriptions and print it. This will be referred to when determining the winner.

3. Create player markers for each player of the game. Determine who will go first.

Gameplay

This game is designed to move quickly and to not last terribly long. You are encouraged to stop and talk about cards, in order to trade and barter. No secrecy or stealth is involved. These are the steps for playing the game:

1. Each player rolls the dice, moves his marker based on the dice roll, and lands on a square. The player is automatically given the inventor or inventor description card that matches the square. The object of the game is to accumulate more inventor-and-description card pairs than any other player.

2. After one player takes a turn at the dice, moves her piece and collects a card, the next player takes a turn.

3. As each player accumulates cards, it becomes apparent who needs which cards to achieve greatness and conquest. Bargaining and bartering for cards will ensue. Life becomes a mad free-for-all. One's knowledge of inventors aids in the ability to bargain and trade for the right cards.

4. After all the cards have been dispersed to players by landing on squares, and the trading is complete, the players add their pairs, and a winner is established.

Creating a Storybook and Board Game

Using one set of scanned photos, you can create both a storybook and a board game. All it takes is a little creativity.

Kids can create stories, one page at a time, by putting a photo on a page and adding a little bit of text above or below the photo, as in Figure 14.19. Then, they can add a title page, sign their name as the author, and enjoy a real sense of accomplishment.

Figure 14.19
A booklet created
with scanned photos.

The Printing Problem

The trouble with creating these little booklets is sequencing the pages for printing. Using 8.5×11-inch paper in Landscape mode means that one page of the booklet will be 8 inches high and 5.5 inches wide. You could print two pages on one piece of paper, and four pages if you use both sides. A nice little eight-page booklet would only require two sheets of paper, printed double-sided.

But the sequencing is tricky. Page one has to go on the right side of what would really be "the back" of the first piece of paper, and the final page must go on the opposite of page one. And it gets more confusing from there.

Inexplicably, most graphics and desktop publishing programs are not that helpful at organizing page output and making it easy to print and assemble booklets. Microsoft Publisher is an exception. If you do the page setup beforehand and have a printer that lets you flip paper halfway through a print job to accommodate two-sided printing, then creating a booklet with Publisher is no harder than creating any other document.

Creating a Booklet

Let's set up a booklet page by using Microsoft Publisher. Publisher lets you add as many pages as you like and adjusts the print job accordingly. We'll use the same pictures that we draw for this booklet in a board game so that you can see how a little creativity and a scanner can go a long way.

To create a booklet, do the following:

1. Open a blank document in Publisher, and choose File>Page Setup. Set the paper orientation to Landscape, and click Special Fold, then Special Size. Choose Book Fold from the drop-down menu (see Figure 14.20).

Figure 14.20
Click Special Fold and Special Size to create a booklet.

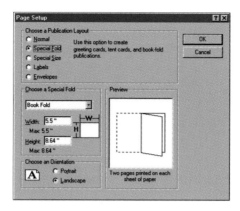

2. Create a title page with your child. Show them the different fonts they can use, how to make the title quite fancy and decorative, and how to "sign" the page with a unique font at the bottom.

3. Set up autonumbering of the booklet's pages. This makes it easy to assemble later, when you print. This is done by creating a small text frame at the bottom of the page, and choosing Insert>Page Numbers (see Figure 14.21). Publisher will place page numbers on each page, no matter how many you add or delete.

Figure 14.21
To avoid confusion while assembling the booklet, add page numbers.

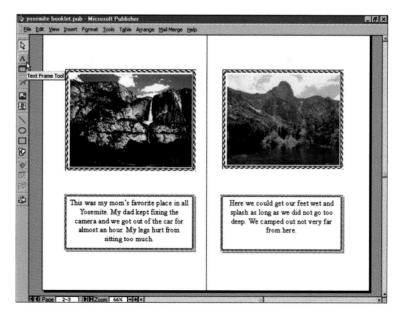

CHAPTER 14

4. The following step depends on your child's age:

    —If your children are old enough, you may want to let them take over, first showing them how to create a text block at the bottom of each page and add one picture at a time.

    —If your children are young and you'd rather not have them searching the hard drive for pictures to include, you can open and insert all the pictures now, setting them off to the side, away from the page (see Figure 14.22). Then, your kids can drag the pictures into place and add text.

Figure 14.22
You can have the pictures readily available in the margins, allowing your children to position them.

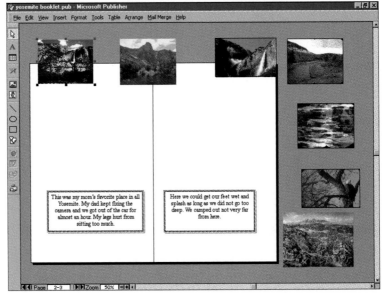

5. Show the kids how to move to the next page, to edit and add pictures and text until their pictures are full.

6. You may want to point out the Shape drawing tools, if they'd like to embellish their work.

7. To print the booklet, select File>Print Setup, and be sure to specify double-sided, or two-sided, printing (if your printer accommodates this feature). Publisher will automatically print each page in its proper sequence.

8. After the document is printed, simply put a few staples in the center fold, and you're done.

For Younger Children

When it comes to activities with scanned photos for children between four and seven years of age, there is one foolproof answer: Kid Pix.

Kid Pix, by Broderbund, is the most beloved and universally enjoyed children's computer drawing program. It has changed little since it was first introduced in 1992, and it still provides just about as much fun as the very young can have sitting at a computer.

Using Kid Pix is very simple, and all kids seem to be able to figure it out for themselves with very little prompting. They simply click a tool on the left side of the screen, such as a Line Drawing tool, a Fill Color tool, or a Special Effect tool. At the bottom of the screen are options for that tool (see Figure 14.23).

Figure 14.23
The venerable Kid Pix screen.

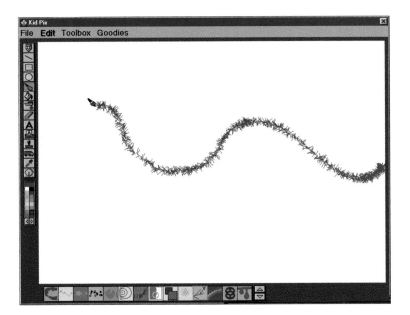

For example, select the Paint Brush tool on the left and click a brush option at the bottom. Kids can paint with odd shapes, bubbles, spider webs, drippy paint brushes, or familiar objects, to name only a few options. Kid Pix also provides big and friendly letters for adding small bits of text to your child's creation.

You can import one of your scanned pictures into Kid Pix, which treats the image as if it were a background for painting. Kids can color and paint on the picture, incorporating it into their own creation, such as the example shown in Figure 14.24.

Figure 14.24
Importing and
decorating a photo
in Kid Pix.

Kid Pix can only import BMP files, so you may have to first open your
image in Paint Shop Pro or some other photo editing program and
convert the scanned photo from its native format to BMP. Kid Pix saves
its picture files exclusively as BMPs, as well.

Kid Pix is a bit old and somewhat hard to find. Many commercial
software stores sell it at a deep discount, because it's rather plain and
unembellished by today's extravagant standards. You can order Kid Pix
from Broderbund's Web site: **www.broderbund.com**.

If you want to experiment with a trialware program very similar to Kid
Pix to see whether this type of software is appropriate for your child, look
online (www.hotfiles.com) for the program Child's Play, by Alston
Software Labs.

Now that you've learned so many uses for scanned images, it's time to
learn how to organize and store those images and retrieve them quickly
when they are needed. In the next chapter, you'll learn how to keep track
of your scans and have them at your fingertips when you want them.

15

Arranging and Archiving Your Files

It's time to talk about what you're going to do with all of those pictures and scans. Not the first twenty-five or fifty, but the first 200, and those that follow. They will add up fast. You need to master several tasks related to organizing your pictures. The pictures you use most often should be the most readily available. Other pictures should be organized according to topic, date, or any other system that enables you to locate them with just a few clicks. And, finally, those pictures that you no longer need immediate access to should be *archived,* grouped together in a way that saves the disk space for more urgent files. They need to be set aside but still be available if you really need them.

First, we'll discuss the need for a plan that states how to begin organizing your files, before so many are accumulated that the task becomes too daunting. Then, you'll learn about thumbnail systems for viewing all of your images quickly, no matter where they are located. You'll learn about programs such as PKZIP that store your files in as small a size as possible, ready to be retrieved later, if you need them. Finally, we'll talk about how to arrange your files for immediate accessibility.

The Need For a Plan

Figures 15.1a and 15.1b show two organizational schemes. You would store your pictures in one of the folders, depending on how they fit into the scheme. Either of these schemes is preferable to saving all of your pictures in one location, because after a while, you'd lose track of anything other than the pictures you scanned most recently.

Figure 15.1a
Organizing your files with a "wide" folder structure.

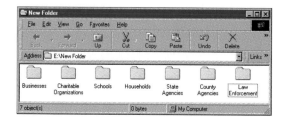

Figure 15.1b
Organizing your files with a "deep" folder structure.

Planning for Accessibility

The best way to organize your files is to think in terms of broad categories first, such as types of files or types of projects, and then get more specific as you create folders beneath those main categories. That way, at the top level of the system, you may see only two or three folders, while at lower levels, the images are stored in subfolders. Don't get too carried away creating deeper levels, however, because each level means more mouse-clicks are required to locate an image. Unless you have many different types of customers or projects that you need to organize, you'll find that one or two levels of subcategories are enough.

Planning for Growth

An important part of your plan is knowing how to expand it. If images do not fit into one of the categories, what criteria do you use to create a new one? Do you create new folders based on the date, type of image, project, customer, or subjects being photographed? And how would the new category fit in with the others? Should you create a new category entirely or just a new subcategory beneath one of the main groups? However you decide to organize your images, use a branching system that will make sense later on, when you have only a short time to retrieve an image.

Organizing and Accessing Your Images with Thumbnails

Let's address the need for quick identification of your files. If you have more than a handful of scanned images in a folder, it's hard to locate a particular picture by its name only. Even if you try to name pictures in a way that jogs your memory ("Joey wins last fall's pumpkin carving contest"), you'll notice that the desktop doesn't display the entire name unless you are viewing your icons in Windows' Detail mode. Too many long filenames can be cumbersome. (To view more information about each file in a folder, select View>Details.)

To make locating images easy, you need to be able to see the pictures before opening them. This requires a *thumbnail* system, which enables you to view a "sheet" of small representations of your pictures, usually fifteen to twenty at a time. Rather than wait for you to open a picture, as soon as you access a folder with pictures in it, the thumbnail program displays all the pictures in that folder, without even being prompted.

Using a Thumbnail System

Thumbnails are usually 1x1.5-inch representations of an image, a size that is big enough to be recognizable, yet small enough to fit a few rows of images on the screen, as in the example shown in Figure 15.2. As part of the setup process, thumbnail viewers ask you to assign a program for each image *type.* That way, you can double-click a thumbnail, and the image will open in the program you have already specified.

Figure 15.2
Thumbnails should be large enough to be recognizable, yet still show four or five rows on a screen.

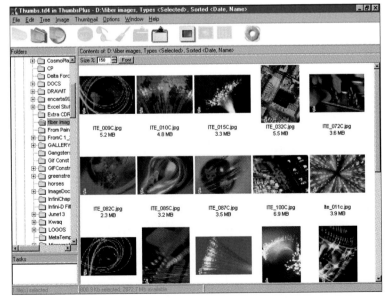

CHAPTER 15

How Thumbnails Work

Thumbnail programs allow you to open an image by dragging a thumbnail onto an already-open program. That way, you can have Paint Shop Pro open, for example, taking up perhaps half of your screen, while next to it, your thumbnail program can be displaying perhaps five or six rows of images. Drag a thumbnail onto the empty Paint Shop Pro screen (or onto the program's own icon on the taskbar), and the full image will open.

Still, the ability to look at all images in a folder is only half an answer. What happens if you need quick access to images that are not all in the same place? You may want to group images by project, client, or date, and not necessarily by file location.

Most thumbnail programs provide several ways of grouping and retrieving images, regardless of where they are found on your hard drive. Here are two ways this is done:

▶ **Galleries**—Most thumbnail programs let you create *galleries,* collections of images that you select from any location you like. You simply name a gallery and then begin searching your hard drive for pictures to include in it. Populate your gallery by dragging the images onto the gallery screen (see Figure 15.3). You are not moving the images to a new location, however. You're merely telling the thumbnail program to create thumbnails. You can gather images into groups and save the Gallery under any name you wish, such as Vacations, Spring Break, or the name of a client. The thumbnails are grouped together in this gallery, like Windows shortcuts. The images themselves are not moved.

▶ **Keywords**—Some thumbnail programs let you assign keywords to images. Later, you can retrieve any image by typing the keyword into a thumbnail search menu. You'll see thumbnails of any and all images associated with that keyword, no matter where they are located. These keywords enable you to group images according to any criteria that makes sense to you (for example, June Vacation, Fall Newsletter, or Clocks).

Cerious Software's ThumbsPlus

Cerious Software's ThumbsPlus (available from www.hotfiles.com) is a sophisticated and easy-to-use thumbnail program that's been around for many years. Figure 15.3 shows ThumbsPlus at work.

Figure 15.3
How ThumbsPlus
is organized.

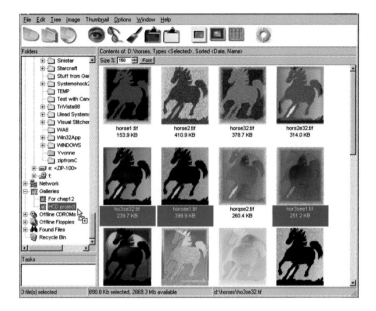

The left side of the screen shows an Explorer-like tree of all the folders on your computer. Click a folder, and the images found inside it will display in thumbnail form on the right. Just like Explorer, click a plus sign next to a folder, and subfolders are revealed. Click a subfolder to see the images inside. ThumbsPlus lets you view all the images in subfolders. This is a nice benefit, because you can open and view many more images without having to "drill down" to that specific folder. To view the images in all folders beneath the one you are currently clicking, right-click the folder and select Show Child Folders.

CHAPTER 15

The right side of the screen shows thumbnails of the images in the selected folder. Click a thumbnail, and it opens in the picture's *native application*. Right-click the thumbnail, and you see a menu that enables you to cut or copy the picture to a new location, view all the full-sized pictures as a slideshow, or even rename or view the file's properties (see Figure 15.4).

Figure 15.4
Here are the Figure properties.

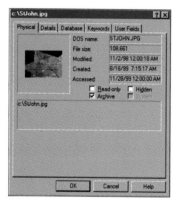

NOTE

A native application is the program Windows associates with that particular kind of file. For example, if Paint Shop Pro is on your computer, many types of graphic files—such as .PCX and .TIF formats—will open in Paint Shop Pro if you click on that file's icon.

Editing Files Globally

The purpose of a thumbnail program is to let you manipulate the image as much as possible without necessarily opening the picture in an image editing program. You can perform tasks such as moving many pictures simultaneously, organizing pictures in galleries, changing the way the pictures are configured in their native application, and even viewing the file full-sized without opening another program to do so.

A thumbnail program recognizes the fact that many graphics-related chores are done globally, meaning that you want to do them to many pictures simultaneously. For example, if you decide to move all of your images that have to do with household items into one specific folder, ThumbsPlus enables you to view multiple folders simultaneously (see Figure 15.5) and then select only the images of interest to you. Then, you can move all of those images related to household items into a new folder.

Figure 15.5
You can select various images even if they are in different folders and move them simultaneously.

Here are examples of tasks that can be grouped together and done "all at once." These are called "batched" tasks, and a good thumbnail program allows you to see the files you want to manipulate as a group, making many jobs much easier.

▶ Changing the file formats of a group of files

▶ Moving a group of files to a new location

▶ Resizing a group of files

▶ Deleting a group of files

▶ Duplicating a group of files as a back-up

Moving Files with ThumbsPlus

To move multiple images to a new folder, even if they originate in different folders, do the following:

1. On the left side of the ThumbsPlus screen, click a folder.

2. If the folder has subfolders beneath it, right-click that same folder and choose Show Child Folders.

3. Choose Edit>Select All.

4. Choose Thumbnail>Make Selected. ThumbsPlus will create thumbnails for all images in every folder at, *and below,* the level you clicked.

CHAPTER 15

5. Drag the scroll bar located toward the center of the screen, so that the folder comes into view where you want to send all these images *to*. Do not click the folder—just make sure you can see it.

6. While pressing the Ctrl button, click each thumbnail you want to move to a new location. Use the scroll bar to view all the available thumbnails. Keep clicking until all the pictures you want to move are selected.

7. While still depressing the Ctrl button, drag the thumbnails from the right side of the screen, across to the destination folder on the left.

8. The images (not the thumbnails) will now be moved to that new location.

Creating a Gallery with ThumbsPlus

To create a gallery in ThumbsPlus, do the following:

1. Click the Galleries icon on the Folders side of the screen (scroll down near the bottom to locate the icon). You'll be prompted to name your gallery.

2. An icon for the gallery you just created appears below the Galleries icon, as shown in Figure 15.6.

Figure 15.6
A newly created gallery.

3. You can now drag any thumbnails you want to that gallery. Use the techniques previously described for viewing folders with images and then dragging them to the gallery.

4. Alternately, you can select all the images you want to display in a gallery and then right-click and choose Add to Gallery (see Figure 15.7).

Figure 15.7
You can populate a gallery by right-clicking an image or group of images and choosing Add to Gallery.

NOTE

When you add thumbnails to a gallery, the pictures themselves remain in their location. You are only creating a new thumbnail in that gallery. Thumbnails in a gallery make it easy to edit, view, print, and change the properties of any grouping of images you so desire. Remember that images in a gallery can be amassed from all over your hard drive, even though they appear to be in one place.

Creating a Slideshow

You can run a slideshow of images in your gallery by clicking the Slide Show icon at the top of the screen. You can configure your show to let it run automatically, move to the next image when a key is pressed, or make each image fill the entire screen. To configure many ThumbsPlus features, including the slideshow , select Options>Preferences.

Printing Thumbnails

You can print sheets of all the thumbnail images you like, either those found in a particular gallery or in a folder or group of folders. To do so, select Image>Print Catalog. You can configure both how large the images should appear on each page (which limits how many can fit on a single piece of paper—see Figure 15.8) and whether you want the filename and path printed with your images. Printing thumbnail catalogs is a great way to avoid losing track of your scanned images.

CHAPTER 15

Figure 15.8
You can specify how large each image should be of a printed catalog.

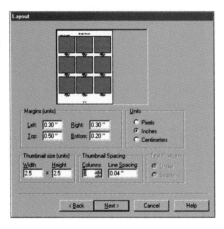

Using Keywords with ThumbsPlus

When you assign a keyword to a thumbnail, you can retrieve that image no matter where it is located on your hard drive. Even if the picture is moved, you can still find it without a long, time-intensive search through folder after folder.

Keywords can help locate one single image or a group of like images. Here's how:

▶ Assign a unique keyword to a thumbnail (Prom Dress, for example), so that one very special picture will always be a click away, no matter where it is moved to.

▶ Group together similar images, making them all instantly accessible as a unit (such as Cats, October Class, Corvette Pics. Please notice that a keyword need not be a single word.)

▶ Assign multiple keywords to an image. For example, if a picture of a Corvette Stingray was also part of your October Class project, you could assign the keywords October Class and Corvette Pics. A search using the October Class keyword would cause that image to display, as would a search using the keyword Corvette Pics.

If ThumbsPlus has generated a thumbnail of an image, you can assign a keyword to it regardless of where it is located on your hard drive. To assign a keyword to an image, do the following:

1. Right-click the thumbnail as it appears in the ThumbsPlus catalog, and choose Assign Keyword>Other.

2. Type a keyword for assignment.

3. Upon assigning a keyword, that image is now associated with it.

It's that simple. The image will be retrieved whenever you perform a database query with ThumbsPlus. Also, that keyword you assigned will now appear in the Assign Keyword drop-down menu, along with all the other keywords, so that you can keep track of all existing keywords and assign those same words to other images.

Retrieving an Image via a Keyword

To locate an image or groups of images by keyword, do the following:

1. Select Find by Query from the Edit menu. The Find Files dialog box appears, as shown in Figure 15.9.

Figure 15.9
The Find Files dialog box.

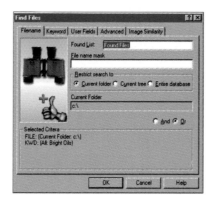

2. On the Filename tab, restrict your search to the current folder, the entire ThumbsPlus database, or the current tree, which includes the current folder and all of its subfolders. To make this choice, click the appropriate check box in the Restrict Search To data box.

3. On the Keyword tab, you'll notice two panels (see Figure15.10):

Figure 15.10
Create a keyword search from the Find By Query dialog box.

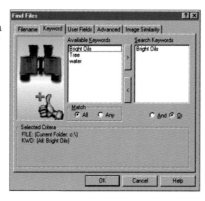

—One panel displays the Available Keywords, which are all the keywords that have been used anywhere in the ThumbsPlus database.

CHAPTER 15

—The other panel displays the keywords that will be used in the current search. Assign keywords to this panel by clicking a word in the Available Keywords list and then clicking the right-facing arrow. The word assigned from the left side to the right side will now be used to search for images.

4. Add as many keywords to your search as you want, using the right-facing arrow to assign them.

5. After you finish assigning keywords for searching, click OK.

6. After searching, ThumbsPlus displays the images in a special folder accessed on the left side of the screen, called Found Files, identified by a binoculars. This folder's contents are displayed on the right, in the catalog area. These are all the files that match your keyword. You can now edit them and open them as you would any other ThumbsPlus thumbnail.

You've now learned how to organize, group, and retrieve images on your hard drive, but what about pictures stored on removable media, such as floppies, CD-ROMs, or Zip disks? That discussion is next.

Organizing Offline Images

ThumbsPlus keeps track of offline images as well. In this sense, "offline" means images stored on a CD-ROM, floppy, or Zip disk that is not currently in the drive. Seems like magic, huh? How can the program keep track of images that are not in their drive? By saving a thumbnail, and not the entire image. When ThumbsPlus searches a CD-ROM, Zip disk, floppy drive, or any type of external drive, it remembers the volume number of the media it searched (see Figure 15.11). The thumbnails are saved. You can view them even after the drive is removed.

Figure 15.11
ThumbsPlus can keep track of offline images.

So, for example, if you offload some of your scanned images onto a Zip disk, you can still use ThumbsPlus to view thumbnails of those pictures even if the Zip disk is not currently in place. To view the actual image, though, you have to insert the Zip disk into the drive. This same principle applies to floppy disks, CD-ROMs, and any other type of removable media.

This feature presents a great advantage to you. After you determine that you aren't going to use certain images for a while, you can offload them to alternative media, such as a recordable CD-ROM or Zip disk, yet still have access to the thumbnails. So, if you suddenly need an offloaded image, you can locate its thumbnail, load the disk on which you saved it, and put it back in circulation. This certainly beats scratching your head thinking, "Where did I put that thing?"

Compressing Image Files Using WinZip

When files are not in use, they can be made very small by using file compression, so that they take up only a tiny amount of hard drive space. If you have files that you know you won't be using any time soon, you can archive them. You can compress them to perhaps as little as one tenth of their current size.

This technology, employed in an application called WinZip, can give you back huge chunks of disk space. Compressing files with WinZip takes between 10 seconds and five minutes, depending on the size of the file to be compressed. You can compress more than one file simultaneously. They can be decompressed, making them usable again, in a little less time than compression takes.

Using WinZip

The best use of WinZip is to compress files that you may need in the future but don't want to offload entirely. Any type of file can be compressed with WinZip. Once decompressed, the file is unchanged. Program files, system files, data files, and graphics files can all be compressed freely. You can compress entire programs and then decompress them later. You can unzip a file or group of files onto another computer. Zipped files are totally independent of the computer you zipped them on. When using the WinZip program, there is no loss of graphic image data or quality loss whatsoever.

WinZip is downloadable as trialware from the Web (www.winzip.com). The program installs in less than five minutes and, in a Windows 9x or NT system, integrates itself into file menus for easy use.

Zipping a File or Group of Files

After the program is installed, the WinZip icon will appear on your desktop. You can zip multiple files simultaneously, including files found in subfolders of the current folder you have clicked. Note that you can zip entire folders and subfolders, not just individual files. Here's how to create a zipped archive and add files to it from many locations on your computer.

1. Double-click on the WinZip icon, and an empty WinZip file interface appears.

2. Open My Computer, Windows Explorer, or any file folder on your computer, and drag a file to the empty WinZip archive interface (Figure 15.12). You'll be prompted to name the zipped archive. This archive can contain many other files from any location on your hard drive. Your zipped archive will be saved in the default location, but the location can be changed by using the Browse menu to select a new one.

3. To add other files to your zipped archive, just drag them from any folder, and the file will appear in the archive.

Figure 15.12
After clicking the WinZip icon, an empty WinZip archive appears, ready for archiving files.

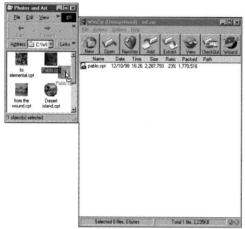

You can also begin a zipped archive by selecting a single file and zipping it. The single file will constitute a zipped archive, although you can add other files to it if you wish.

1. Select one or more files to zip, as follows:

   —To zip one file, right-click it.

   —To zip multiple files, select all the files you want to compress, and then press Shift + F10.

2. From the shortcut menu that appears, select Add to Zip.

3. The Add menu appears. You can accept the default options or make adjustments. If you have selected folders and subfolders for zipping, or if you've selected files found in different folders and there may be duplicate files in your selection, place a check by both options in the Folders panel of the Add dialog box.

4. In the Add drop-down menu, select Add (and Replace) Files. If you want the files automatically erased after making zips of them, select Move Files. This option saves the zipped files and immediately erases the originals. The Add option leaves the original files intact.

5. After selecting any or all options, click the Add button.

6. WinZip compresses the file. A blue bar moves from left to right at the bottom of the screen, denoting zipping progress.

7. When the file is done zipping (compressing), you can close the Zip menu by clicking the X in the upper-right corner of the screen.

8. The zipped file now appears in the same folder where the original file was located. If you selected Add (and Replace) Files, then the originals are still where they were (see Figure 15.13). If you selected Move Files, then the originals will be erased. Only the zipped files remain.

Figure 15.13
The zipped file as it appears in the same folder with the other files it compressed.

Zipped file

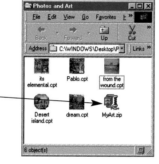

All files zipped from other folders will be found in this one big Zip file that you just created. If you "group zipped" folders from several locations, you will not have lots of little zipped files in those other folders. Those files are now stored in this one large zipped file. If you placed a check by both options in the Folders panel, then when you unzip your files, they will all be returned to their original locations.

Unzipping Files

To restore a zipped file or files, right-click the Zip file and select the second Extract To option (see Figure 15.14). This option restores the files to their original location. Selecting the first Extract To option lets you choose which folder to restore. This is helpful if your computer's configuration has changed and the folder that originally contained this file (or files) no longer exists. This option is also important if you are unzipping these files onto another computer.

Figure 15.14
To decompress the files to their original location, select Extract To.

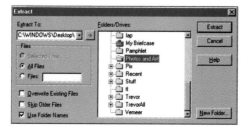

CHAPTER 15

Appendix A
Scanning and the Law

This appendix briefly reviews the legalities of scanning. It is not meant as legal advice but to create awareness that this issue is important. The information presented here is included because, as technology makes it easier to reproduce images and text, rules regarding intellectual property are going to matter more and more.

Scanning *is* reproducing. This is a touchy subject among photographers, artists, graphics designers, and others who make their living by having control over how their reproduced images are sold.

Who Owns an Image?

Let's say you've purchased an illustrated book on gardening. What have you bought? You have words and pictures you can read and look at. You can apply the knowledge those words and pictures supply. And you can use the pieces of paper they are printed on for anything you like. But you have bought only a single copy of those words and pictures. You have not bought the rights to reuse them or make additional copies. This distinction points out the difference between owning something printed in a book or magazine and owning intellectual property.

NOTE

In the United States, the copyright for an original work lasts for that person's lifetime, plus an additional fifty years. The copyright on a "work for hire"–an image that was made while in the employ of someone else (for example, a logo created by an employee of a company)–lasts for one hundred years from the time of its creation, or seventy-five years from its first publication.

Guidelines for Legal Use of Images

Two bits of technology can undermine a creator's ability to earn his or her fair share from intellectual property: the ease with which anyone can download an image from the Web–and scanners.

Web-Based Images

It's usually not legal to download an image from a Web page unless express permission to do so is granted. Many Web sites that display images post warnings not to download the images. However, even in the absence of such warnings, you are still prohibited from doing so.

Scanned Images

When using a scanner, here are some basic guidelines:

▶ You may never scan a copyright-protected image for the following uses:

—Placement in a product brochure or to reproduce on items for sale

—Placement in a business logo

—As part of your own creative endeavor

▶ You cannot affix someone else's image in any way to an item, such as a T-shirt or calendar, and then sell it.

▶ Scanning trademarks, such as the Coca-Cola symbol, is prohibited.

▶ When using an image, you must credit the owner of the image.

▶ You may never give the impression that someone else's image is your own.

NOTE

When you scan images of living, famous people, you have to contend with two issues: the celebrity's property rights and that person's sensibility. Most celebrities are very protective about how their images are used. Take these factors into consideration when contemplating scanning images of the rich and famous. Bear in mind that anyone has rights to how his or her image is used for commercial purposes.

The Fair Use Rule

Images protected by copyright law nonetheless are subject to the rule of "fair use," which recognizes some instances in which you may make a copy of an image, such as the following:

▶ Research, such as referring to a work in a scientific publication

▶ Reporting, journalism, and criticism, such as printing a still shot from a movie while reviewing it

▶ Teaching, which includes using a picture as an example of art from a particular period or using a photograph with subject matter that is genuinely instructive to students

In such cases, you may not be required to get written permission from the image owner in order to use the image. If you are ever unsure whether your use of an image will be considered fair, seek the owner's permission.

However, commercial viability and profitability supersede the application of the fair use rule. The fair use rule is not a license to undermine someone's ability to use their image profitably.

Using Royalty-Free Images

At times, you may need to supplement your own scanned photos with other pictures for your projects. How can you do that legally? You can purchase collections of royalty-free photos.

Royalty-free collections come in all sizes and price ranges. They're found wherever software is sold. Those huge clip-art packages often include thousands of photos. Very pricey collections of royalty-free photographs can be ordered through magazines that cater to graphics professionals. The more professional royalty-free collections will include large, high-resolution photos shot with more creativity and personality than the collections you'll find as part of a clip-art package.

What is meant by royalty-free use? You may use these images in any way you please, without obtaining written permission from the owner of the image. However, if the image is central to the product you create, and you are actually marketing the image in some way, you still need written permission. For example, if you use a photograph on a brochure for a real estate company, it's the *services of the company* you are selling, not the image. However, if you display photographs on coffee mugs, calendars, greeting cards, or T-shirts, you are marketing the image.

Scanning and Reproducing Text

You may scan text according to the rules of fair use, if you are referring to the text as part of research (properly credited, of course), in a review or critical article, or as part of classroom instruction or educational use.

Different rules apply depending on whether you are scanning short quotes, forms, large excerpts, or comments by individuals:

▶ **Quotes**—The rules for scanning and reproducing short bits of text are mostly concerned with maintaining accuracy. For example, lots of people use Oscar Wilde's pithy quotes to spice up their articles (such as "Living well is the best revenge.") However, accurately quoting a famous statement ("Those who forget history are doomed to repeat it," for example) is more of an ethical responsibility than a legal one. Yet if a quote is misused, misconstrued, and its alteration is deemed to cause harm, the issue can become legal.

▶ **Speeches**—You may scan and use quotes from public officials or other individuals deemed to be in the public eye. Lengthy excerpts are also fair game. You have to credit the source from which you obtained the quote or excerpt. You may not quote or scan and reproduce the words of private individuals without their written consent.

▶ **Forms**—You may not scan and use forms that a commercial entity is selling or marketing in some way. Some companies, such as loan agencies, invite you to download, make copies, or scan their forms. This is fine.

▶ **Text excerpts**—If you scan and quote large sections of classic literature, such as excerpts from *Romeo and Juliet,* your obligation is not to the deceased author. Rather, your obligation is to the book publisher who published the book you scanned the excerpt from. The book publisher owns the way the words were laid out on the page, the footnotes, and other formatting, even if it does not own the words themselves. You need to contact the publisher before you make copies of its book's pages. Keep in mind that the heirs of an author's estate may well carry the rights to use of published material of the deceased.

Repercussions

Violating copyright laws can result in the following repercussions:

▶ A warning to refrain from such violations in the future

▶ Fines levied for violation of copyright laws

▶ Damages awarded to the owner of the images in the amount that may have been lost as a result of the infringement

Other laws may apply as well, such as laws that apply to selling counterfeit CDs or videos. These could include interstate trafficking of counterfeit merchandise or fraud, depending on the seriousness and scope of the violation. For more information, check out www.copyright.com This site is a clearance center for all types of copyright information, as well as assistance in registering copyrights.

Appendix B
Your Scanner and Your Mac

The Mac has been involved in desktop publishing and creative design since its inception by Apple in the early 1980s. Scanners have been part of the Mac environment for almost as many years, and although some of the hardware elements of the Mac environment are different, on the whole, the experience on the Mac is largely identical to that on the PC. The main reason for the compatibility is that much of the software actually originated on the Mac platform before it migrated to the PC. The packages that you are most familiar with—OmniPage, Photoshop, and many others—were first developed on the Mac.

Although many of the features of Mac scanners are the same as those on PC scanners, some important differences exist that haven't been covered yet that you need to be aware of when installing, setting up, and using your scanner on the Mac. Those differences are covered in this appendix.

Mac Installation Tips

Installing your scanner involves two phases:

1. Connect the hardware
2. Install the necessary software

After you select the right kind of scanner for your computer, the physical aspects are quite straightforward. Fortunately, the software installation on the Mac is also quite easy. Nothing is ever as easy as it should be, however, and you need to take care when installing and connecting your scanner.

In all cases, after you purchase your scanner, your first port of call is the user manual that came with it. If you've yet to choose a suitable scanner, or you are having problems, then use the information in this section as a guide to smoothing the selection process and identifying many of the installation traps.

Before you start, the recommended specification for your Mac machine is as follows:

▶ Quadra- or Centris-based 68K Mac; or any PowerPC-based Mac

▶ 16MB RAM for 68K; 32MB RAM for PowerPC

▶ System 7.5 for Quadra or Centris (68K); or MacOS 8 or later (PowerPC)

▶ 50MB of hard disk space

▶ Built-in video; or a video card capable of supporting thousands of colors (millions preferred)

Hardware

Choosing the right scanner for your needs is very important. Aside from the decisions about image quality, scan resolution, and bit depth (refer to Chapter 2), you also need to think about the connectivity between the scanner and the Mac. Most scanners for the Mac are based on the SCSI interface. The first Mac used SCSI as the interface for supporting hard drives, and since then, the SCSI system has been a central part of the Mac environment. You already know that SCSI allows the connection of a number of devices to the same chain. There is, of course, no difference between the specification on the two platforms. The end of the SCSI chain must be terminated, and all devices on the chain must have their own unique ID.

All Macs, from the old 68K-based machines such as the Centris and Quadra, and most PowerPC machines have a SCSI interface as standard. The exceptions to this rule are the "Blue and White" G3, the G4, iBooks, and iMacs. We'll return to the available solutions for those machines shortly. For those Macs equipped with SCSI interfaces as standard, you need to use a SCSI scanner. Newer Macs have dropped the SCSI interface, using a different technology for connecting the hard disk and CD-ROMs (IDE), and external connectivity is handled by the USB and FireWire ports. No FireWire-based scanners exist yet, but the inclusion of USB on the iMac has triggered an explosion in the market for USB scanners and other devices.

Using SCSI

The SCSI connector on a Mac is a 25-pin D-Type connector (see Figure B.1), identical to that used for serial and parallel port connections on a PC. Generally, connections to the scanner are via a 50-pin Centronics-style connector (see Figure B.2). Your scanner should come with the correct cable. However, if you have other devices, such as Zip, Jaz, CD-R, and external hard drives, you need to purchase a separate cable. Where possible, you should get the shortest possible cable—there is a maximum limit to the size of the SCSI chain, which is about ten feet (three meters).

Figure B.1
The 25-pin SCSI port
available on most Macs.

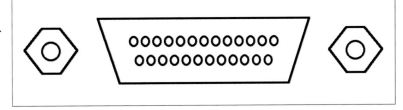

Figure B.2
The 50-pin Centronics
interface used by most
peripherals.

Some scanners come with only one SCSI interface, instead of the normal
two, which means that you cannot easily daisy chain the scanner in
between other devices or attach the required terminator. For these
situations, you should have been supplied, or will have to separately
obtain, a "two-headed" SCSI cable. This is similar to a normal cable,
except that on one end you get two connectors, arranged so that one side
connects the scanner, and the other side allows you to plug in a normal
50-pin Centronics cable from other devices. See Figure B.3 for an
example of what a two-headed SCSI cable looks like.

Figure B.3
A two-headed
SCSI cable

When setting the SCSI ID, remember the following:

▶ SCSI IDs can be set to a value between 1 and 6; ID 7 is the ID given to
the CPU.

▶ You cannot set the SCSI ID "live"; you must switch the machine off
and then back on after setting the ID.

The desktop G3 and G4 machines do not have SCSI interfaces as
standard, but they support USB, so the immediate solution appears to be a
USB scanner. USB scanners are fine for home and small office use, but
they can be a bit slow when scanning the high-quality images used for
inclusion in a company magazine or brochure. Since we can also use USB
scanners with iMacs, iBooks, and PowerBooks, and the G3/G4 desktops,
they make an ideal solution that should work with a variety of Macs.

Instead, because the G3 and G4 machines have three spare PCI slots, for high-quality scanning, a better solution may be to purchase a separate SCSI card and use a SCSI-based scanner. On the Mac, fitting a SCSI card is as easy as opening the box and inserting the card—most cards do not need any special software to be installed, since the Mac already supports the SCSI standard and includes SCSI drivers within the operating system.

The recommended card for SCSI scanner connections is the Adaptec 2930U PCI card, although there are many other SCSI cards that will allow you to connect SCSI scanners. Most cards provide a 50-pin Micro-D connector (refer to Figure B.3). You must ensure, however, that you purchase a "Narrow" SCSI card, not one of the "Wide" SCSI cards. Scanners use Narrow connections, using the 50-pin connectors, whereas Wide SCSI devices and cards use 68-pin connectors. Adapters are available to connect 50-pin Narrow devices to wide SCSI channels, but these add extra levels of complication that can sometimes cause crashes.

Using USB

For iMacs, iBooks, and other machines that support the USB interface, a USB scanner is probably the best solution. Using a USB scanner is simply a case of connecting the USB cable to your keyboard or to the spare USB connector on the side of your iMac or the back of your G3/G4 machine. If you already have other peripherals connected to your Mac, then you probably need to purchase a USB hub, which provides four or eight additional USB ports.

For the current crop of G3 PowerBooks, you are in the unique position of being able to support either SCSI- or USB-based devices. The PowerBook has a 30-pin HDI (high-density interface) connector, so you will need a special cable, available from Apple or your local Apple dealer. The PowerBook also has two USB ports, supporting the full 12Mbps speed. Since a PowerBook is designed to be picked up and moved around, it's unlikely that you will also want to take your scanner with you everywhere you go. However, when you return to your desk, connecting a single USB cable is much more convenient than SCSI and other cables, especially since you should turn the machine off (or at least put it to sleep) before connecting.

You cannot "hot-connect" SCSI devices to your machine, because you risk damage either to your computer or to the devices that you are connecting. You can connect the SCSI cable to the PowerBook while it is asleep or powered down, but this is not always convenient. Therefore, for a PowerBook, you should ideally use the USB rather the SCSI interface. This will allow you to connect the scanner even while the machine is switched on.

There is one final solution available to you if you have a USB-capable Mac and want to use a SCSI scanner. The iMac and iBook do not support any additional expansion cards, so connecting SCSI devices seems impossible. However, a few companies, notably Adaptec, produce a USB-to-SCSI interface. This connects to your USB port and provides a SCSI connector so that you can attach scanners and other SCSI peripherals to your Mac. In ideal conditions, the USB interface supports a transfer rate of 12Mbps—most SCSI scanners support a transfer rate of only 5 or 10Mbps, the lowest speeds available within the SCSI specification.

Although not an ideal solution, these USB-to-SCSI interfaces can allow you to use your legacy SCSI scanner with your iMac and iBook. You can even use it with your PowerBook in place of the onboard SCSI to allow hot-plugging of your SCSI devices, without any of the normal dangers associated with connecting SCSI devices while the computer and device are switched on.

Quick Guide

Table B.1 gives a quick rundown of the recommended scanner for the type of machine you have.

Table B.1
Recommended interfaces for different Mac platforms.

Machine	Scan Type	Scanner
Quadra/Centris Mac	Any	SCSI
PowerMac (not B&W G3 or G4)	Any	SCSI
B&W G3 or G4	Home/small office	USB
B&W G3 or G4	High-quality for magazine or brochure	SCSI (needs PCI card)
iMac/iBook	Any	USB or SCSI with B-SCSI adapter
PowerBook	Any	USB or SCSI

To install the software required to use your scanner, insert the CD-ROM that came with your scanner into the CD-ROM drive and then run the installation application on the CD-ROM. You might want to disable any virus checking software that you have installed, to ensure that the installation process doesn't trigger the checking system and prevent you from installing the software.

APPENDIXES

If you are using MacOS 8.6 or higher, a better solution is to start up with the standard set of Mac extensions. To do this, open the Extensions Manager control panel, select the MacOS 8.6 Base (or similar setting), and then restart. This configures your machine only with the extensions and control panels required for a basic operating system, including the CD-ROM drivers required to use the CD-ROM. This eliminates any third extensions or control panels that might otherwise affect your installation process.

After you start the installer, follow the onscreen instructions, which normally ask you to select a disk to install the software onto and which may also ask you to agree to a license agreement and enter an unlock or serial number to validate your software. With a few minor exceptions, all the software that you need in order to use your scanner should be installed in one step. You will need to restart your machine after the software has been installed and reset your extension set in the Extensions Manager to your normal setting to ensure that your Mac restarts properly. Note that you may need to select the extensions and control panels installed by the software, to ensure they are loaded correctly.

Mac software generally consists of three main elements:

▶ Extensions and/or control panels

▶ Application software

▶ Plugins and adapters

The extensions and control panels are installed into your System Folder in the appropriate folders. For most SCSI devices, these extensions are included here purely to provide a central location and interface for software to communicate with your scanner. For a SCSI scanner, no drivers are required for the OS to identify the scanner. Software is just installed into the System Folder so that the scanning software and application extensions, such as Photoshop plugins, know where to find the drivers required to use the scanner.

For USB scanners, the story is quite different. When you attach a USB peripheral, the OS looks for some driver software so that the application software on your machine can communicate with the scanner over the USB interface. The USB software must be installed when the scanner is connected, even though the drivers for the scanner will not be loaded until the scanner is switched on and attached. However, the basic principles for other software installed in the System Folder are the same as for SCSI scanners—the System Folder provides a central location for software to find the drivers required to use the scanner.

Irrespective of the scanner-specific driver that is installed, most scanners also include TWAIN drivers. TWAIN is a standard that allows any TWAIN-capable application to obtain an image from any TWAIN-compatible scanner or other device, such as digital cameras. Unlike Windows scanners, which often use the TWAIN system in preference to their drivers and interfaces, most Mac scanners use their own rather than TWAIN, largely because TWAIN is a relatively new system to the Mac platform; although it is supported, it is not always reliable.

TWAIN can also place restrictions on the types of scans that can be made. For Mac designers and creative people, the limitations of the TWAIN system mean sacrificing scanner capabilities in preference to cross-application compatibility. Since most scanners come with their own special software that allows full control over the scanner, the requirement to use TWAIN is much lower on the Mac.

All Mac scanners install their own software application to allow you to scan documents with your scanner. These applications are unique to either the manufacturer or, in some cases, even the scanner model. In addition, some companies install some additional packages, such as OmniPage Lite for optical character recognition (OCR) or an image management tool such as ImageAXS. Finally, some scanners also come with image manipulation and publishing tools, such as Adobe Photoshop, Photoshop LE (which has reduced features), Adobe PhotoDeluxe, or Adobe PageMill.

In all cases, your scanner should come with suitable extensions and plugins to allow you to make scans directly within applications such as Photoshop. The interfaces normally supported by these plugins are identical to the interfaces available within the standalone applications also supplied with your software. The advantage of using these plugins is that you can scan and then immediately edit the image without having to save the file and use two different applications.

Traps for the Unwary

Most problems relating to scanners on the Mac platform are associated with the physical aspects of the scanner connection, such as the SCSI interface, rather than the software. To identify what sort of problem you have, use the following guidelines.

Solving SCSI Problems

If you are experiencing any of the following problems, then you probably have a problem with the SCSI connectivity somewhere:

▶ The machine freezes on startup

▶ The machine freezes when you try to use the scanner

▶ The scanner software can't see the scanner

All of these problems are related to the SCSI chain. If you suspect a problem with the SCSI chain, you should check the following items before continuing:

▶ Make sure the scanner and computer are switched off before connecting the scanner to the computer

▶ Before booting a machine, switch on the scanner and any other external devices before you press the power key to start the machine

▶ Check that the scanner has a unique SCSI ID

▶ Check that the SCSI chain is terminated

If you are still having problems after checking all of this, and you have other devices on the SCSI chain, then you may need to play with the order of the devices connected to the SCSI port. From experience, scanners often work best at the end of the chain, with removable storage devices closest to the machine.

To resolve any conflicts of SCSI ID numbers for the individual devices, you need to use a piece of software that lists all the IDs in use on the SCSI chain. If you have MacOS 8.5 or later, you can use the *Apple System Profiler* to display the devices attached to your machine. We'll look at using the Apple System Profiler later, since it also allows us to look at the USB connectivity. If you don't have MacOS 8.5 or later, then the best-known software for checking the SCSI bus is *SCSI Probe,* available from Adaptec (**ftp://ftp.adaptec.com/pub/BBS/PowerMac/scsiprobe5.1.1.hqx**). SCSI Probe scans the SCSI bus and asks each device it finds for an identifier. You can see a heavily populated SCSI chain in Figure B.4.

Figure B.4
The SCSI Probe ID
checker.

If your scanner does not appear in the list, then it probably means that the scanner is switched off, has the same ID as another device on the chain, or is faulty. Switch off other devices on the chain and rescan the bus—the scanner should appear. If it doesn't appear in the list, check the SCSI ID again and then switch the scanner off and then on—check one last time. If the scanner still doesn't appear, then the scanner likely is faulty—return it to your supplier so it can be checked it for you.

When scanning with a SCSI-based scanner, if you get a message such as "Trouble Communicating with Scanner, check connections," then the problem is either a faulty cable or excessive traffic on the SCSI chain. It is best not to be scanning while simultaneously copying information from an external device or performing other high-volume transfers, such as writing a CD. Although, in theory, this shouldn't make any difference, it can sometimes affect the process. When scanning, a lot of information is transferred from the scanner to the computer. Due to the way the scanner works, the information is normally sent in one long stream of data as the scanner scans the page. An interruption, such as writing to CD, causes an interruption in the flow of data from the scanner, which confuses the scanner software and interrupts the scan.

USB Problems

Connecting a USB scanner poses very few potential problems. The connectivity, termination, and addressing that cause problems with SCSI are automatically configured by the USB system. This means that we can isolate USB problems into three areas:

▶   The scanner is not switched on

▶   The cable is not connected

▶   The software is not installed

The first two problems should be obvious to check. If you are using the scanner in combination with a USB hub, make sure that the hub is powered. You can check the USB devices that are connected to your machine by using the Apple System Profiler, available on MacOS 8.5 and later. Under the Devices and Volumes tab, the Profiler shows all the different devices attached to your machine—the USB section is shown at the top of the window.

When you switch on the machine or connect the scanner while the machine is switched on and a "Missing Driver" message is displayed, then it probably means that you have not installed the USB drivers. Alternatively, it may mean that the USB drivers have been deleted, corrupted, or disabled. Before you try reinstalling the software, check your System Folder for the extensions. All USB drivers should start with "USB"—you can find the USB drivers within the Extensions folder of the System Folder. If you are uncomfortable with getting this close to the System Folder, then use the Extensions Manager to locate the drivers.

Software Problems

If you can see the scanner and no errors are reported during the startup process, then it probably means that the software is installed correctly. Any further problems will be software-related. Software problems can be isolated into one of two categories:

▶ Problems with the extensions installed into the System Folder

▶ Problems using either the supplied scanner software or the plugins for Photoshop and other applications

Identifying extensions and control panels that are causing problems is very difficult—often, it is not individual extensions that are causing problems but rather a combination of extensions or the order they boot in. The only way to isolate these problems is to disable individual extensions apart from those related to your scanner and then restart—if the error reoccurs, then you should be able to identify which extension is causing the conflict.

If the scanning process fails halfway through the process, then either the disk is full or you have not allocated enough memory to the application. To increase the amount of memory given to the application, find the application in the Finder, select File>Get Info and increase the Preferred Size by 500K. If you are scanning very large files, consider increasing the size even further—some images can be as much as 40MB in size.

One final thing to check if you are still having problems is that the disk itself does not have any problems. Sometimes, areas of the disk can become corrupted, and when you try to save information to the disk, the machine crashes because it doesn't know how to avoid the corrupted portion of the disk. Use Norton Utilities, System Tools Pro or a similar program to verify and repair the integrity of your disk.

You can also check your machine by using the Disk Tools floppy disk that came with your machine. New PowerMacs come with a Software Install or Restore CD-ROM. In both cases, the floppy and the CD-ROM include a program called Disk First Aid that can check and fix most problems on your hard disk.

Performing a Scan

Let's have a look at the scanning process using the VistaScan software that comes with the Umax range of scanners, including the Umax 1220U, the most common scanner used with the iMac. Figure B.5 shows the main window used for scanning either via the VistaScan software or via the supplied Photoshop plug-in. We're currently working in Beginner mode, which makes the process of selecting the type of scan you want much easier.

Figure B.5
Scanning with the
VistaScan software.

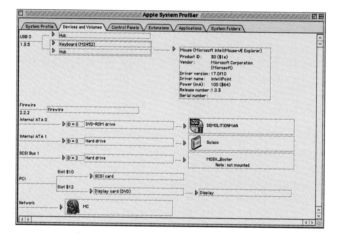

The area on the left gives a preview of the image you are about to scan—you can update the image by clicking the Preview button on the right side. In Beginner mode, we are given a number of choices as to where the image can be sent once it has been scanned and what quality of scan should be made. Figure B.6 shows the available destinations. They are, from left: disk, another application (copies to the clipboard), direct to a printer (so the scanner operates like a photocopy), via fax (so the scanner works like a fax machine), and by e-mail.

Figure B.6
Selecting a destination.

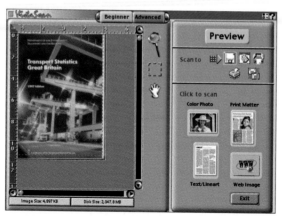

Obviously, you can print the scanned document only if you have a printer, and fax it only if you have suitable fax software, such as the FaxSTF system that comes with iMacs, iBooks, and G3/G4 desktops. After you decide where you want the scanned image to go, you need to select the quality of the image you are scanning. Figure B.7 shows the available options.

Figure B.7
Selecting the
image quality.

The VistaScan software will automatically set the resolution and bit depth settings for you, according to the type of image you are scanning. If you want more control over the specific settings, then you can switch to Advanced mode. This enables you to individually select the resolution and other settings (see Figure B.8).

Figure B.8
Advanced settings
with VistaScan.

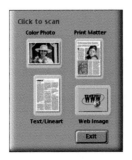

Recommended Software

Because the Mac has always been a serious creative-design machine, the range of software for home users is somewhat limited compared to that available on the PC. However, in comparison, the range of professional-quality software is much greater, especially if you include the range of plugins and adapters that are useable with Adobe Photoshop. We'll have a quick look at some of the software packages you can use for different tasks on the Mac.

Image Editing/Viewing

After you scan the image, you will probably want to clean it up and perhaps even modify or adjust it slightly for your needs. Surprisingly, the number of packages for editing images is relatively small, mainly because Adobe Photoshop managed to set a standard that still has yet to be beaten. That said, there are some packages, either free or shareware, that can perform at least some of the elements supported by Photoshop.

Adobe Photoshop

The premiere commercial image editing tool is Adobe Photoshop. All the features are identical on the two platforms, so our previous forays into the Photoshop arena apply just as much to the Mac version of the product as they do to the PC version. One of Photoshop's primary strengths lies in its ability to modify images, using either the built-in tools or external plugins that provide additional facilities such as blurs, embossing, and even image stretching. There is a whole industry based on the provision and development of these plug-ins.

For photo editing, the most popular tools are the paintbrush, airbrush, and the rubber stamp tools. The former tools are obviously when you want to modify the contents of an image. The rubber stamp is a bit different. You can use this to duplicate one portion of an image somewhere else, including the colors and textures within the photo. Unlike a simple cut/copy and paste, you can duplicate the effects anywhere on the image as if you were using a rubber stamp. This is exceedingly useful where you want to be able to replace lost portions of an image. You can see Photoshop in action in Figure B.9.

Figure B.9
Photoshop in action.

GraphicConverter

GraphicConverter from LemkeSoft (**www.lemkesoft.de**) is a shareware product that is designed as an inexpensive version of Adobe Photoshop. Many of the basic image editing features supported by Photoshop are also supported by the GraphicConverter application. These include the usual Pencil, Rubber, Magic Wand, and Rubber Stamp tools, in addition to some complex image and color manipulation facilities included so that images can be optimized for use in different situations.

For example, using GraphicConverter, you can reduce the file size of an image so that it includes only the colors actually contained in the image. For many images, this can more than half the file size, without losing any detail in the image. This particular feature is most useful when down-sampling an image for display on the Web as a GIF rather than as a JPEG image.

Another favored feature of the GraphicConverter package is that the onscreen information supplied to the user is much improved over that supplied by Photoshop. Additional floating windows show the statistical information, such file and image size, while another window displays a zoomed version of the image directly under the cursor. This is incredibly useful when cropping an image, because you find the edges so precisely, or when editing, because you can be so much more precise without zooming in so far that you don't see the surrounding area. This is further augmented by the OverView window, which displays a thumbnail version of the image at all times. See Figure B.10 for an example.

Figure B.10
Using GraphicConverter to crop an image and save it as a GIF.

GraphicConverter can also be used to perform batch conversions of a number of images from one format to another. For example, you may have been given the images for a slideshow that needs to be put on the Web. Manually converting any reasonable number of slides is a very time-consuming task. With GraphicConverter, you can select the files you want to convert, specify the destination format, and then let the application do all the conversions automatically. If you register and purchase a copy of the software, you can go one stage further, not only performing file conversions but also automatically cropping, resizing, or resampling images.

QuickTime 3.0/4.0

Apple's QuickTime software includes an application called *PictureViewer*, which allows you to display most image formats onscreen. Although you cannot scan using PictureViewer, using it when simply viewing an image often is quicker than using Photoshop or GraphicConverter. PictureViewer also supports some very basic image viewing capabilities, including rotating, inverting, and zooming in on the image.

Finally, because PictureViewer uses QuickTime, the application not only can read images, it can also save them back in a number of different formats. This can be useful if you want to quickly convert a TIFF into a GIF for display on a Web page. However, if you want a more professional job, you should use the facilities offered by PhotoShop or Graphic-Converter. Figure B.11 shows a sample image and the save process.

Figure B.11
Using PictureViewer to view and convert an image.

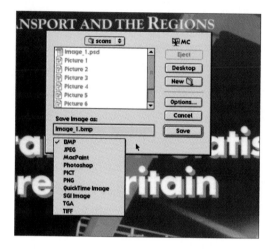

Optical Character Recognition

Numerous programs for identifying characters and turning scanned documents into text have appeared over the years, but there is really only one contender for the role of OCR software for the Mac: OmniPage from Caere. Most scanners include a copy of OmniPage LE, a limited version of the full OmniPage Pro software.

OmniPage is incredibly easy to use and has a claimed success rate of 99 percent, although, from experience, the actual rate is somewhat lower, depending on the text source. Scanning laser or professionally printed output is normally quite successful, but scanning documents printed on an inkjet printer can be a little haphazard. You can see a sample recognition process with OmniPage LE in Figure B.12.

Figure B.12
Using OmniPage LE
to recognize text.

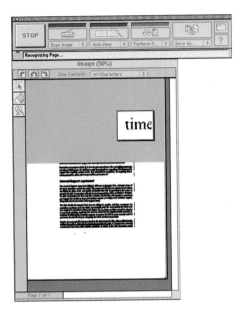

APPENDIXES

Faxing/Copying

There is no software available that directly supports copying and/or
faxing using a scanner, although many of the software packages that come
with scanners provide such capabilities. We looked earlier at the Umax
VistaScan that supports the ability to send a scanned image directly to a
printer or to fax software, such as FaxSTF and 4-Sight Fax.

Both of these fax technologies also allow you to fax a document by
accepting them as a print job. You print to a special printer and, instead
of coming out on paper, you are asked to provide the fax number of the
person to whom you want to send the scanned document. This means
that you could potentially fax the document from any application—
including Photoshop!

Alternatively, if you are just printing, you could simply scan the
document and then print it using Photoshop or GraphicConverter (or
other image acquisition software). You have to do the scanning and
printing one page at a time, but it's still an option.

Publishing

Once the image has been scanned, you can save the file in a variety of
formats so that it can be incorporated into documents. The main format
used for production-quality images on the Mac is TIFF and EPS which
can be imported and placed directly by packages such as QuarkXpress,
Adobe PageMaker, and Adobe InDesign. Aside from scanning, you
shouldn't need to perform any other actions when scanning documents
and images for inclusion in this way.

You can also import images directly into other applications, such as AppleWorks and Microsoft Word. However, the TIFF format is rather large for displaying within a normal text document. Instead, scan the image at a lower quality and save the image as a PICT rather than a TIFF.

Document Storage

When using a scanner as a method of recording paper documents electronically, it's useful to have some form of database in which to store the information. There are many types of databases available, from simple standalone databases, to those used on a network, which allow many users to submit, catalog, and retrieve images. At the simpler end of the range are products such as Presto PageManager, supplied with Umax scanners. At the opposite, professional end of the spectrum are products like Canto Cumulus, a product that is often used by slide and image libraries to catalog their collections.

The following sections look at two midrange products. Extensis Portfolio has simpler abilities but can be installed in a networked environment. ImageAXS Pro is a professional-quality multimedia cataloguing system that is designed for use on a single machine. Both tools share some common features, such as the ability to record additional keywords and other data with files and the ability to display a slideshow from the files contained in the catalog.

Extensis Portfolio

Extensis Portfolio is a cataloguing system that appears to have only simple features. Portfolio allows you to import most of the different image file formats, and because it supports QuickTime, you can also include formats supported by the QuickTime system, including movie and audio files such as MP3. Portfolio is also cross-platform-compatible, so databases created on a Mac can be opened and used by Windows-based machines running Portfolio software. For people who are in a cross-platform environment or for companies that supply image catalogs on CD-ROM, this is an invaluable feature.

The other major advantage of Portfolio over many other cataloguing applications is that you can migrate from the simple standalone version right up to a network-based client/server catalog. Having the catalog available on the network enables you to import, edit, and update images within the catalog directly from within Photoshop and other packages, without ever opening a file using the Finder. See Figure B.13 for a screenshot from the package.

Figure B.13
An Extensis Portfolio
database.

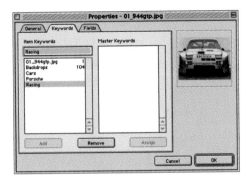

You can download a demo version of the application from the Extensis
Web site, **www.extensis.com**.

ImageAXS Pro

ImageAXS Pro is supported by Caere, the same people responsible for the
OmniPage software. As well as allowing you to store image files,
ImageAXS Pro will catalog video and audio data and can be configured to
automatically obtain images from a connected scanner using the TWAIN
interface system. Unlike Extensis Portfolio, ImageAXS Pro is a
professional package designed for the single user.

ImageAXS Pro is much more like a database that supports the ability to
store and acquire scanner-based images. The database used to store meta
information about the files—such as the contents, keywords, and other
data—is extensive, with fourteen customizable fields, ten freeform fields,
two number fields, and two date fields, in addition to the standard image
information (size, resolution, and so forth). The database even includes a
"long" text field so that you can attach longer, article-style notes to the
data. Another useful database feature is that, as well as grouping
individual images within the same database or with the same keyword,
you can create image sets within a database file. For example, imagine
that you have one large database with all of your images stored within it.
You could group all the landscapes together, allowing you to browse
through only those images with landscapes, without having to perform a
keyword search, which might pick up other images not directly related.

APPENDIXES

You can see a sample database in Figure B.14.

Figure B.14
ImageAXS Pro
in action.

As part of the integration process, ImageAXS Pro also includes plugins for Photoshop and a contextual menu extension. The Photoshop plugin enables you to obtain an image from a database and start editing it immediately within Photoshop. The contextual menu item allows you to add an image to the database directly from the Finder.

Presto BizCard!

Taking a completely different tack to the task of recording information, Presto BizCard! allows you to scan business cards and then have the information instantly recognized and placed into a customized contact manager. This makes BizCard! much more than just an image cataloguing system—it also makes it a good database manager. When you get someone's business card, instead of manually entering the information, put it in the scanner and let BizCard! do the rest.

You can get more information on Presto BizCard! at **www.newsoftinc.com**.

Family Fun

The Adobe PhotoDeluxe product fills many of the gaps left by other software. You can open an existing image or acquire one directly from a scanner, digital camera, CD-ROM, or the Internet. After you open the file, you can clean it up by adjusting the colors and size, and you can even remove the red-eye effect that can occur in some camera pictures. Once you have the image you want, you can modify the image, applying a number of special filters and modifiers, and automatically format the image so that it is suitable for use within greetings cards and for other special output options.

You can see the Special Effects that are available in Figure B.15. In this instance, we've done a page curl on an image.

Figure B.15
Adobe PhotoDeluxe Special Effects.

Figure B.16 shows our page-curled Porsche image converted into a greeting card.

Figure B.16
PhotoDeluxe cards, calendars, and other features.

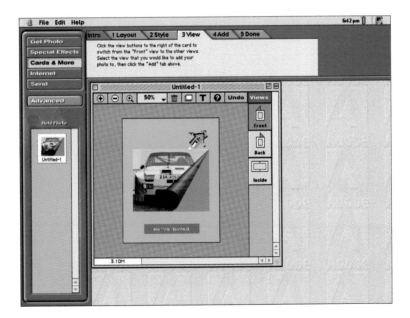

Web Publishing

When you are scanning images for display within a Web page, you need to be more careful about the image you are creating. The GIF format, the one most widely used for images on the Web, supports only 256 different colors and is specially optimized for displaying computer-generated graphics. The JPEG format is great for photos, but it can produce a slightly blurred image if the wrong settings are used when saving the file. Other concerns include the number of colors that are supported by each platform and the number of those colors which are actually available for public use once you have taken into account the window and desktop colors.

Adobe ImageReady

Adobe ImageReady is a kind of stripped-down version of Adobe Photoshop. Whereas Photoshop is aimed at designers who want to edit photographs at high-resolution, ImageReady is designed for editing images that will only be viewed onscreen, either during a presentation or within a Web site. Many of the same tools exist—you can paint, draw, or duplicate areas of the image. However, when it comes to saving the image, you have ultimate control over the bit depth, image size, and format in which the file is saved. ImageReady also allows you to create animations (which are saved as animated GIFs) and other Web page effects, such as rollover images, where an image can be made to look recessed as the button is pressed. You can see a sample screenshot in Figure B.17.

Figure B.17
Adobe ImageReady.

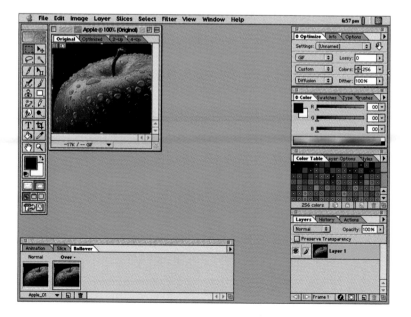

Equilibrium DeBabelizer

Although included here under the "Web Publishing" section, DeBabelizer is, in fact, a simple image conversion package. However, it is targeted at optimizing the images that you want to use in Web sites, to make them as small and as quick to download as possible. You can translate any file into any of the supported formats, modifying the color table and the aspect ratio (Macs and Windows use two different aspect ratios for many resolutions). The translation window is shown in Figure B.18.

Figure B.18
Adobe ImageReady.

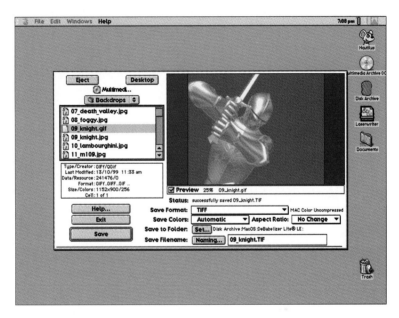

A trialware edition of the software, which only supports BMP, GIF, PICT, and TIFF formats, can be downloaded from the Equilibrium Web site, **www.equilibrium.com**.

Index

INDEX

INDEX

INDEX

Order Form

Postal Orders:
  Muska & Lipman Publishing
  2645 Erie Avenue, Suite 41
  Cincinnati, Ohio 45208

On-Line Orders or more information:
  http://www.muskalipman.com
Fax Orders:
  (513) 924-9333

Title/ISBN	Price/Cost		Title/ISBN	Price/Cost

eBay Online Auctions
0-9662889-4-7
  Quantity _____
  × $14.95
  Total Cost _____

Digital Camera Solutions
0-9662889-6-3
  Quantity _____
  × $29.95
  Total Cost _____

MP3 Power! with Winamp
0-9662889-3-9
  Quantity _____
  × $29.99
  Total Cost _____

Scanner Solutions
0-9662889-7-1
  Quantity _____
  × $29.95
  Total Cost _____

Paint Shop Pro 6 Power!
0-9662889-2-0
  Quantity _____
  × $39.99
  Total Cost _____

Subtotal _____

Sales Tax _____
(please add 6% for books
shipped to Ohio addresses)

Shipping _____
($4.00 for the first book,
$2.00 each additional book)

TOTAL PAYMENT ENCLOSED _____

Ship to:

  Company _____

  Name _____

  Address _____

  City _____ State _____ Zip _____ Country _____

Educational facilities, companies, and organizations interested in multiple copies of these books should contact the publisher for quantity discount information. Training manuals, CD-ROMs, electronic versions, and portions of these books are also available individually or can be tailored for specific needs.

Thank you for your order.